YOUR ULTIMATE SECURITY GUIDE:
WINDOWS 7 EDITION

JUSTIN CARROLL

**YOUR ULTIMATE SECURITY GUIDE:
WINDOWS 7 EDITION**

By Justin Carroll

All rights reserved. No part of this book may be reproduced in any form or by electronic or mechanical means including information storage and retrieval systems without permission in writing from the author.

First published: 26 April, 2015

The information contained in this book is on an "as-is" basis, without warranty. The author has taken great care in the research and writing of this book but assumes no responsibility for errors or omissions. Further, he assumes no liability for damages, consequential or inconsequential, arising from the use of the material or programs contained herein.

Rather than use a trademark symbol with every occurrence of a trademarked name, the names within this book are used only in an editorial fashion and to the benefit of the trademark owner with no intention of infringement on this trademark.

Library of Congress

Copyright © 2015 Justin Carroll

All rights reserved.

ISBN-10: 150864778X
ISBN-13: 978-1508647782

CONTENTS

Introduction 1

PART I: BASIC BEST PRACTICES

1   OS HARDENING AND GENERAL SECURITY   9
    User Accounts and PLP   10
    OS Updates   12
    Application Updates   14
    Antivirus   15
    Anti-Malware   17
    Windows Firewall   20
    Microsoft EMET   21
    AutoPlay   23
    Best Practice: Displaying File Extensions   24
    Best Practice: Scanning Removable Media   26
    Best Practice: Removing Bloatware   27
    Best Practice: Sleep, Hibernate, or Shut Down?   30
    Best Practice: Limit Startup Applications   32
    A Word on BIOS Passwords   33
    Summary   34

2   USER AUTHENTICATION   35
    Password Managers   36
    Host-Based Password Managers   37
    Web-Based Password Managers   44
    Usernames   45
    Passwords   48
    Password Vulnerabilities   49
    Other Password Issues   53
    Two-Factor Authentication   55
    Checksum Calculators   60
    Summary   62

PART II: DATA-AT-REST

3	SECURING DATA-AT-REST	65
	Encryption Basics	65
	TrueCrypt	68
	DiskCryptor	73
	7Zip	76
	Bitlocker/EFS	77
	Backups	78
	Summary	83
4	SECURE FILE DELETION	85
	Secure File Deletion Basics	87
	Eraser	89
	CCleaner	92
	CCEnhancer	95
	Darik's Boot and Nuke	96
	Defragmenting	97
	Managing Data Leakage	99
	Summary	101

PART III: DATA-IN-MOTION

5	SECURING DATA-IN-MOTION	105
	SSL and TLS	105
	Virtual Private Networks	108
	Wi-Fi Security	112
	Wi-Fi Settings in Windows 7	113
	Basic Router Setup	115
	Best Practices for Untrusted/Unsecured Networks	120
	Considerations for Air Gaps	123
	Summary	125
6	INTERNET BROWSER SECURITY	127
	Browser Setup – Firefox	127
	Firefox Add-Ons	133
	Epic Privacy Browser	139
	Tor Browser	140
	Browsing Best Practices	142
	Summary	145

7	SECURING ONLINE ACCOUNTS	147
	Online Accounts Best Practices	147
	Banking Accounts	150
	E-Commerce Accounts	150
	Email Accounts	151
	Email Encryption	159
	Social Media Accounts	165
	Cloud Storage Accounts	166
	Online Messaging Systems	169
	Summary	170
	Conclusion	173
	Index	175

Dedicated to the memory of Master Sergeant Thomas A. Saunders

"Have a good 'un!"

JUSTIN CARROLL

INTRODUCTION

This book is intended to walk you, the end-user, through the best practices for securing both a personal computer running the Windows 7 operating system (OS) and your personal digital footprint. Though this book does cover the basics, my intent is to provide tools and techniques that allow the reader to far surpass a mere "basic" level of security and privacy. My goal is for the reader to have the advanced tools and knowledge to be in the top tier of security- and privacy-minded users.

To accomplish this goal, this book is intended to be read and implemented from start to finish. The original idea for this book was to create the book I wish I had had years ago: a guidebook to setting up a brand new computer, from start to finish, with security and privacy as the primary goals. Though this is perhaps most easily implemented on a brand new machine (or clean installation), all of the techniques covered here can be applied to a machine that is already in use. Various sections in this book will reference material previously covered, so it is perhaps best to take it in order, but the user may use this book as he or she sees fit.

There are several concepts that will be referred to constantly and consistently within these pages. The first is redundancy. Many of the ideas expressed here may seem to overlap each other and you may wonder why I recommend so many steps that seem duplicative of previous effort, but this is by design. Computer security is not simple, nor is it easy, and redundancy is required. Massive vulnerabilities are routinely discovered in security software and protocols that are assumed to be secure. For example, in early 2014 the so-called "Heartbleed" vulnerability was discovered in the SSL protocol, a system of encrypting Internet traffic that had been assumed to be secure for years. Users who relied on the SSL protocol alone to protect their sensitive Internet browsing sessions potentially had vast amounts of information exposed online. Had these users implemented a second, redundant form of encryption for their Internet traffic, the Heartbleed vulnerability would not have been nearly so alarming. For this is the reason I recommend a sound defense-in-depth with overlapping security measures. When working with security programs I always work with the underlying assumption that one or more of the protocols or applications I am using is compromised. Though this may seem paranoid, the concept has proven itself time and time again.

The second concept to which this book will continually refer is the idea that convenience and security are inversely correlated. To wit, the more convenient a system is, the less secure it is. This is, in my opinion, the reason computers are not more secure than they are. End users are typically unwilling to give up convenience for the sake of security and are constantly seeking more and more convenient systems (a concept the market validates by offering increasing convenience at the expense of security).

If the previous statement does not apply to you, and you are willing to sacrifice some convenience on the altar of security, then this is the book for you. Following the steps here will take time and patience, and will doubtlessly make your system somewhat less convenient to use, but the process will also make it far more secure. My intent, however, is not to *purposefully* make the system inconvenient. Where possible, I have tried to simplify and render security measures as painless and transparent to the user as possible without sacrificing security. It is up to each individual to find his or her own personal "sweet spot," that ideal balance of inconvenience you are willing to endure and the corresponding level of security that you are comfortable with.

WHY THIS BOOK MATTERS

With the inconvenience and time investment inherent in securing a computer, many wonder why bother. I hear it all the time: "Why would anyone want to get into my stuff?" or "Why would anyone care about me?" And the honest answer is they probably wouldn't. But what if your computer was stolen from your home or hotel room? What if your computer is borrowed by your child and lost or forgotten at school or on the bus? What if you were mugged and your briefcase were stolen? What if any of a thousand scenarios occurred that resulted in you losing physical control of your computer? In any of these instances the new "owner" of the computer may try to take a look at your data. What will they find there?

On my fully encrypted computer they will find nothing but a blank screen prompting them for my password. My entire hard drive, including even the operating system, is encrypted and the device will not boot without correctly entering this password. But replace my computer with that of most home users (and, unfortunately, many business users) and the answer is likely to be credit reports, medical documents, résumés and job applications, family photos, saved logins, credit card and other financial information, internet browsing history which may reveal interests, hobbies, sexual affinities, and so on. All of this information may be used to harass, blackmail, extort, or further exploit you, or to steal your identity, open credit, or commit crimes in your name, leaving you to clean up the mess. Though it is almost a certainty that no one is after *you* specifically, it is very possible that under the right circumstances you may become a target, and victim, of opportunity.

I am also frequently informed that "no one would want to hack my computer." Again, this may be somewhat true. It is unlikely anyone would want to hack *your* computer specifically, but a hacked machine can take on a life of its own. Botnets (groups of thousands of hacked computers) are frequently used to carry out sophisticated distributed denial of service (DDoS) attacks unbeknownst to their owners. Hacked PCs are used as spam servers, captcha solving zombies, and in the most shocking and frightening cases, child pornography servers. Even if one cares little whether his or her own files are "hacked," securing a computer is in the best interest of society at large.

The other rejoinder I frequently encounter (especially in regard to comments regarding the government surveillance apparatus) is the "I have nothing to hide" line. Individuals employ the logic that they have done "nothing wrong" to justify an indifferent attitude toward security, generally, and privacy, specifically. Obviously I do not agree with this logic. Though I am completely law-abiding and theoretically have "nothing to hide," I still believe in the individual right to personal privacy, and despite their protests to the contrary, so do most of those in the "nothing-to-hide" camp. I will borrow Glenn Greenwald's technique here: If you truly have nothing to hide, I would ask that you email the username and password to your personal email account to:

5moii@notsharingmy.info

I doubt I will get many responses (if any), proving the point that most of those with "nothing to hide," probably have more to hide than they think.

DISCLAIMERS

A couple more points that I want to make within this introduction: This book is not intended to help you commit any unlawful act, nor am I especially worried that it will. While there are those who will undoubtedly say that encryption and privacy tools enable criminals and terrorists, I would submit to them that so do automobiles, smartphones, and occasionally, hammers. Any tool can be applied to either side of the law, and the applications and techniques presented in this book are merely tools.

I would also like to point out that none of these tools will make you invisible to the United States government's invasive surveillance apparatus. Though the tools promoted in this book will make you much safer from surveillance (government or otherwise), the Snowden documents have elucidated the vastness of the US collection effort, and it would be folly to believe otherwise. In fact, I would be remiss for not pointing out that using these tools (or any encryption or privacy-enabling tool), or even researching them online, may make you a target of surveillance, as has also been indicated by the Snowden documents.

Though I mention numerous products and applications by name, I would like to point out that I have neither received nor sought any form of compensation, direct or indirect, from any company or individual for the placement of their products in this work. The products that appear on these pages are not here because they profit me in any manner. They are here because they are the best (or in a few cases the *only*) tool for the job.

Where possible, I have attempted to find a free solution to every security and privacy problem, and for the most part I think I have done a pretty good job. Unfortunately, there are a very small number of services recommended in these pages that require a paid subscription, though this is not necessarily a bad thing. Free services have set the business model for monetizing the internet: surveillance. Collecting ever-broadening swaths of data has hurt us all. It has hurt us by making far too much personal information public, and by desensitizing us to constant, pervasive, and invasive surveillance. It is time that we recognize that paying for services isn't necessarily a bad thing; we will pay for it in one way or the other, and when necessary or prudent I have no problem paying for it up front.

It is also important to note that there are two types of "free" in the software/computer/internet service world. The first is the ideologically motivated open-source community that believes in security and privacy, and in an open internet, and creates their products in accordance with this philosophy. This community gives freely of its work to our collective benefit. The second is less pure, and is motivated by profit: companies that offer you "free" services such as email accounts that are not actually giving you a product because you *are* the product. By joining their services, you have given yourself over to the company to be a product that they market to their *real* customers: data brokers and advertisers. Discerning the difference between the two can be challenging, and I have attempted to make this distinction apparent in the tools that I recommend.

USAGE NOTES

The operating system version used during the writing of this book is Windows 7 Home Premium. Users of other versions should still have all of the capabilities mentioned in this work, while users of the Professional, Enterprise, and Ultimate versions will have some expanded functionality, such as the ability to use Microsoft's Encrypting File System (EFS) and Bitlocker (these programs are only packaged with the top-tiered versions).

For standardization's sake, whenever I reference the Control Panel and provide directions to navigate to a particular setting, I am using the control panel in **Category view**. While all of these options can be accessed from all other views, the exact directions apply only to the Category view as shown on the following page:

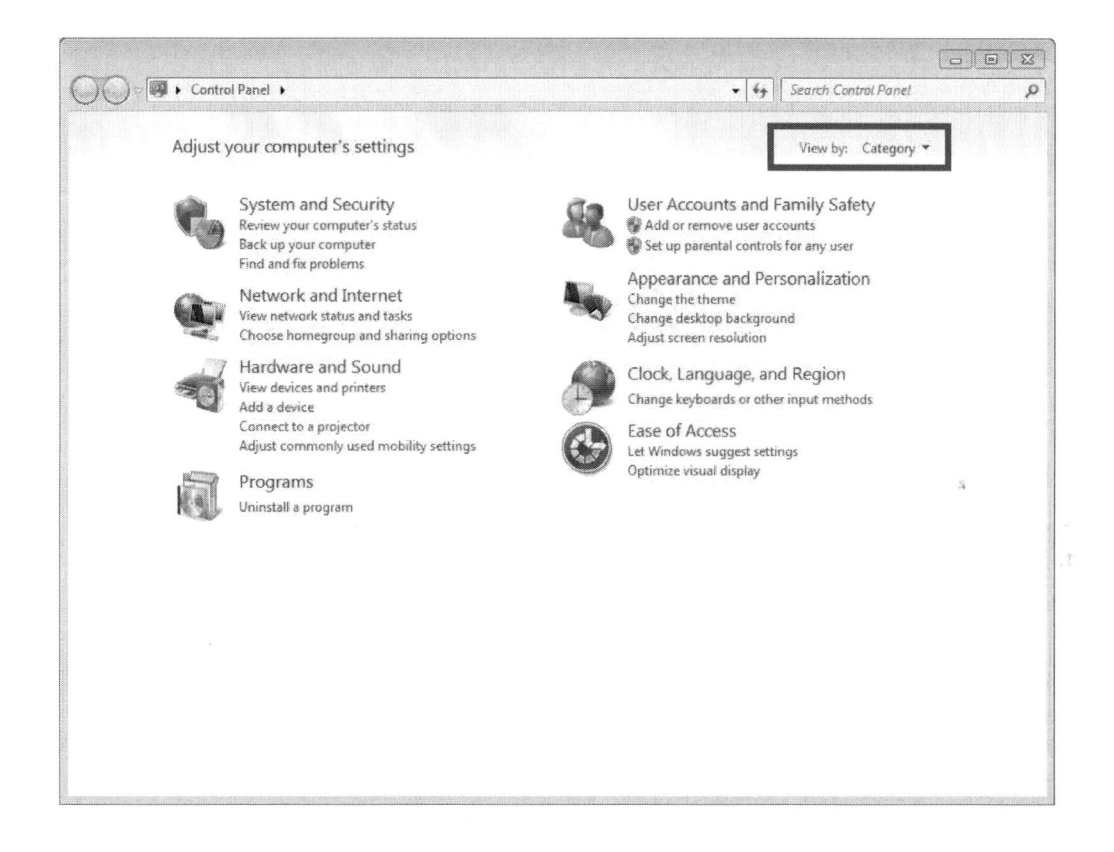

PART ONE:
BASIC BEST PRACTICES

JUSTIN CARROLL

CHAPTER 1:
OS HARDENING & GENERAL SECURITY

The Windows 7 operating system (OS) has been incredibly successful. Though it is two generations old and aging, Windows 7 still has extraordinary market penetration and remains the most popular OS on the planet. Indeed, it is the operating system upon which I rely on a daily basis for tasks large and small. Its popularity and near universality prove to be both a boon and a bane, however. The good news is there are a breathtaking number of products available for Windows 7, including a wide array of very capable and feature-rich security applications. The bad news is Windows 7 has an enormous attack surface and malicious hackers and software engineers are constantly writing new exploits for Windows 7, precisely because of its popularity and near-ubiquity. The more machines that may be affected by an exploit increase the value and desirability of that exploit.

Because there are so many threats against the Windows 7 OS, users must take special pains to secure the computers running it, and computer security should begin at the operating system level. Though there are numerous security applications on both the commercial and free/open source markets, there is much you can do just by making some minor adjustments to the way your operating system behaves. Most of these changes will have only a very minor impact on the convenience of your system, but will have a disproportionately large positive impact on the security of your device.

In addition to OS hardening, this chapter will also cover some basic best practices, and some very basic security applications. The applications covered in this chapter, though of the most basic variety (antivirus and anti-malware, for instance) are incredibly important for users, from the casual personal user to the heavy-duty enterprise user. Ultimately it is the user, not the settings or a magic suite of software, that will make a computer secure. Understanding best practices like the Principle of Least Privilege (see the next section of this chapter), and employing the computer in a manner that supports the software and settings, is at least as important as the software and settings themselves. This requires an aware and thoughtful user, as most of you reading this book will certainly be.

USER ACCOUNTS & THE PRINCIPLE OF LEAST PRIVILEGE

Though it is a phrase that is normally applied to the corporate or government sectors, personal computers should also employ and adhere to the Principle of Least Privilege (PLP). The Principle of Least Privilege is a concept stating that any user should have only the permissions necessary to do his or her job. In the corporate world this prevents users from "privilege escalation" (performing tasks that are not within their scope of work). For the home-user it applies to the operating system itself through Windows 7's User Access Control (UAC). At the home-user level this means creating and using a Standard User account rather than performing day-to-day operations on an Administrator account. Using the Windows Administrator account is perhaps one of the most common errors I see committed by home computer users, and one that has caused me endless frustration in "fixing" friends' computers that have become thoroughly infected with malware.

Windows 7 has two different types of accounts: Standard User and Administrator. A Standard User account has all of the necessary privileges for most of us to do the jobs we do on home PCs. Even though I work at a computer daily, I only rarely log into an Administrator account. User accounts have the privileges necessary to do most day-to-day tasks including creating, opening, editing, and saving documents, browsing the Internet, etc. There are a very small handful of things a User account does not have the privileges for, the most important of which is installing programs.

Because Administrator accounts have the necessary privileges to install programs, executable files may be able to run on an Administrator account without having to ask permission. If permission is required, malicious executables are sometimes capable of tricking the user into agreeing to install the program. Standard User accounts have fewer permissions, and the most important permission a Standard User account lacks is the ability to install programs without permission from the administrator. When a malicious program attempts to install itself on a Standard User account, a prompt will appear asking for permission from the Administrator (and the administrator's password if the account is password protected). Seeing a password prompt alone should be enough to make a user question whether he or she really wants to allow the executable to run.

When you purchase a new Windows computer, the only account that is enabled by default is an Administrator account. Many home users will never create another account, choosing instead to work only inside this account. This is problematic as it makes the computer more susceptible to malware and viruses. To set up a user account, navigate to: **Start** >> **Control Panel** >> **User Accounts and Family Safety** >> **Add or Remove User Accounts** >> **Create a New Account**.

Figure 1.1: The Windows 7 Control Panel dialogue allowing the creation, deletion, and modification of accounts. All of these functions can be done within a Standard User account with permission from an Administrator in the form of a correctly-entered password.

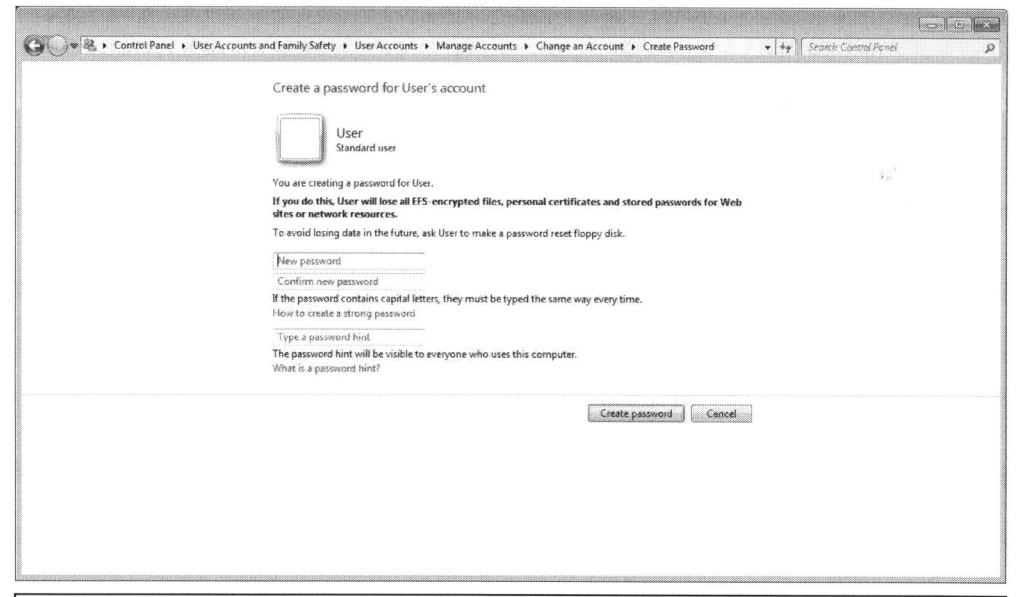

Figure 1.2: The dialogue for creation of a password for a Windows 7 Standard User account. Even though these accounts offer only a modicum of security overall, they should be password protected.

Both User and Administrator accounts should be password protected. To set up passwords for these accounts, navigate to: **Start** >> **Control Panel** >> **User Accounts and Family Safety** >> **Add or Remove User Accounts**, then click on the icon for the selected account as shown in Figure 1.1. When the expanded menu for that account appears, select **Create a Password**

The passwords for administrator accounts and user accounts should be different, and passwords will be discussed at length later in this book. Though I recommend using long, complex passwords in most cases, I recommend (and use) easily memorable passwords that are quick and easy to type for the Administrator and User accounts. This is because the password protection on these accounts offers very little actual security, but having a password can hinder anyone attempting to install malicious software on your device.

User and Administrator Account names: There is a tendency to give Standard User and Administrator Account distinctive names; for instance, a family of four might name their accounts Justin, Sarah, David, and Ashley. Unfortunately, these unique account names associate themselves with many things. For example, Microsoft Office records the creator of file by recording the User account name under which it was created in the metadata. If you send out files (of any type) this may leak information about you or your family. For this reason I strongly encourage using bland generic names such as Administrator, User 1, User 2, and so on

OS UPDATES

Keeping your software up-to-date is another incredibly important step in securing a computer. As software ages, security holes are discovered in it, and attacks are written to take advantage of these holes. Though software updates are occasionally released to add features and to deal with bugs, they are very often written specifically to patch security holes. If your software is outdated it is vulnerable to holes that are, in addition to everything else, well-publicized by virtue of the fact that a patch exists to fix them.

Microsoft releases updates to Windows on "Patch Tuesday," the second (and occasionally the fourth) Tuesday of each month. If a serious security vulnerability is discovered critical updates may fall outside of this cycle. There are several options for how you update Windows: You can allow all the updates to take place automatically in the background (the easiest option), download all the updates and individually choose which you will install and when you will install them, or download and install fully manually. There are some advantages to fully automating and some to doing it yourself.

When installing updates automatically you enjoy several advantages; this is the method I recommend for most users. First, all of the updates will be installed at the earliest possible opportunity, meaning the computer will spend the minimum time running outdated software. I also like the idea of fire-and-forget solutions; updating happens on its own and you don't have to worry about it. On the other hand, downloaded updates that install automatically will install the very next time your turn your computer off. If this happens to be an inopportune time (i.e., moments before you leave work) and these updates take a great deal of time to install (as they occasionally do), you may be stuck for a while waiting for them. Also, not all of the updates may be necessary or desirable for you.

The downside to going fully manual (searching for, downloading, and installing updates manually) is that important updates may not be installed in a timely manner or may be missed altogether. Further, I like the idea of the computer doing things for me when possible, but on the other hand I like the freedom of being able to choose which updates I install and when.

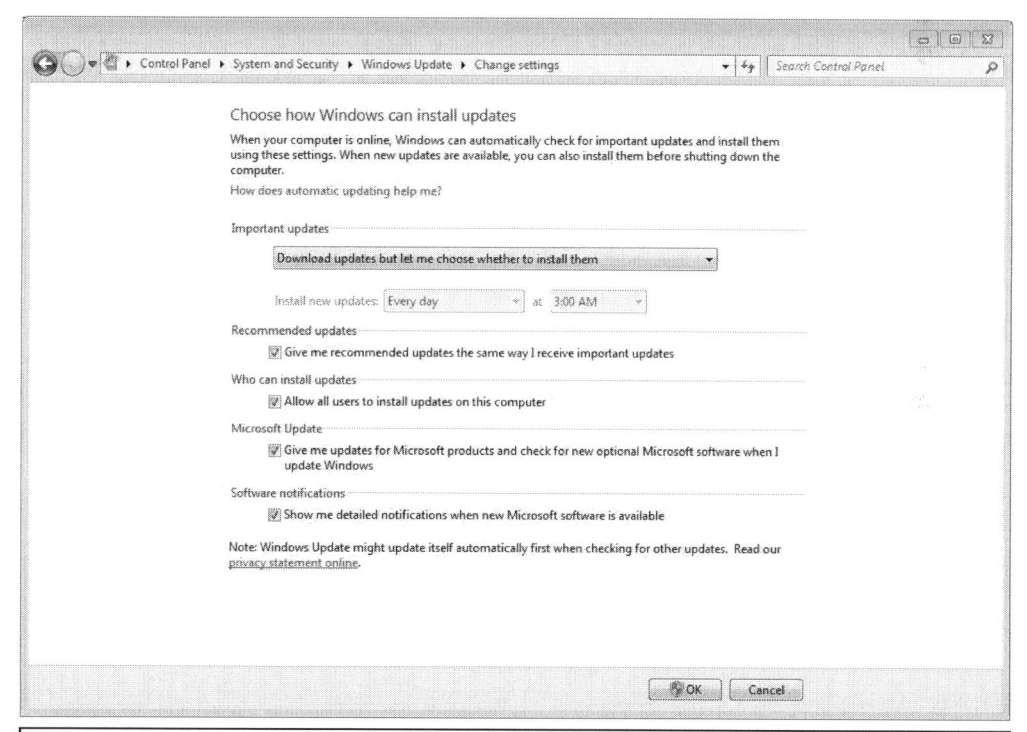

Figure 1.3: The Control Panel dialogue allowing you to change how updates are downloaded and installed. For power users I recommend allowing automatic downloads, but choosing which ones to install.

The solution I prefer is to split the difference: I have Windows check for updates, download them all automatically, and then I can choose which ones to install. If an update is of questionable use to me I will read the bulletin and decide whether or not I need to install it (I will always install security updates and you should, too). Once they are downloaded I can choose to install them at the time that is most convenient for me.

To change update settings, navigate to **Start>>Control Panel>>System and Security>>Windows Update** and select **Change Settings** from the left sidebar. Open the dropdown menu. If you want to go fully automatic (Windows downloads and installs updates as soon as they are available) choose **Install updates automatically (recommended)** as shown in Figure 1.3. If you prefer to go with my technique, choose **Download updates but let me choose whether to install them.**

APPLICATION UPDATES

Just as vulnerabilities in the operating system may be exploited, so, too, can security holes in your installed applications be used as attack vectors. It is important to keep all software up-to-date.

Patch My PC Updater: Patch My PC is a very simple application that scans all of your software for updates. Patch My PC runs live so it does not need to be installed to work, a feature that I greatly appreciate. Simply download the application, allow it to execute by entering your Administrator account password, and it will scan all of your programs for available updates. Once the scan is complete you can download and install all necessary updates through Patch My PC as shown in Figure 1.4.

Patch My PC also has a number of other options. There is a menu from which you can select programs to not check. For instance, I run a legacy version of Eraser and do not want it updated (see Chapter 4 for more information on Eraser). It also includes an uninstaller for removing programs, and it can be used to remove programs that launch on startup. I run this application once per week to ensure my programs are not outdated.

Patch My PC is available at: https://patchmypc.net/download

Secunia PSI (Personal Software Inspector) is another option if you want a second opinion. Simply open the application, enter your Administrator password (Administrator privileges are required to run it), and click "Scan Now." Similar to Windows Update, Secunia allows the user some discretion in downloading and installing updates. The options are to "Update programs automatically (recommended)", "Download updates but let me choose whether to update", and "Check for updates but let me choose whether to download and update (not recommended)." Again, I prefer the flexibility of the second option; any necessary updates will be downloaded, but I still have the option to choose when to install them.

Secunia PSI is free and available at: http://secunia.com/vulnerability_scanning/personal/

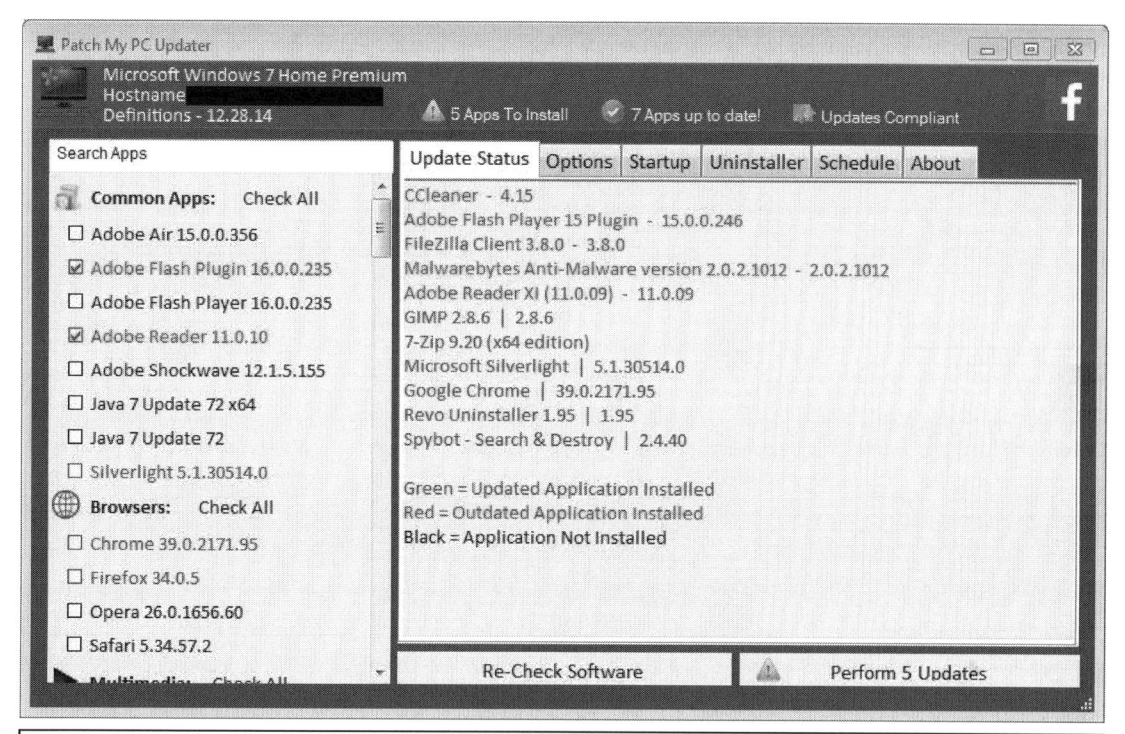

Figure 1.4: The results of a Patch My PC Updater Scan on my computer. Clicking "Perform x Updates" (lower right) will download and install all the needed updates quickly and easily.

ANTIVIRUS

At this point it seems that nearly everyone, and certainly everyone with an interest in computer security, is aware that a computer running Windows 7 should also run an antivirus application. Literally thousands of viruses are written and deployed on a daily basis to exploit the Windows 7 operating system, and the consequences of your computer becoming infected with one are potentially dire. Viruses and malware come in all degrees of seriousness; they can range from merely annoying to posing serious threats to the user's personal privacy, financial information, data integrity, and more.

Anti-virus tools are primarily preventative in nature, detecting viruses and other malware programs before they have a chance to be installed on the host machine, and there are various paid anti-virus tools on the market. Though paid antivirus applications do a good job (and some have very comprehensive suites that perform a great many functions), I still prefer free antivirus software. Fortunately there are numerous, free antivirus options available that compete very well against the premium, paid suites. Whether using a free or paid solution, antivirus definitions (the list of malicious software and behaviors it scans for) must be kept up-to-date for the program to be effective. All of the antivirus software listed here is free, and offers a good level of protection.

SOFTWARE SOURCING

Software is expensive. It is tempting to download or torrent cracked versions of expensive software and get them for free. But what are you really getting when you download a pirated version of an expensive application?

The answer is probably a version that looks and performs similarly to the original software but whose code has been modified. This is an extremely popular attack vector for malware and though it hurts up front, I recommend actually purchasing a copy of any software you must have on your machine. Of course the most secure option is to limit the number of applications on your computer to the absolute minimum. The more applications you have, the more potential security holes your system has. These security holes may be legitimate errors in the code or intentionally placed malware.

Avast Free Antivirus: This is my preferred antivirus program. Avast is easy to set up, offers excellent real-time scanning, and consistently performs at the top of independent tests for detection of viruses in the wild. Although Avast is feature-rich and allows power-users a good range of settings to modify, it is still amply capable in the default configuration and requires very little intervention, which is perfect for inexperienced or disinterested users.

Avast gives users real-time protection against viruses, and is very responsive in handling those threats. In addition, Avast offers on-demand scanning of specific files, drives, or devices. It also offers network scanning that will examine your home wireless network to alert you to vulnerabilities within it. Avast works on a freemium model; paid versions of Avast offer a number of other features.

My biggest complaint about Avast is its annoying voiceover audio alerts, which can be loud and unexpected (and in my opinion are usually completely unnecessary). Although an alert is desirable if an infection or attack is detected, many of them are simply to let you know that the virus definitions have been updated, or some other mundane task has been completed. The good news is that you can easily turn these alerts off by opening the Avast interface, and clicking Settings at the bottom of the left sidebar. Under General Settings, scroll down to Sounds and uncheck the box that says "Use voiceover sounds."

Avast Free Antivirus is available at: http://www.avast.com/index

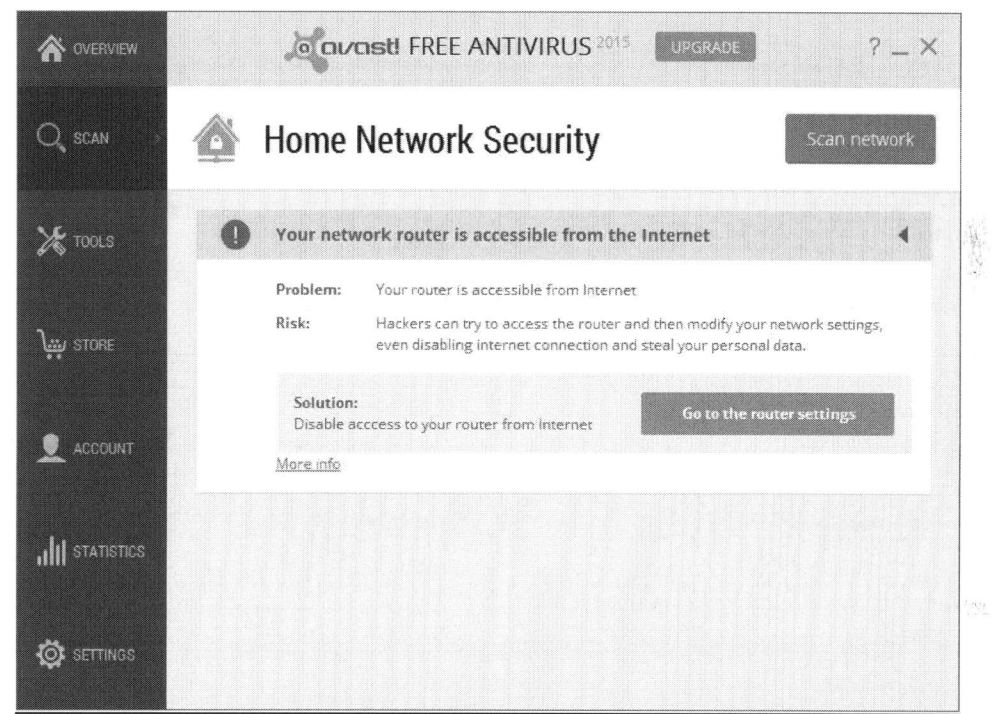

Figure 1.5: The results of a Home Network Security scan with Avast Free Antivirus. This is an incredibly useful feature and one that I use frequently. Note the simplicity of the graphic user interface.

Bitdefender Free: This is a very lightweight antivirus application, and what I would consider a total "set it and forget it" solution. Performing extremely well in independent testing but lacking many of the bells and whistles (that may be desirable to power-users) of larger antivirus tools, Bitdefender Free still has an excellent track record. This is, in my opinion, the perfect tool to install on older machines or the computers of less technically-literate friends and family members.

Bitdefender Free is available at: http://www.bitdefender.com/solutions/free.html

A word on **Microsoft Security Essentials**: I love the idea of an antivirus software that is made expressly for its host operating system, and Microsoft Security Essentials (MSE) is Windows' answer. The MSE user interface is extremely user-friendly, making the program enticing. Unfortunately, in 2012 and 2013, MSE did not perform exceptionally well at detecting viruses in the wild. In fact, it performed exceptionally poorly, and I would not recommend it for this reason. That doesn't mean it won't improve, and I still have a lot of hope for MSE, but at the time of this writing much better options are available.

IMPORTANT NOTE

All of the antivirus and anti-malware applications listed below require you connect to the internet to download them before installation. Absolute best practice says never connect to the internet without running antivirus which presents a catch-22. In reality it is probably ok, but I recommend one of the following:

Either connect to the internet and navigate **directly** to the links provided here and antivirus applications, or (for the truly paranoid) download the software onto another computer and transfer it via removable media such as a DVD/R (best) or USB flash drive. Immediately upon installing the application, connect the computer to the internet and allow the antivirus definitions to update so it can begin providing real-time protection against current threats.

ANTI-MALWARE

I frequently get asked by friends and family members to "take a look" at a computer because they think it might have a virus. The symptoms are usually the same: the computer is running slowly, they get tons of pop-ups, and/or instead of their internet browser going to Google.com, it instead goes to some other search engine homepage (like Search Conduit or Vosteran), etc. While the computer *may* actually have a virus, what it much more likely has is a pretty good set of some other forms of malware. Malware is a general term, and though a virus is technically malware, not all malware is a virus.

There are various types of malware including viruses, Trojans, worms, adware, nagware, ransomware, and spyware. Many of them are merely annoying, and present themselves in the form of undesired search engines and home pages, internet browser toolbars, popups, and in other disagreeable ways. Some can be much more than a mere annoyance. Cryptoware, for instance, is a form of malware that installs itself and begins encrypting all your files. Once all of your files are encrypted, a ransom is demanded in exchange for the decryption key to your files. If you don't pay, all your files may be lost forever.

Some malware allows its controller to access your computer directly. Depending on the capabilities of the malware, the attacker may be able to watch and listen to your webcam and microphone, log every keystroke you make (capturing your login information, content of your emails, internet search terms, etc.), or harvest information like contact lists and calendars off of your machine. Your computer may be turned into a "zombie" or a "bot," a remote server that carries out the bidding of the botnet controller. Not only may this slow down your machine considerably, it also makes your computer a participant in distributed denial of service (DDoS) attacks, a spam server, or even a child pornography server. If your computer is compromised it may take on a life of its own, and this could have very real consequences for you, the owner, in real life.

Anti-malware differs slightly from antivirus. While antivirus software scans in real-time for viruses and other malware and is primarily preventative in nature, anti-malware scanners are primarily *reactive* in nature and scan for a broad array of threats that may have slipped through the antivirus suite or were inadvertently installed. Once the infections are discovered, these programs also have the capability to fully remove them from your system. Anti-malware scanners typically scan on an on-demand basis: whenever you elect to run a scan, simply open the anti-malware application, update its definitions, and allow it to scan your system. I recommend running one of these scans at least once a week. Although some of the programs mentioned below offer premium paid versions with real-time scanning, the free versions I recommend are not standalone and should always be used in conjunction with a real-time antivirus software like Avast.

There are three anti-malware scanners that I employ in my personal life, and install on the computers of friends who ask for my help. I use all three of them because each one has slightly different definitions, and each may catch something the others missed. This is not indicative of any one being better than the others; all of them are highly capable, but again, definitions vary, so I choose to build redundancy into my malware defenses. All three of the programs listed below are free.

Malwarebytes Anti-Malware (MBAM): Malwarebytes is perhaps the most user-friendly anti-malware application I have found, and it has an excellent, well-deserved reputation. Malwarebytes is consistently at or near the top of every independent test of anti-malware scanners.

Malwarebytes is free and available at: https://www.malwarebytes.org/mwb-download/

Spybot Search and Destroy: Spybot has been around for a long time. I remember using Spybot on my first computer back in the early 2000's. Like MBAM, Spybot has an extremely simple, user-friendly interface, and is extremely adept at finding and removing malware infections.

Spybot is free and available at: http://www.safer-networking.org/spybot2-own-mirror-1/

Comodo Cleaning Essentials (CCE): Comodo Cleaning Essentials is the most robust anti-malware application that I employ, and it also takes the longest to run. Some malware is programmed to adjust the definitions of antivirus programs so the malware remains undetected, and some malware will not allow antivirus or anti-malware applications to install. To bypass this tampering, CCE uses a live application that does not need to be installed to run; instead, it can run directly from its location on the hard drive. Once it is initiated, CCE updates its definitions and then shuts the computer down. Upon restart, CCE will scan for rootkits, which are deeply embedded infections that install very early in the boot process and that can remain undetectable to other anti-malware applications.

CCE is free and available at: https://www.comodo.com/business-security/network protection/cleaning_essentials.php

---

SCANNING ON A SCHEDULE

Using all three of the anti-malware scanners I recommend below consecutively would take a considerable amount of time, and using them all at the same time may cause conflicts between them. For this reason I use each one independently, using the following monthly schedule.

First Sunday:	Malwarebytes
Second Sunday:	Spybot Search & Destroy
Third Sunday:	Comodo Cleaning Essentials
Fourth Sunday:	Avast (using the on-demand scanner)

This schedule allows me to use all three of the anti-malware applications, plus the on-demand feature in Avast ensuring excellent coverage. For each one of these I run a full system scan, scanning every single file and application on the computer. This may seem like overkill to the average user; at a minimum I recommend choosing one of these programs and running it weekly.

WINDOWS FIREWALL

A firewall is an application that monitors and restricts the traffic coming into and going out of a computer's Internet connection. Though there are various free and paid firewall applications out there, the firewall packaged with Windows is extremely flexible and capable, and I see no need for third-party firewall applications. And, conveniently Windows Firewall comes turned on by default in Windows 7.

The Windows Firewall blocks incoming connections by default when you are connected to a public network. For this reason, I prefer to set all my networks up as Public (see Chapter 5 on Wi-Fi Security). There are many more features to Windows Firewall that advanced users can take advantage of, including the ability to block outbound traffic, force all traffic for certain programs through a VPN, etc. Though some of these advanced techniques such as using VPNs will be addressed more thoroughly later in this book (see Chapter 6), I feel a firewall is an important component of basic security and that it should be acknowledged early on.

If you would like to verify the settings in Windows Firewall, navigate to **Start>>Control Panel>>System and Security>>Windows Firewall**. The basic settings I recommend are shown in Figure 1.6.

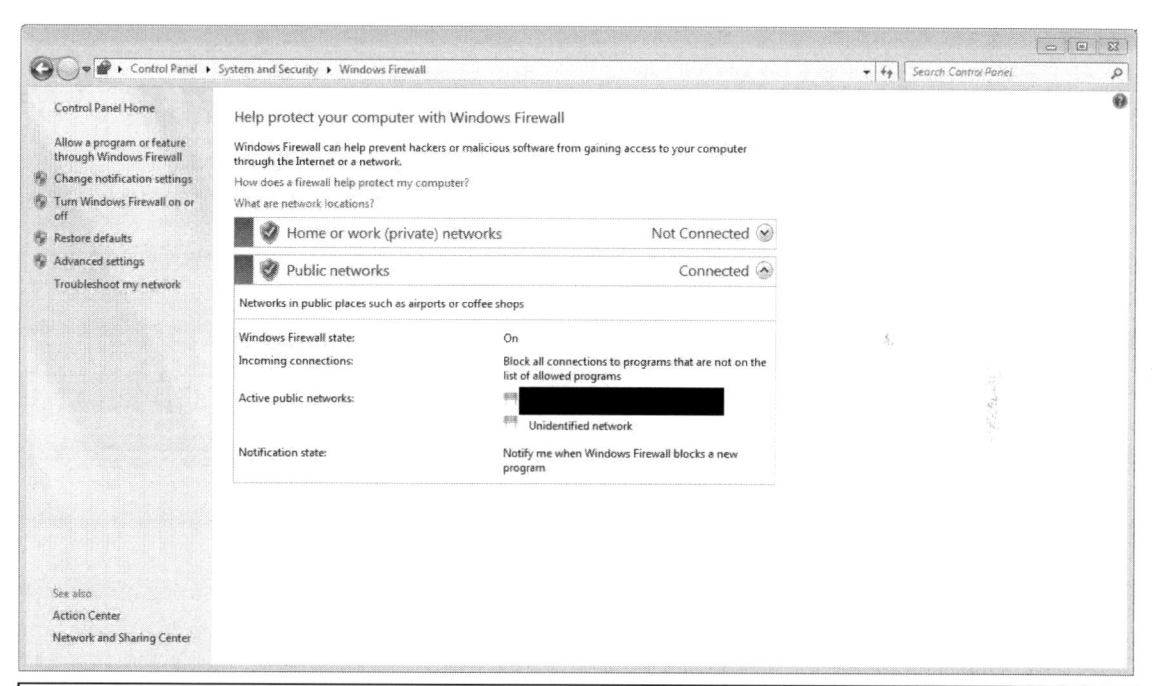

Figure 1.6: The basic configuration for Windows Firewall. The Firewall State is ON, Incoming Connections are set to block all except those that have been previously allowed, Active Networks should display the networks to which you are currently connected, and the Notification State is set to notify you when a new program is blocked.

MICROSOFT EMET

Microsoft's Enhanced Mitigation Experience Toolkit (EMET) is a very powerful, advanced application. Few laymen know about it, however, because it is intended primarily for use by administrators of large networks, but EMET can be used by individuals to secure their computers as well. EMET prevents infections, though not in the same way as an antivirus program. While an antivirus watches for certain types of behavioral signatures, EMET mitigates the very vulnerabilities these behaviors exploit in certain vulnerable programs (including Microsoft Office, Adobe Reader, and Oracle's Java) before they can fall victim to malicious exploits.

The EMET does so by providing protections, such as Data Execution Prevention (DEP), Mandatory Address Space Layout Allocation (ASLR), and Attack Surface Reduction (ASR). DEP, for example, is designed to prevent buffer overflow attacks by marking potentially vulnerable sectors of memory as non-executable. ASLR randomly shuffles application and system libraries in memory. This prevents attacks by making normally predictable file locations in memory unpredictable. Even if an attacker finds a vulnerability in your software, EMET may prevent the attack against it from being usable, and EMET can also work to minimize potential exploits through ASR. Attack Surface Reduction works to minimize the presence of exploitable programs; for example it can allow internet browsers to load without enabling the Java plugin, or allow Microsoft Word to load while still disabling Adobe Flash (the Java and Flash plugins are common attack vectors).

In addition, EMET also provides Structured Exception Handler Overwrite Protection (SEHOP), Heapspray Allocations, Null Page Allocation, Export Address Table Access Filtering (EAF), Bottom-Up Randomizations, and a number of Return Oriented Program (ROP) Mitigations. The scope of this book does not allow me to delve deeply into each of these mitigations, but the EMET User Manual offers explanations of each.

EMET is free from Microsoft, and the download includes a very good, 38-page user manual. To use EMET, download it from Microsoft's Technet site, install it. Out-of-the-box EMET offers a good degree of protection, especially for Windows applications. Many other applications on your computer may be secured with EMET, however. The configuration panel (see Figure 1.7) will list the programs that EMET can protect, and allow you to choose the options you wish to enable for each. Be aware that some options may render some programs inoperable, so a period of trial and error may be necessary until you are protected to the extent possible while still having the full, desired functionality of programs. Once installed and running EMET is very unobtrusive.

EMET is free and available at:: http://technet.microsoft.com/en-us/security/jj653751

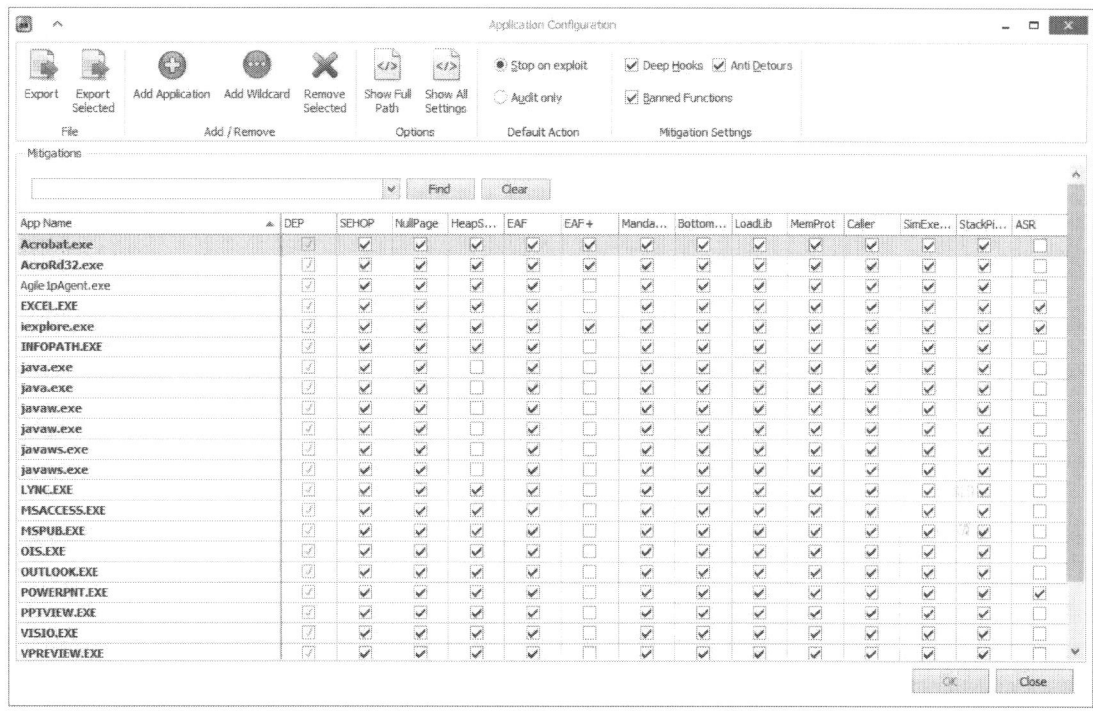

Figure 1.7: The list of applications and configuration options in Microsoft's Enhanced Mitigation Experience Toolkit. By default this application will protect many of your programs. It is both highly configurable and unobtrusive.

AUTOPLAY

Autorun and Autoplay are features in the Windows operating system that automatically start accessing and playing content when a removable hard drive, flash drive, or CD or DVD is inserted into the computer. This is a convenience feature designed to allow the operating system to record your preferences for various types of media. For example, if you insert a music CD Autoplay allows music to begin playing from the CD with no further input. Unfortunately this also introduces a vulnerability. If the CD in question (or SD card, flash drive, hard drive, or any other type of removable media) contains a malicious program, AutoRun and AutoPlay can allow the code to execute without asking for permission first. Disabling this feature is the first line of defense against this attack vector. AutoRun and AutoPlay should always be disabled by default; this is especially important if you use removable media across multiple devices.

To disable AutoPlay and Autorun, navigate to **Start>>Control Panel>>Hardware and**

Sound>>AutoPlay. This will open a Windows Explorer dialogue allowing you to choose what action the OS should take for various types of media. The first action you should take within this dialogue is to uncheck the box at the top that states "Use AutoPlay for all media and devices". Next, in the drop-down menu for each type of media, select "Take no action" and click Save. Your computer should no longer AutoPlay, but may ask you to make a decision if a form of media that the computer has not previously encountered is connected.

It is important to note that disabling AutoPlay does not completely entirely eliminate the threat of a USB device executing malicious code. It is still possible that malicious files can execute automatically upon the insertion of a USB device. For this reason caution is strongly recommended when using USB devices. I personally recommend never using a USB device that you do not personally own and control; hot-swapping USB devices is a significant cause of infections and helps them spread.

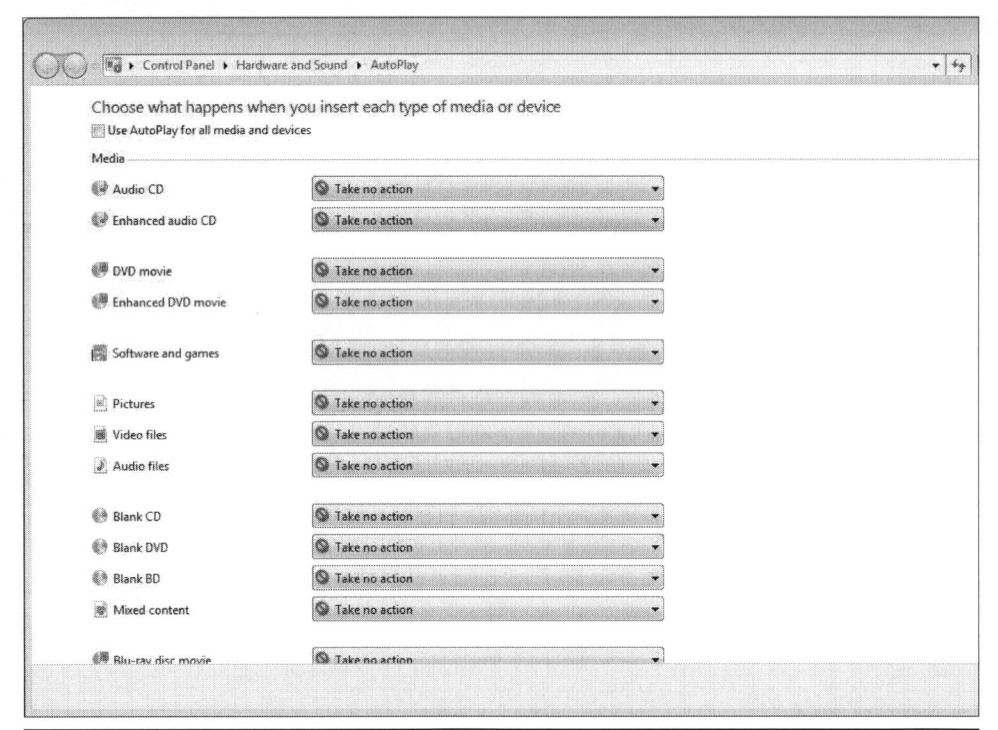

Figure 1.8: Turning off AutoPlay in Windows 7. Selecting "Take no action" will allow you to make the choice what to do with media each time it is connected. Also ensure the "Use AutoPlay for all media and devices" is unchecked.

BEST PRACTICE: DISPLAYING FILE EXTENSIONS

By default, Windows hides the file extensions of most files from its users. The filename extension is the three- or four-letter appendage at the end of most file names (such as .pdf, .jpeg, or .docx), and it is there simply to inform Windows of the encoding of the file which is commonly used to determine which program will be used to open it. I am not sure of the reason Windows hides these, other than out of a (largely correct) assumption that most of its customer base doesn't care about the file extension or need to see it. For security reasons, it is a good idea to keep file extensions visible.

An attacker who wants you to open a file containing a malicious payload will likely wish to make the file look like one that you would usually open. For example, let's say an attacker wants the file to look like a text file created in Notepad. The usual file extension would be .txt, so he or she could simply name the document MALWARE.txt. If file extensions are not displayed on your computer, you cannot see the real file extension and may only see the "fake" one that is part of the root name of the file. The full filename, including the extension, would make clear that something was wrong with this document: MALWARE.txt.exe. Further, attackers can easily make the malicious file's icon appear to be a standard Notepad icon (even though the file is an .exe), making it reassuring to the recipient, and increasing the likelihood it will be opened and ran.

Displaying file extensions is an important step, but it does little good if the user does not take the time to verify the file extension before opening a file. Pay close attention to the file extension, especially when opening a file downloaded from the Internet or received from a questionable source. If the file is questionable, consider scanning it with antivirus and anti-malware software as described in the next section.

To display filename extensions, open any folder on your computer; at the top right-hand side of the folder are several drop-down menus. Click **Organize**, and within this menu click **Folder and search options**. This will open a new dialogue called Folder Options. In this dialogue, click on the **View** tab and scroll down to **Hide extensions for known file types** as shown in Figure 1.9. Uncheck this box and click **Apply** to accept this change.

BEST PRACTICE: SCANNING REMOVABLE MEDIA

Universal Serial Bus (USB) devices are incredibly convenient, and none are more popular, omnipresent, or common than the USB flash drive. Because of this, flash drives are also a popular attack vector. They are plugged in and swapped between machines frequently in an office environment which lets them spread viruses, Trojans, and other malware freely. Even a USB flash drive that is not infected can become a vector if it is plugged into an infected computer. Flash drives can be targeted at the employees of a company by being "lost" in a place they will be found and affixed with an enticing label (imagine finding one on the floor of your office labeled "employee performance reviews" or "year-end bonuses"…or perhaps, better yet, "pR0n"), almost guaranteeing they will be plugged in and used. Further, many people cannot resist the simple allure of a free USB flash drive.

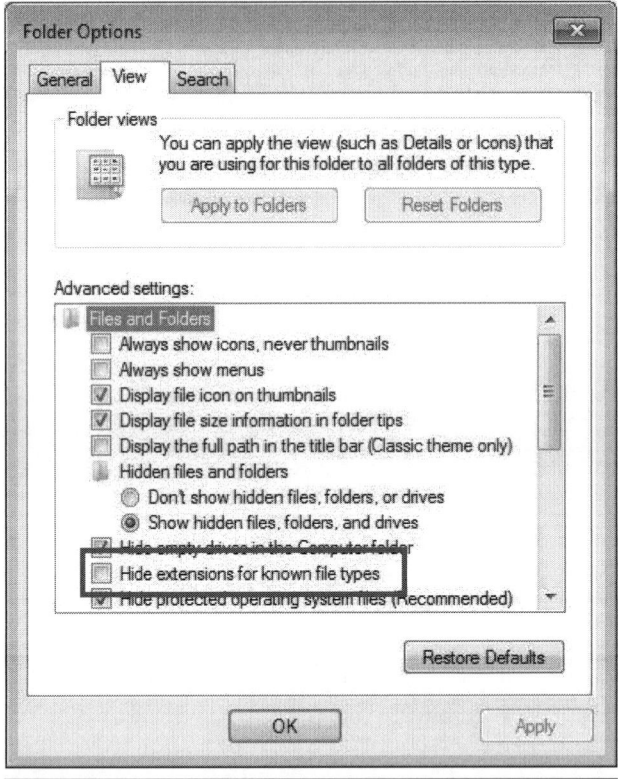

Figure 1.9: The Folder Options dialogue allowing you to display extensions for known file types.

The absolute best practice for found USB drives is to avoid using at all. Any USB devices that *are* used should be scanned beforehand. With AutoRun and AutoPlay disabled, the likelihood of malware executing is greatly reduced, but not totally guaranteed. Before you open the drive or the files on it you should scan the drive for malware with your antivirus suite. This is fairly easily accomplished from the right-click context menu.

When you insert a USB device, SD card, CD/DVD, or other removable media into your machine, and it is recognized by the computer, navigate to My Computer, locate the device, and right-click on it. If you are using Avast Free Antivirus, a prompt will appear in the context menu to "Scan F\:" (or whatever drive letter it is assigned). Depending on the size of the device, this may take some time as the antivirus software scans all the documents and applications on the drive against its virus definitions. Additionally, Spybot Search and Destroy may be configured to show up in the right-click context menu, allowing it to be used to scan removable media as well. I am a fan of the redundant approach to security, and though it may seem onerous to scan a flash drive, hard drive, or SD card with two separate applications, it is cheap insurance

Though it is probably not a bad idea to scan *all* removable media every time, it is also probably not necessary. However, there are a couple of instances in which it is crucially important. The first is instances of new media being added to your computing ecosystem, whether a brand new device you own, a friend swapping some files with you, or an office environment in which files are being shared more or less constantly. Each time a new device or one that has been used on another computer is plugged into your machine, it should be scanned. The next is when previously "trusted" media have been used outside of your closed ecosystem and may have picked up an infection. Took your external hard drive to work? It should be scanned before trusting it again.

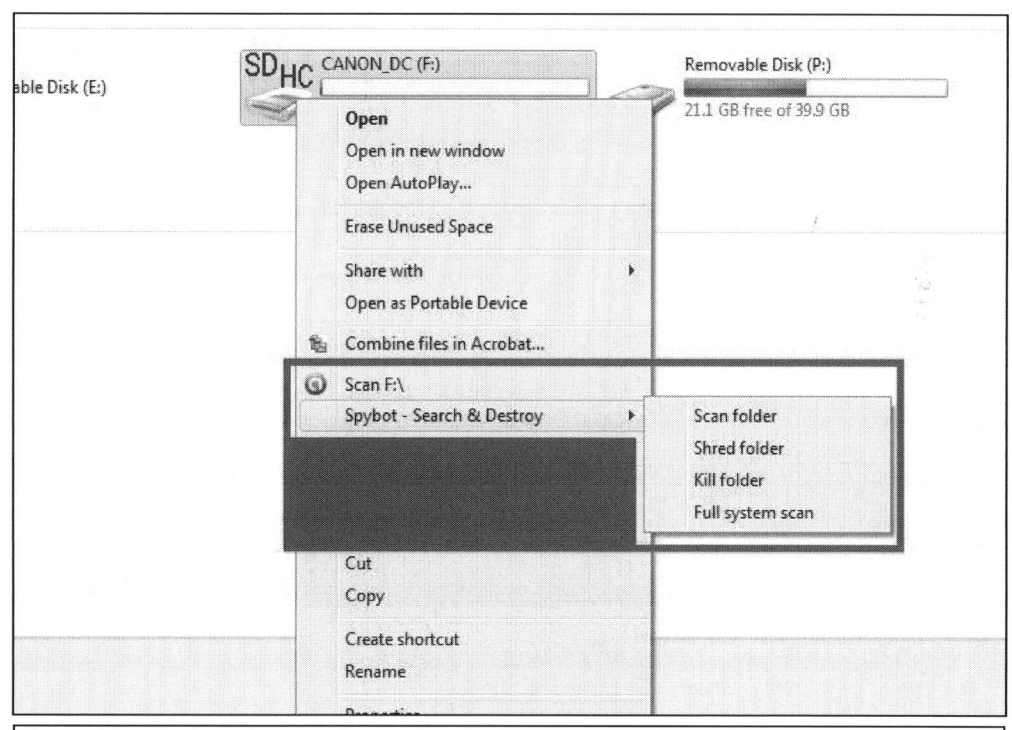

Figure 1.10: Options for scanning an SD Card (or any other type of media). The card can be scanned for malware with Avast (top) or several other options can be selected with Spybot Search and Destroy as shown in the expanded menu at right.

BEST PRACTICE: REMOVING BLOATWARE

If you purchased your computer from one of the major manufacturers, there is a very good chance that it is clogged with bloatware. Bloatware is the almost universally useless third-party software packaged with Windows by hardware manufacturers. Though all of this software is intended to at least *appear* helpful, there are a number of disadvantages to bloatware. The first is system performance: more applications running at once require more processor power, leaving less processor power to do what you really want to do. Superflous programs also create system "clutter," slowing your computer and its startup process by adding thousands of lines of code to the registry.

The next disadvantage of bloatware (and the one I find most abhorrent) is its effect on privacy. Many of these programs are intrusive, constantly prompting you to register your device, send information to the manufacturer, etc. Registering the computer is unnecessary (your receipt is legally acceptable proof of purchase for warranty purposes), and sending information back to the manufacturer is just a data-mining and marketing scheme that benefits them, not you.

A shocking and frightening example of this was revealed during the writing of this book: A prominent PC manufacturer had shipped computers between October and December of 2014 with an ad-serving software called Superfish. Superfish automatically and quietly breaks all HTTPS connections made over the computer (more details on HTTPS vulnerabilities are available in Chapter 5). This program was purportedly included in the OEM software load to allow the manufacturer to serve advertisements on encrypted web pages (which by necessity allows them to see the page). As if this weren't bad enough, it also exposed the user to potential third-party, man-in-the-middle attacks. Superfish is not limited to these particular machines; your computer may contract it elsewhere, but this is an incredibly shocking example of a machine that has shipped from the factory with what amounts to pre-installed malware.

Bloatware can be avoided altogether through a couple different methods. Computers purchased through small companies that custom build computers typically don't package bloatware into the OS. Another option would be to purchase a clean, OEM version of Windows 7 separately. This is the surest, though most costly option, as operating systems are not inexpensive, especially when added to the cost of a computer that already has an operating system. The third, and most cost effective option, if you already own or are purchasing a laptop from a major manufacturer, is to remove the offending applications yourself. Though you may not get all of them, you should try. If you have any questions about whether you should remove a particular application or not, do a quick Internet search on it. If it isn't critical to the OS, get rid of it.

Applications can be removed manually by navigating to **Start>>Control Panel>>Programs>>Uninstall a Program**. Each application can be culled individually, allowing you to selectively remove them one at a time. When doing this, it can sometimes be difficult to tell which application is bloatware, and which ones are required by your system. When in doubt, do some research before uninstalling a program that may be necessary for the operating system to function correctly. This is not my favorite method of cleaning; it is difficult to catch everything, some programs resist being uninstalled, and it can be difficult to sort the necessary from the unnecessary. It doesn't all have to be done manually, however. There are some programs out there that can help.

Decrap My Computer: Decrap would be my choice for cleaning a brand new computer. Decrap is a very simple, intuitive program that scans your computer for *all* unnecessary software. If run in fully-automatic mode, it will remove everything that is not critical to the function of the machine. Even when running on a brand new computer, I would still use Decrap in the manual mode, allowing me the opportunity to select programs to remove rather than having it done automatically.

Decrap is free and available at http://www.decrap.org/

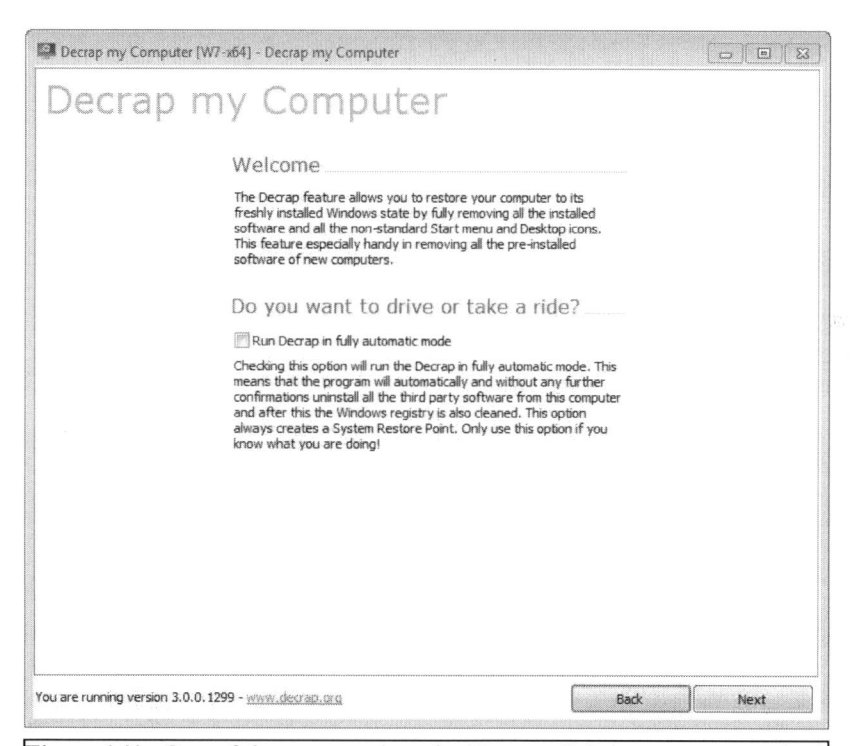

Figure 1.11: One of the setup options for Decrap. It is important to uncheck the "Run Decrap in automatic mode" button unless you are on a brand new machine as some of your programs may be uninstalled.

Revo Uninsaller: Some programs simply do not want to be uninstalled. The programs that make uninstallation purposefully and exceptionally difficult usually do so for a reason: they are probably malware in some form or fashion. When I find programs like these, I use a Revo Uninstaller to remove them. Revo is a powerful, dedicated uninstaller. Not only does it remove the unwanted program, it also gets rid of the remnants of the program that are typically left behind by the Windows Uninstaller. Revo is also much faster than the Windows uninstaller, has a clean interface, and is simple to use. Revo offers a more feature-rich, paid professional version as well.

Revo Uninstaller is free and available at:
http://www.revouninstaller.com/revo_uninstaller_free_download.html

BEST PRACTICE: SLEEP, HIBERNATE, OR SHUT DOWN?

The Sleep, Hibernate, and Shut Down functions all make your computer's fan stop and screen go dark, but beyond that they all do significantly different things. Because of the differences in what each of these modes do, they all impact security slightly differently.

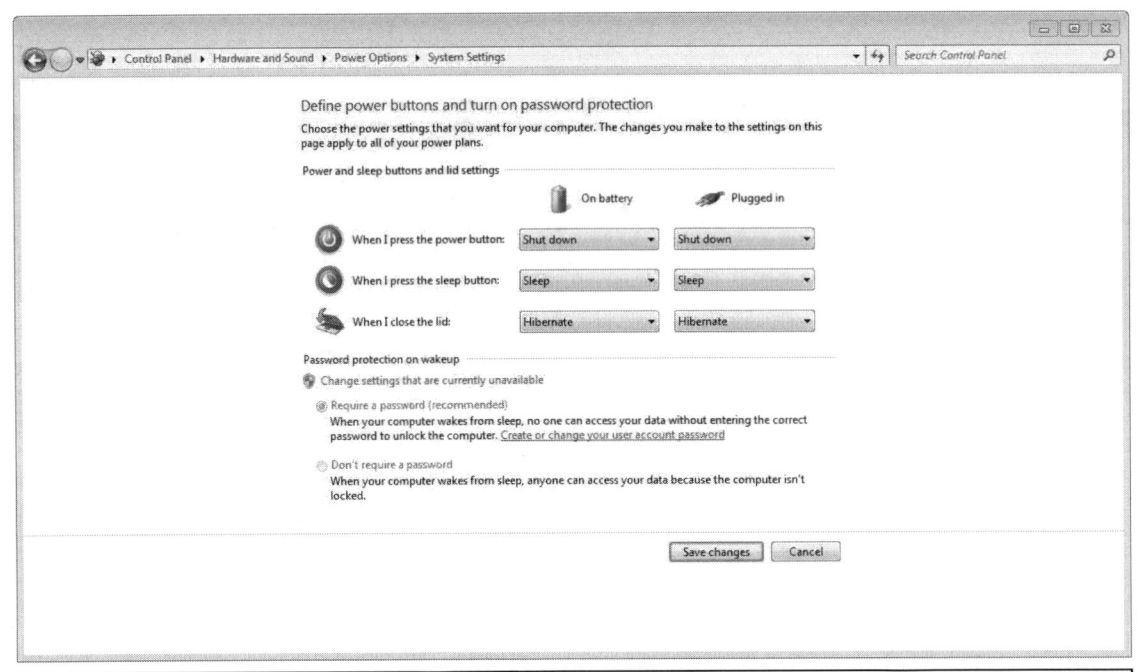

Figure 1.12: Windows 7 power options defining what action is taking upon pressing the power button, sleep button, or closing the lid. Be aware of the security implications of each of these decisions.

Sleep: Sleep mode is the most convenient and allows you to quickly "wake" the computer with a mouse click or key stroke, but it also consumes the most power. When the computer is in sleep mode the hard drive is shut down, but power is still supplied to the RAM (Random Access Memory) so programs can be kept open and unsaved modifications to documents can remain in volatile memory. Anyone with physical access to your machine and the ability to access your User account can access any programs and documents that may be open.

One possible benefit to the Sleep mode is that many applications for cracking or bypassing Windows account passwords require rebooting the computer. Rebooting the device would close any programs that were open, as well as risk losing any unsaved information. If your attacker is worried that his or her actions may be discovered, shutting down a sleeping machine may be an unacceptable risk. For this reason it is important to know your threat profile. If your adversary is highly sophisticated or does not care if his or her actions are revealed, this may offer very little actual security.

Hibernate: Hibernate is somewhat less convenient than the Sleep mode. In this mode the device's power button must be pressed and held to wake it. Upon "waking" the computer you will have to enter both the full-disk encryption password (if your computer is full-disk encrypted; see Chapter 3) and the account password, similar to a full reboot (though waking from Hibernate is typically somewhat faster). Hibernate mode uses very little power. When waking from Hibernate mode the computer will restore all documents and applications that were open when you entered Hibernate mode, but not by storing the data in RAM. Instead, it will write this information, unencrypted, to your hard drive. If your computer is subject to a forensic examination later, it is very likely that this information may be located and retrieved, provided the full-disk encryption key is compromised and access to the machine is gained. Because information is written to non-volatile memory (the hard drive), I always run an erasure of all free space after my computer has hibernated (see Chapter 4).

Shut Down: When a computer is fully Shut Down the hard drive is powered off, the power to RAM is removed (allowing its contents to be lost), and the computer is turned fully "off". Shut Down uses the least power, but requires the longest startup period when the computer is booted back up. Shut Down also encourages you to close all applications and save all data prior to executing, which, while inconvenient, ensures that you delete it or save it to a secure (encrypted, see Chapter 3) location. Upon reboot the full-disk encryption password is required, as well as the password for the account that you wish to open. From a security standpoint, this is the safest mode provided your device is fully encrypted.

Regardless of which of these options you choose to employ on a daily basis, there is one that should *not* be chosen: leaving your computer running and connected to the Internet. The more time your computer spends running with a live internet connection, the greater its attack surface and the risk that it may be compromised by hackers. If you do choose to leave your desktop running at all times, you should kill its internet connection when it is not in use. This can be done manually on the machine, or through router settings that automatically disable Internet connectivity at predetermined times (see Chapter 5).

You can choose which of these three actions are taken when you press your computer's power or sleep button (if your computer has one, or close the lid of your laptop). Navigate to **Start>>Control Panel>>System and Security>>Power Options**. On the left-hand menu, select "**Choose what the power buttons do**". Upon taking any of these actions, the computer may be instructed to sleep, hibernate, or shut down.

BEST PRACTICE: LIMIT STARTUP APPLICATIONS

Many of the applications installed on a Windows 7 computer will attempt to run on startup. This is ostensibly to allow you faster access to the application when you need it since it will already be running in the background, and to allow the program to be "always on" so it can pull updates, etc. In some cases, these applications running in the background may capture information about your Internet usage and browsing habits, compromising your privacy. In many instances, these programs may be sending information over the Internet, which can potentially compromise your security. And in all instances, having an excessive number of programs running on startup will slow your machine, making it more difficult to know what processes are running, and if they *should* be running at a given time.

I recommend paring down the number of applications that automatically launch at start up to the bare minimum. Before you can begin removing these programs you have to see what they are. To do so, open the Windows start menu and type in "cmd.exe" (without quotation marks). This will open up a windows command terminal into which you can type commands directly. Then type "msconfig" (again, without quotations). This will open a new, tabbed interface. Click on the startup tab to see the list of programs that launch when booting Windows.

Each application that runs on startup will have a check in the box beside it. To disable an application from launching on boot, uncheck this box. When you have finished, click the "Apply" button at the bottom of the interface. At this point it is worth mentioning that you should not uncheck startup applications unless you are absolutely certain they are not needed. Mistakenly disabling the driver for your keyboard, touchpad, or monitor may make your computer very difficult to use until you fix the issue. If you are in doubt, conduct an internet search on the name of the application to find out what it does and whether it is necessary before disabling it.

I should also point out that I do want certain applications to launch on startup. Eraser, a secure file deletion program that will be discussed in Chapter 4, is nice to have on startup so I can use it natively in Windows Explorer. If the application is not necessary for the sound functioning of my machine, or not one that you have chosen to execute on startup, disable it.

CCleaner (discussed in Chapter 4) can also be used to remove programs from startup.

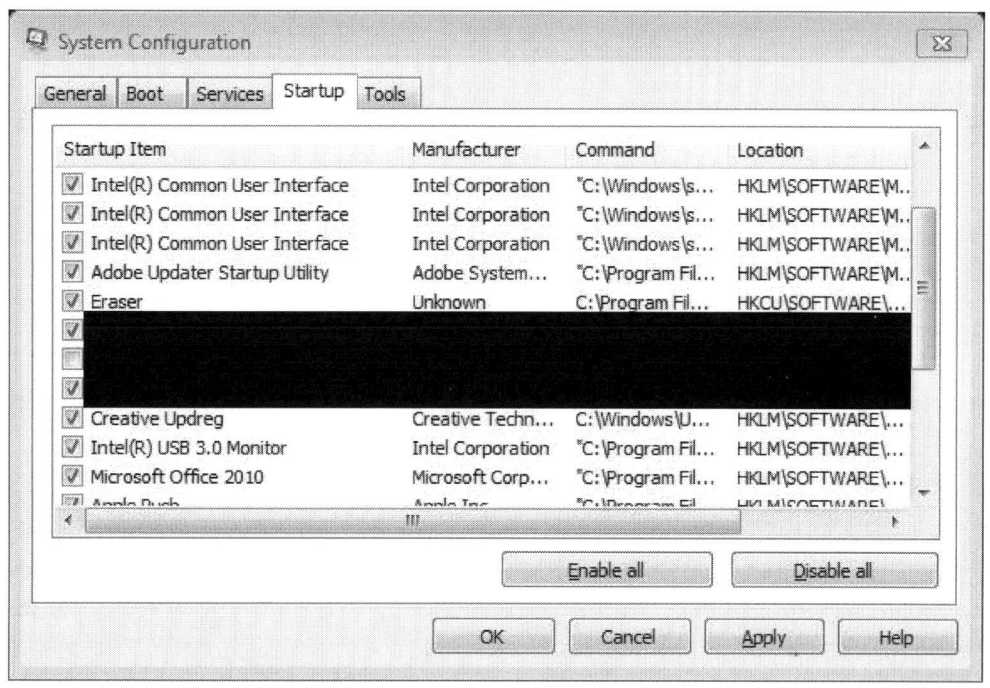

Figure 1.13: The applications that run by execute on startup on a Windows 7 computer. This list should be kept to an absolute minimum.

A WORD ON BIOS SECURITY

Some security experts recommend using a password to protect the BIOS. The BIOS frequently offers password protections that prevent the computer from booting without entering a password, or prevent anyone from changing the boot order of the machine without a password (preventing it from being booted from a USB drive or optical disk). Though this is some protection, I consider it a fairly soft one relative to full-disk encryption. Because of this, I do not cover BIOS passwords or other BIOS security measures as I consider them superfluous.

If you do not choose to enable full-disk encryption (covered in Chapter 3), I strongly recommend setting a BIOS password (tutorials with specifics for your make/model device can be found online). Be aware that there are multiple ways to bypass or break BIOS passwords; the security they provide is minimal.

SUMMARY

The steps taken in this chapter are merely the basics, the absolute minimum effort that <u>everyone</u> should put into securing their computer. These steps will make your computer safer, minimize your risks of being contracting malware, and keep your machine running well. If you do nothing else listed in this book, take the steps listed in this chapter:

- o Set up and user a Standard User account, and password protect all accounts
- o Keep your OS and applications updated
- o Run antivirus and scan with anti-malware applications on a regular, scheduled basis
- o Ensure your Windows Firewall is enabled
- o Use Microsoft's very powerful EMET
- o Disable AutoPlay
- o Display file extensions and verify the file extension before opening a file
- o Scan removable media before transferring files from them
- o Understand the differences between Sleep, Hibernate, and Shut down and choose the one(s) that make the most sense for your security situation
- o Limit the applications that launch automatically on boot

A thorough understanding of the basics is necessary for a strong security posture. Without the basics, the security of the advanced tools and techniques to follow is in doubt. The following chapter will cover some more basic best practices that should be widely employed and must be discussed before delving into more advanced topics.

CHAPTER 2:
AUTHENTICATION

Authentication is the process of verifying that a user is who he or she claims to be. In the Windows 7 operating system, the "claim" made about identity is the account you attempt to log in to. If you are attempting to log in to that account, Windows assumes you must be the owner. The authentication process is complete when the correct password has been entered. On a website login, however, the claim of identity is the username and the authentication is again, typically, the password. Though passwords receive the most attention as a security measure, I prefer a more thorough and comprehensive approach to online account security, beginning with the username, then discussing passwords, and finally two-factor authentication.

Though a fairly tedious topic, I consider authentication an important one. Because we are so intimately familiar with usernames and passwords many of us tend to have many, deeply ingrained bad habits. I consider this section a necessity and one that should be covered very early on. Developing effective passwords, and to a lesser extent, usernames, is an important step in many of the future techniques we will employ. Without doing these things well many of the advantages of encryption are lost and securing online accounts becomes far less likely.

This chapter will also cover another facet of authentication: verifying the integrity of applications before trusting them. Programs (especially security-related applications) are vulnerable to minor modifications that, while transparent during normal use, can render the software insecure. These modifications may include "backdoors" that allow unauthorized access to information protected by the program, or they may reduce the efficiency of applications preventing the clean execution of their intended functions or otherwise weaken their security. Checksums will allow us to verify that a downloaded program has not been modified or altered, and is the original, trusted version.

JUSTIN CARROLL

PASSWORD MANAGERS

It has been suggested that the strongest password is the one you don't know. Humans are notoriously poor at developing effective passwords because we are limited largely by the constraints of memory and the desire for convenience. Later in this chapter I will discuss how to create effective, difficult-to-crack passwords that are still memorable and usable. I will further recommend, and explain why it is a good idea that you use a different username and password on all your online accounts. This may seem terribly difficult, exceedingly inconvenient, and impossible to remember, and generally I would agree. With only the benefit of human memory it would be nearly impossible to remember and use more than just a few passwords of the recommended length and complexity. For that reason, I have chosen to begin this chapter with a discussion of password managers, one of the single biggest and most important tools you can employ to strengthen your digital security posture.

I have been using password managers for years, and cannot imagine going back to *not* using one. Password managers solve many of the problems inherent in password development and use. A password manager can "remember" my passwords for me so that I don't have to. This allows me to use a different password (and username) on all my online accounts. It also allows me to assign passwords that are randomly generated, and of the maximum allowable length and complexity. Further, with a password manager, I can change my passwords as often as I like without fear of forgetting them and most offer some other convenient features, as well.

Because password managers store all your passwords in one place, they are an "eggs-in-one-basket" situation. It should go without saying that a password manager should be protected by an extremely strong password, and, if at all possible, two-factor authentication (see successive sections of this chapter on passwords and two-factor authentication). If you can only take the time to remember one very strong, very complex password, you should do so for your password manager. Be exceedingly careful not to lose or forget this password. Password managers are designed to not let you back in without the correct authentication credentials. This could result in the loss of all passwords for all your accounts, an unenviable situation in which to find yourself. It should also go without saying that your password manager should be backed up. If you are using a host-based manager and your computer crashes you must have a way to recover the information it contained (see the section of Chapter 3 that deals with backups) or risk being locked out of, and potentially losing, dozens of accounts.

There are two basic categories of password managers, host-based and web-based. Although this section will discuss both, my recommendation is to use a host-based password manager. While web-based password managers are strongly encrypted, they are significantly more risky because they store your passwords in the cloud and are a target by nature because of the wealth of information they store. Though a certain amount of confidence is placed in all online account providers, an extraordinary amount is required to entrust the passwords to all your accounts to an online service.

> **HOW MANY PASSWORDS DO YOU REMEMBER?**
>
> I am constantly asked, in what seems to be a mix of amazement, skepticism, and concern, "how do you remember all of those passwords?" Because password managers do so much of the work for you, when using one you should only have to remember a handful of passwords. The only passwords that I actually know and enter manually are:
>
> 1. Full disk encryption password (required to boot my computer) (very long and complex)
> 2. Password for volume encryption of files (very long and complex)
> 3. Encryption Password for backed up files (very long and complex)
> 4. Password manager password (very long and complex)
> 5. Windows User Account Password (very simple and easily memorable)
> 6. Windows Administrator Account Password (very simple and easily memorable)

HOST-BASED PASSWORD MANAGERS

A host-based password manager is an application that runs locally on a single device. All the information that is stored in a host-based password manager is stored locally, and is not sent to the cloud or otherwise transmitted. This is somewhat less convenient than a web-based password manager as your passwords are only available on your computer or device. That is to say, you may have difficulty logging into many of your online accounts from other computers. This is not an issue for me since I am reluctant to log in to an account from a computer I don't trust. But for some accounts, you may prefer a solution other than a host-based password manager. The advantage host-based managers enjoy over web-based password managers is security. I have an instinctual, inherent distrust in cloud storage, and prefer to keep my passwords stored safely on a device that I physically control.

PASSWORD SAFE

Password Safe is my favorite host-based password manager for Windows operating systems. Developed by cryptographer and security icon Bruce Schneier, Password Safe is free, uses very strong Twofish encryption, and is widely known for its simplicity and ease of use. The first step is to download the application and install it on your machine. Upon first opening the application you will be required to build a database, the file that stores your passwords. By default, Password Safe will build a folder called "My Safes" in the My Documents folder on your computer. To increase the security of my Password Safe database and its backups, I store them in an encrypted TrueCrypt volume (TrueCrypt is covered in Chapter 3). To do this, simply navigate to the location of your choice when creating your Password Safe database.

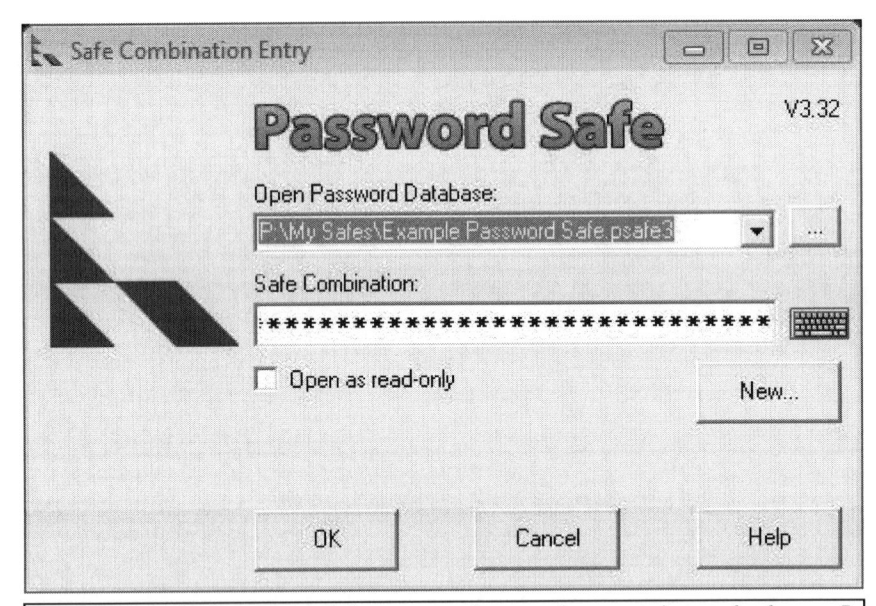

Figure 2.1: The Password Safe prompt shown when opening a database. In addition to allowing password authentication, Password Safe also offers two-factor authentication using the YubiKey USB token.

Once you have created your database (it will save as a *.psafe) and created a "Safe Combination" (what Password Safe calls the master password—use a good one!), you will be allowed to create entries in the database. Each entry, when opened, contains several tabs. The "Basic" tab is displayed by default when an entry is opened and contains the login information for the account. It also has several fields to allow you to customize the entry. These fields are the group/subgroup into which the entry is to be placed, the title, username, and password (with a build-in password generator). The Basic tab also contains a field for the URL, the email address associated with the account, and notes.

Though it may be tempting to only fill in the basic information, I recommend filling in all of these fields as thoroughly as possible. I use the Title as an organizational tool and typically number my accounts to order them efficiently for my day-to-day use. Filling the URL field allows Password Safe to open your browser to the desired webpage when clicking on the "Browse to URL" button at the top of the application. Filling the URL field with the exact URL may also provide some protection against redirect attacks. I also fill in the email account field because I use a very large number of email addresses and it is helpful for me to remember which account is associated with which email

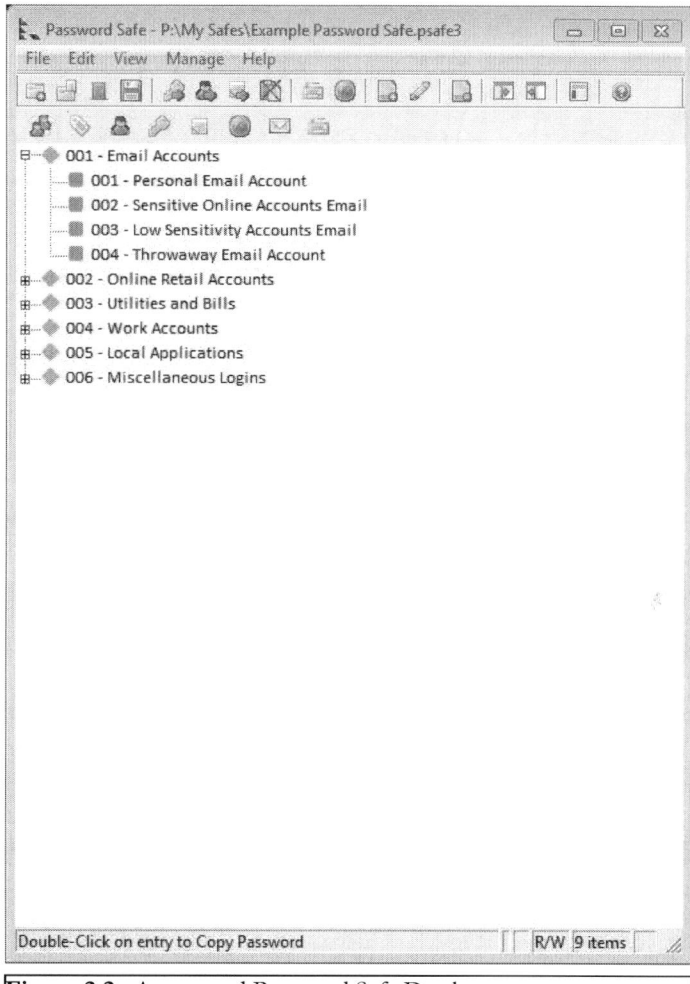

Figure 2.2: An opened Password Safe Database.

address. Finally, I use the Notes section for any additional information relevant to the account. If the account in question is a Gmail account, for instance, I will use the Notes section to store the phone number associated with the account as well as the backup two-factor authentication codes. If it is an account that requires password reset questions, I use notes to record the answers to these questions. This places all the relevant information about an account in one single, easy-to-access location that is heavily and safely encrypted.

The "Additional" tab allows you to make several customizations to the shortcuts in Password Safe. These options give you the ability to change mouse and keyboard shortcuts and the ability to choose how many legacy passwords are stored for the entry. In my opinion, it is a good idea to store at least two or three, especially if you change passwords frequently. There have been a few occasions where I have changed a password on a website and updated the entry in Password Safe. Only later did I realize the entry was not saved on the website, and I still needed access to the old password. The Additional tab is where I go to get it, as I save the last five passwords for each entry. The vast majority of these old passwords will never be used, but it is nice to know they are there should I need them.

DOUBLE-CLICK AND "SHIFT" DOUBLE-CLICK

One of the most convenient features of Password Safe is the ability to copy a password just by double-clicking the entry. By default, double-clicking on an entry will copy the password to the clipboard, allowing you to paste it into the necessary field. Double-clicking while holding "Shift" will then copy the username, allowing it to be pasted, greatly speeding the process of logging into a site.

I always copy and paste in this order, by the way: password first, then username. This is a very small measure but ensures that my password is stored in the clipboard only for a few seconds before I copy the username. This reduces the risk of inadvertently pasting a password in an insecure location such as the body of an email or in a Word document. Should someone else gain access to my computer this also ensures that a password is not readily available in the clipboard.

The "Dates and Times" tab allows you to set password expiry which will remind you to change the password on a specific date or after a set period of time (which may be recurring or not). This tab also provides some statistical information about the entry, including the dates and times it was created, last accessed, and the last password change.

Finally, the "Password Policy" tab allows you to select from a very comprehensive set of parameters for password generation for each account. The first option allows you to choose a password policy (see Password Safe Options below). You can create as many policies as you like, allowing you to quickly and easily switch between very long and complex policies to shorter, simpler policies for logins that restrict password length or complexity. If you choose not to use a pre-defined policy, you can set up a custom policy for each entry.

The details you can assign when creating a custom policy are password length, character sets (allowing or disallowing upper- and lowercase letters, numbers, and special characters), and the minimum number of each character type to be included in each password. These options also allow you to exclude ambiguous characters, create pronounceable passwords, or use hexadecimal digits only, though I don't recommend any of these for day-to-day use, as reducing the pool of characters from which passwords are constructed inherently weakens them.

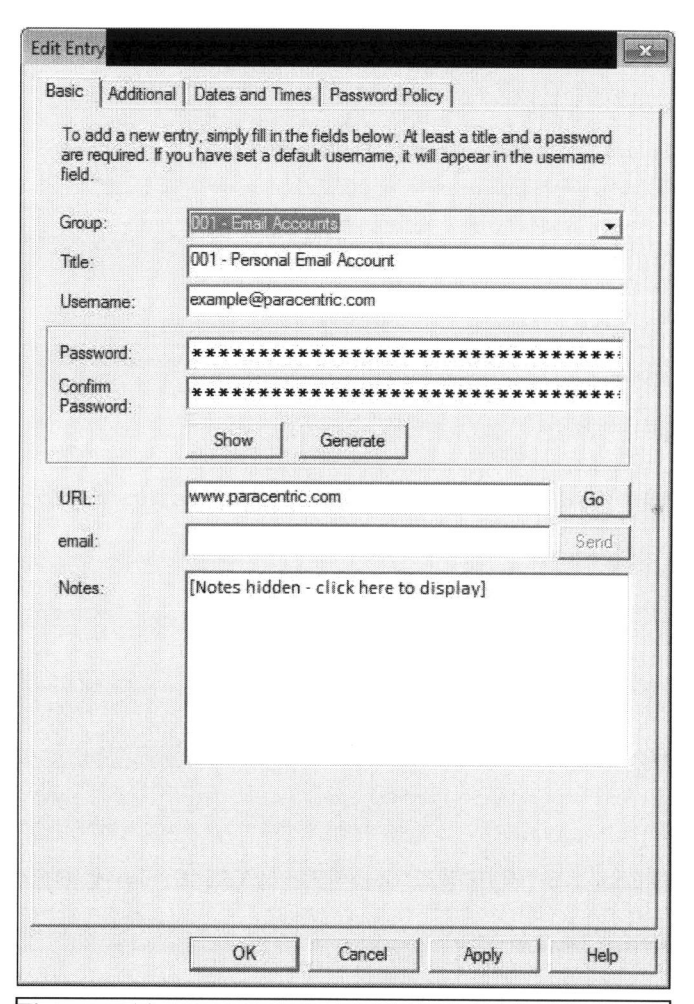

Figure 2.3: The dialogue for inputting or editing a Password Safe Entry. Note the tabs at the top of the entry; these all contain fields allowing the customization of that entry.

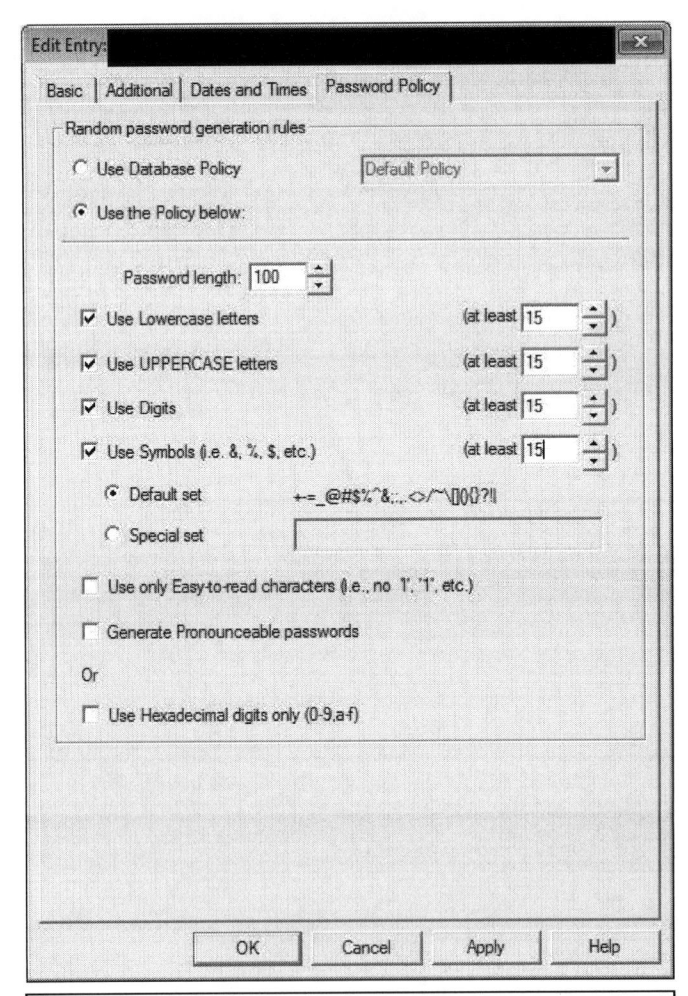

Figure 2.4: A Password Safe Password Policy. Password Safe allows the user to customize passwords to the desired length and complexity, as well as negating the need to remember complex passwords.

Global Password Policies: Though each database entry allows you to define a custom password policy, Password Safe does offer the ability to define global password polices, or policies that can be used across all entries in the database. This saves the time and hassle of defining a new, custom policy for each database entry. Opening the Password Policies dialogue allows you to create as many global policies as you like, all of which will appear as options when building a new entry. It is a good idea to take the time early on to build several policies that will accommodate most of your requirements, though occasionally you may still have to build a custom policy for logins that disallow certain characters, or exhibit other password idiosyncrasies. I recommend having the following global policies at a minimum:

\multicolumn{4}{c}{RECOMMENDED POLICIES FOR PASSWORD SAFE}
Policy	Length	Character Set	Uses
Standard Policy	60+	All	Most websites and logins
Long Policy	99+	All	Sites allowing very long passwords
Short Policy (or policies)	12-16	Customized to site restrictions	Sites disallowing very long passwords; sites disallowing the use of certain characters in passwords
Username Policy	24	Uppercase letters and numbers only	Creating random usernames for sites where user-selected usernames are allowed (see section below in Usernames)

Password Safe Options: Password Safe is highly customizable to the needs of its users. There are a great number of options you can customize to make Password Safe work better for you. I will cover only two of those options here: Security and Backups. To reach the Security options, open the **Manage** drop-down menu and navigate to **Options**. In the Options dialogue select the **Security** tab. The security tab allows you to adjust certain security measures in Password Safe. The ones I recommend are as follows: check the boxes for Clear clipboard on minimize, Clear clipboard on exit, Lock password database on minimize, and Lock Password Safe after __ minutes idle. I recommend setting this last option at no more than 15 minutes idle, after which you will have to restore Password Safe and reenter your authentication credentials to access it.

The other tab that deserves some attention is the Backups tab. Password Safe will automatically save backups of your database in the same location as your database. For this reason, the folder containing your database may appear cluttered with a bunch of unsolicited *.ibak files. These are the backup files and should be kept. Should you change a password that is unsaved in the database, you can revert back to one of these backups. By default, Password Safe will only save the most recent three backups, deleting the oldest one when a new one is added. If you desire more backups (I save the last 10) or want to change the location to which the backups are saved, go to **Manage >> Options >> Backups**.

Password Safe is available at: http://passwordsafe.sourceforge.net/

WEB-BASED PASSWORD MANAGERS

A web-based password manager is a cloud-storage application that stores all of your passwords online and allows you to access them from anywhere. Web-based password managers are very convenient as they allow the user to access them from any computer or device with internet access and the appropriate browser add-on or app installed. Though web-based password managers do offer robust encryption, two-factor authentication support, and other security features, they are primarily focused on convenience. While this convenience is nice, I remain unconvinced that being able to access my passwords from *anywhere* is a good thing. One benefit of web-based password managers that cannot be denied, however, is the inherent safety (*safety* is not the same thing as *security*) in having them stored offsite. If your computer crashes, is destroyed, or rendered otherwise inoperable, you will still have access to your passwords and the accounts they protect.

I will offer a warning here about accessing your web-based password manager from an untrusted computer: if you do not have control of the computer, it is possible for the owner of the device to capture your master password which would then grant access to *all* your passwords. Even if the owner of an untrusted device is not intentionally logging your keystrokes he or she may not have taken the necessary pains in securing the device and it may be infected with keylogging software or other malware that could compromise your password. Because I trust neither computers that I do not personally control nor cloud storage, I am very cautious about web-based password managers (and you should be, too) and the information I will place in their care.

I do use one for accessing a few accounts that are relatively unimportant and that contain little or no sensitive information. The convenience of some of these accounts is important and their compromise would do me little actual damage.

LASTPASS

LastPass is my preferred web-based password manager. LastPass has a strong reputation for being very secure. LastPass offers the user the ability to utilize a number of two-factor authentication schemes including the app-, hardware-, and paper-based systems, all of which are described in detail later in this chapter. Passwords stored in LastPass are encrypted locally on your machine, then uploaded to the LastPass' cloud servers. From there they can be accessed from any Windows, Mac, or Linux with a simple browser add-on for the Chrome, Firefox, Opera, Safari, and Internet Explorer browsers, or from an Android, Blackberry, iOS, or Windows mobile device via the LastPass app.

In addition to being very secure (which is certainly a prerequisite for cloud-based systems), LastPass is also very user friendly. LastPass has auto-fill and auto-login functions that will automatically fill the login fields and log the user in as soon as you browse to a site requiring a login. In addition to this, and storing all usernames and passwords, LastPass has a secure notes function that allows you to record small bits of information securely.

One problem endemic to web-based password managers is that they are sometimes difficult to use with logins consisting of more than a username and password. For example, some logins require a username, password, and some other identifier before allowing access. When working with sites like these, LastPass can usually fill two of the three fields, but often does so poorly. If LastPass consistently has a problem with a site with three or more fields, I will typically place the login credentials in a secure note with LastPass, and copy and paste each one individually.

As I have previously mentioned, I do not fully trust all my passwords to the cloud. For this reason, I consider LastPass only a small part of my password management strategy. There are a select, few non-sensitive logins that I need access to on the go, none of which would cause great harm to my privacy or finances if compromised. These are the only ones I store with LastPass. Additionally, I always use a hard-to-guess username, a very strong password, and two-factor authentication.

LastPass is a freemium service. The desktop version that is available as a browser extension is free, as is LastPass Pocket, which offers you the ability to store a local, offline copy of your LastPass password vault. LastPass Premium costs $12.00/year and allows you to access LastPass from mobile devices.

    LastPass is available at: https://lastpass.com.

USERNAMES

With password managers to keep up with all of your login information, it is now possible to elevate your security posture significantly without a corresponding increase in the amount of work required. Usernames are generally overlooked in the discussion of online security. I think this is a mistake, and I think usernames should be carefully chosen and considered the very first line of defense for such accounts. Most websites require at least two things to log in: a username and a password. If the attacker cannot find your username, your account is that much more secure as the attacker does not know which account to attack in the first place.

A predictable username has several problems, the first of which is susceptibility to guessing. If an attacker is targeting an attack against a specific individual, he or she will attempt to guess the target's usernames to various sites based on known information about that person. This information can be gathered online from social media sites, personal blogs, people search sites, and public records. Predictable usernames are most commonly generated from a combination of first, middle, and last names, or initials and dates of birth. Once the username has been discovered, the attacker can now target that account and attempt to break the password. Conversely, the attacker can never begin targeting the account if it cannot be located.

The second problem with predictable usernames is that they are typically used across multiple sites, especially when the email address associated with the account is used as the username. Using the same username across several of your accounts correlates those accounts, making them easier to locate, and leaks information about you such as your social media presence, interests, the online services and commerce sites you use, etc. This can expose a great deal of information about you. After locating your username, the attacker in this scenario may user a service like Know'em (http://knowem.com/) to locate other accounts you have. If a common username and password combination are used across multiple accounts, hacking one account can very quickly lead to the compromise of multiple accounts with disastrous consequences. Though you may not care if your throwaway email account or an old social media profile is hacked, it could lead to your bank account being hacked if they share a username and password.

Finally, when breaches occur, the username and password combinations are usually sold or posted online in massive databases. If you use a username or email address that correlates to your name, a breach can reveal personal information about you, especially if you have an uncommon name. As an example, let's assume your name is Harrison Tang and your username to a site is harrisontang83, an obvious and easily guessable username based on your name and year of birth. Let's also assume that a large password breach occurs at a given site, and the usernames and passwords are posted online. Anyone seeing this database would easily recognize your name and with some research could probably confirm that user is you. This reveals information about you and your personal interests: it could be a dating site, a bank, an ecommerce site, or an online service of some sort. This would reveal to anyone seeing this database that you use this dating site, bank, online retailer, or service, leading to further avenues of exploitation.

To combat this, we should consider the username a security measure. If the usernames on your accounts happen to be obvious, change them. If a particular site does not allow you to change your username, consider opening a new account using a non-obvious username. There are several ways to create difficult-to-guess usernames.

Random Generation: When setting up an account that lets me choose any username I want, I will use a random string of letters and numbers in the maximum allowable length, generated by a password manager. An attacker may know a great deal of personal information about me and use it to guess my username if the username is personally relatable to me (or more commonly, my email address), but it is unlikely in the extreme that he or she will guess a randomly generated username. A string of characters has several advantages beyond being difficult to guess. First, it will not be easily memorable to anyone should they happen to see it. Second, if someone did find this, the likelihood that they would even recognize it as a username is low. Finally, if that username were leaked in a breach, it would not point directly back to me because it is not personally relatable to me.

An ideal username would look something like this: **532T4VYL9NQ54BTMDZI1**. Though this would be extremely difficult to remember (especially if the account bearing it was used only on an occasional basis), a password manager solves the memory problem for us. Additionally, such a complex username can make even locating your account difficult. Some online accounts will allow you to choose a username up to 60 characters in length; you should do this wherever it is allowed. Unfortunately, many online accounts do not allow you to choose your own username, and will use your email address as the username by default. If this is the case, there are several ways in which you can still have a difficult-to-guess username.

Gmail Address Modifiers: One of my favorite techniques for creating unique usernames for multiple accounts, while still having all emails go a single inbox is available through Gmail. Gmail allows you to add a "+" in your email address, immediately before the "@gmail.com". After the "+" you can add a modifier to make this email address unique, even though Gmail will resolve it back to your email account. For example, if my Gmail address is paracentricbook@gmail.com, I would add the "+" and an additional modifier after "paracentricbook," like this:

paracentricbook**+example**@gmail.com

The modifier can consist of letters and numbers, and can be unique for each online account you wish to associate with that email address. To reap the maximum security benefit from this technique, I recommend making the modifier a random set of characters rather than something easily guessable. For example, if I were going to set up an Amazon.com account using this Gmail address, I would add a short, random, modifier like this: paracentricbook+3uc8i@gmail.com rather than paracentricbook+amazon@gmail.com. Though "+amazon" is easy to remember it is also easily guessable, which defeats the whole purpose for using this technique.

With a single Gmail address, a user has an infinite array of email addresses at his or her disposal (I have successfully used modifiers as long as 30 characters), and can use a unique email address for each online account owned. Be aware that these should not be considered anonymous, as a human seeing these addresses could very likely be aware of this technique and quickly figure out your "real" email address. It should also be pointed out that some services do not recognize an email address with a modifier as valid.

Multiple email addresses: Though this is the most time-consuming method of setting up multiple usernames, it is perhaps the most secure. See Chapter 7 for more information on structuring these accounts, and for information on email forwarding services

> ## WHY GMAIL?
>
> Google gets a very bad reputation in the privacy community, and for good reason. Google collects a large amount of information about you through your online activity, the content of your emails, etc. So why do I recommend Gmail? Simply put, Gmail is an excellent product and Google offers excellent security.
>
> Security and privacy differ, and where Google may not be ideal in terms of privacy, it excels in security. Google allows very long passwords (up to 99 characters), two-factor authentication through several different mechanisms, and an HTTPS connection during your entire session. Google has set the bar very high for secure accounts, and this will be discussed in more depth in Chapter 7.

PASSWORDS

Passwords are a phenomenon much like keys: we all carry them and use them daily, but few realize the threats against them or the concepts underlying a good one. As an example of how poorly understood passwords are, I recently had a new television installed in my home. The television is Internet-capable and required my Wi-Fi password for setup. After the installer typed my very long, very complex password into the television he remarked in a frustrated tone, "You really should change that." I replied that although it's an inconvenience now, once all my devices are set up I only rarely have to enter the password. He responded with reasoning that left me speechless: "Well, if you have guests over it's easier to give them a shorter password…" Needless to say, I changed the password immediately after he left, though not to a shorter one.

The television installer mistook the point of a password, considering it a convenience feature rather than a security measure. Passwords aren't very exciting, but good passwords are an absolutely crucial component of digital security. The ability to design and implement strong passwords will be extremely important to the proper execution of many of the techniques discussed in the remainder of this book. The password techniques that I recommend here produce extremely long, complex, and difficult to crack passwords. Unfortunately, this makes them somewhat inconvenient to input and slightly more difficult to remember, but the security they provide is well worth it.

Though password managers provide most of the memory I need, there are still a handful of passwords that I need to manually enter on a day-to-day basis (see sidebar on page 37). Not only do I want these passwords to be memorable, I need them to be incredibly strong as the compromise of these passwords could lead to the compromise of all of my sensitive data. For this reason, I still need to know how to develop a strong password that I can remember and enter manually.

Password Basics: Before we discuss how to build a good, strong password it is critical to understand what comprises one. There are two factors that make (or break) a password: length and complexity. Length and complexity both exponentially increase the difficulty in breaking a password.

Password length is uncomplicated. With today's computing power, 20 characters is a prudent minimum length (if your site does not allow a longer password). When passwords are cracked using brute force techniques, powerful processors run through millions or billions of possible passwords per second. Every possible combination of a very short password could be tested in a matter of minutes with strong enough computing power, and computers are growing faster every day.

When using a password manager, I will use passwords that are much, much longer than 20 characters, sometimes exceeding 100. If this seems like overkill, consider this: Regardless of whether my password is 1 character or 100, with a password manager, both require the exact same amount of effort on my part, so why not go with the longest allowable password? If the site you are registering with does not allow a longer password, think twice before registering with that service.

Complexity can be a bit trickier. Password complexity is created by following some basic rules. Ideally a password will contain characters from the full ASCII suite, including: upper- and lower-case letters, numbers, special characters (!@#$%^&*_+=-/.,<>?;'":[]{\|}), and spaces. Spaces are very important as they are not commonly used in passwords, and as a result are not commonly searched for by password-cracking programs.

PASSWORD VULNERABILITIES

You may be wondering why such extreme measures are needed to develop an effective password. The reason complexity is desirable is that passwords are not typically cracked by "dumb" brute force methods alone, like starting at lowercase "a" and going all the way through "ZZZZZZZZZZZZ," and testing everything in between. Though brute force attacks exist, they are not the most popular or effective method of cracking a password, as they can take an immense amount of time. Time is the enemy of the password cracker, and your goal in designing a password should not be to make it unbreakable as nothing is truly unbreakable given enough time, but to make it take an unacceptable length of time. Passwords are typically cracked in a much more timely manner by understanding how people make passwords and designing a dictionary attack to defeat it. Dictionary attacks rely on two things: specific knowledge of the target and heuristics.

Knowledge of the target is useful when cracking a password because personal information is frequently used as the basis for human-generated passwords. An individual may use his or her birthday (or birthdays of a spouse, or children, or a combination thereof), favorite sports team or player, or other personal information or interests. This information can be input into programs like the Common User Password Profiler (CUPP), an application that takes such tedious personal data as birthdays, names, occupation, and other keywords, and generates thousands of potential passwords based on the data. This list of passwords can then be programmed into a custom dictionary attack against the target machine or account.

Dictionary attacks work through a trial and error approach. First, a list of passwords is entered into a password-cracking program. This list might be customized against the target (through applications like CUPP as described above), or it may be more generic. Even though "generic" lists are not tailored to a specific target, they are still far more successful than they should be. These lists are based upon the heuristics of how people develop passwords. These lists are developed with the knowledge that many people use the techniques explained in the following list of password pitfalls.

Never use a dictionary word as your password. Almost all dictionary attacks will include a list of dictionary words in a number of languages. Do not use a dictionary word with numbers/characters at the beginning or end (e.g. password11 or 11password), and do not use a dictionary word with simple obfuscation (p@ssword). These are the most common methods of adding complexity to a dictionary word-based password, and combinations such as these would be tested in any decent dictionary attack.

Never leave the default password on your devices (Bluetooth devices and wireless routers are notable offenders in the retail market). Default passwords for any device imaginable are available through a simple web search, and would absolutely be included in an attack against a known device. Also, never use information that is personally relatable to you. As we have discussed, information that is personally relatable to you can be used in an attack that is customized to target you specifically.

The inherent problem with complexity is that it makes our passwords difficult to remember, though with creativity it is still possible to create passwords that are very long, very complex, yet still memorable. Below are two of my favorite techniques to develop strong (and memorable) passwords.

The Passphrase: A passphrase is a short phrase instead of a single word and is my preferred technique. Passphrases work like passwords, but are much, much more difficult to break due to their extreme length. Additionally, if appropriate punctuation is used, a passphrase will contain complexity: upper- and lower-case letters and spaces. A shrewd passphrase designer could even devise a phrase that contains numbers and special characters. An example of a good, solid passphrase might be:

> *"My sister rode her bicycle last evening!"*

An even better example might be:

"We were married on 07/10/09 on Revere Beach."

Both of these passphrases are extremely strong and would take a long, long time to break. The first passphrase contains 42 characters, including letters in upper- and lower-cases, special characters, and spaces. The second is even longer at 46 characters, and it contains numbers in addition to having all the characteristics of the first. Additionally, neither of these passphrases would be terribly difficult to remember.

A variation on the passphrase is the "XKCD method". This method is a variation on the passphrase but rather than inventing an actual phrase you simply choose four, five, or six (the more the better) random words. Like passphrases, this is a good method for developing passwords that are long, though it eschews the use of numbers and special characters. The example in the infamous comic (which can be found at http://xkcd.com/936/) is "correct horse battery staple"; other examples are nearly infinite, but be careful not to use information that could be easily guessed about you. Further, hackers have noticed the uptick in popularity of this method in recent years and have designed dictionaries and heuristics-based attacks that take advantage of this.

THE CONCEPT OF GRADUAL COMPLEXITY

Creating long, strong passwords can be a pain, especially if you implement them all at once. If there is a particular application for which I actually need to remember a password, I will start with a short password that I can remember fairly easily and gradually increase its length and complexity by adding three or four characters every couple of weeks.

One place that I have done this time and again is with my smartphone. Every month I add four characters to the passcode until I have reached what I believe to be an acceptable length (and everyone else thinks is ridiculously long). I could not remember such a string of characters all at once, but by adding only a few to an already familiar sequence it becomes ingrained in small pieces.

It should go without saying that when using this technique I will not store sensitive information behind the password until it has reached an acceptable strength. This requires some consideration and planning on the part of the user but is, in my opinion, worth it in the long run.

The "First Letter" Method: This method is a great way to develop a complex password, especially if it does not have to be terribly long (or cannot be because of site restrictions on password length). For this method select a phrase or lyric that is memorable **only** to you. Take the first (or last) letter of each word to form your password. In the example below I use a few words from the Preamble to the Constitution of the United States:

We the people of the United States, in order to form a more perfect union, establish Justice, insure domestic Tranquility…

>WtpotUSiotfampueJidT

This password contains 20 characters, upper- and lowercase letters (the letters that are actually capitalized in the Preamble are capitalized in the password), and does not in any way resemble a dictionary word. This would be a very robust password. The complexity and length of this password could be increased greatly by spelling out a couple of the words in the phrase, and more complex still by replacing a letter or two with special symbols:

>We the People of the United States, i02famPu,eJ,idT

Figure 2.5: The above password tested on https://howsecureismypassword.net. This is an excellent indicator of password strength but I recommend against inputting your *actual* passwords into it.

Containing 51 characters, this is the strongest password yet, but would still be fairly easy to remember. The first seven words are spelled out and punctuated correctly, and the last fifteen words are represented only by a first letter, some of which are substituted with a special character or number. This password is very long and very complex, and would take eons to crack with current computing power. To give it a bit more punch, it is also the method currently recommended by security expert Bruce Schneier.

OTHER PASSWORD ISSUES

Even if all your passwords are strong, there are some other issues to be aware of.

Multiple Accounts: Though this is covered elsewhere in this book it is worth reiterating: each of your online accounts should have its own unique password that is not used on any other account. Otherwise the compromise of one account can lead quickly to the compromise of *many* of your accounts. With a password manager doing all the work for you there is no reason not to have different passwords on every single online account.

Password Reset Mechanisms: Most online accounts feature a password recovery option for use in case you forget your password. Though these are sometimes referred to as "security" questions, in reality they are convenience questions for forgetful users. Numerous accounts have been hacked by guessing the answers to security questions or answering them correctly based on open source research, including the Yahoo! Mail account of former Vice Presidential candidate Sarah Palin.

The best way to answer these questions is with a randomly generated series of letters, numbers, and special characters (if numbers and special characters are allowed). This will make your account far more difficult to breach through the password-reset questions. If you use a password manager the answers to these questions can be stored in the "Notes" section of each entry, allowing you to reset your password in the event you become locked out of your account.

If you are prompted to enter a password "hint" I recommend using purposely misleading information. This will send the attacker on a wild goose chase if he or she attempts to discover your password through the information contained in the hint. You should never use anything in the hint that leaks any personal information about you, and if you are using a strong, randomly generated password the hint should have nothing at all to do with the password itself. Some examples of my favorite purposely misleading hints might be: *My Birthday, Miami Dolphins, Texas Hold'em,* or *Password,* none of which have anything at all to do with the password at which they "hint."

Password Lifespan and Password Fatigue: Like everything else, passwords are vulnerable to the ravages of time. The longer an attacker has to work at compromising your password, the weaker it becomes in practice. Accordingly, passwords should be changed periodically. In my opinion, they should be changed once per year *if no extenuating circumstances exist*. I change all of my passwords much more often than that, because as a security professional, I am probably much more likely than most to be targeted (not to mention much more paranoid, as well). If you have any reason to suspect an online account, your wireless network, or your computer itself has been breached you should change your password immediately. The new password should be drastically different from the old one.

If you are using a password manager, a practice I strongly recommend, changing passwords is not difficult at all, as remembering them is a non-issue. If you choose not to use a password manager, or you have more than one or two accounts for which you prefer to enter the password manually, you may become susceptible to password fatigue. Password fatigue is the phenomenon of using the same four or five passwords in a rotation if you change them, or are forced to change them, frequently (as you may be required to do on your company computer). This impacts security negatively by making your password patterns predictable, and exposes you to the possibility of all the passwords in your rotation being cracked.

With modern password hashing techniques, changing passwords frequently is typically unnecessary. The corporate practice of requiring a new password every 30, 60, or 90 days is a throwback to the days when passwords were predominantly stored in plaintext and there was significant risk of the entire password database being hacked. If passwords are being stored correctly (that is, with a correctly-salted hash), they should be secure from the vast majority of breaches. With that being said, I am more paranoid than most and regularly change the passwords on all of my accounts. Though it takes a bit of time and patience to update passwords on multiple sites, doing a few each week in a constant rotation can ease the tedium a bit.

Password Recycling: When the time comes to make a new password, it is often easier just to change a few characters (especially if they are numbers) than it is to remember a whole new password (for example: Timothy77, Timothy78, Timothy79, Timothy80, etc.). This is known as password recycling, and unfortunately this makes your passwords very predictable. If one in the series is compromised, successive ones can be guessed rather easily. When you change passwords, the new and old ones should be totally unrecognizable from each other. You should never reuse a previous password.

Online Password Checkers: There are dozens of online password checkers that offer you a field into which you may type your password. The password will then be analyzed and you will be told how long it would take to crack the password using brute force. These sites can be useful, and give you an idea how strong your password might be. Additionally, by entering a password and then modifying it slightly, you can instantly see the effect that small changes can make (add a semicolon and a space and see how much harder it makes the password to crack, and so on).

You should be aware that password checkers have access to the passwords that you give them. For this reason, I will never give a password checker one of my real passwords. I have no control over how, or if, they use it, and no control over how it is stored. Additionally, it is being transmitted over the internet where it is vulnerable to interception. For this reason, the closest I will come to testing my actual password is to test one that is similar in structure.

You should also be aware that password checkers do not paint an entirely accurate picture. Password testers are based on the premise of brute force, and some will allow you to select the number of passwords tested per second. If your password is based on personal information about you that can be used in a custom dictionary attack, all bets are off: the password may be broken in a matter of minutes. Likewise, if you are using a password that has made it into a more common dictionary, your password may be broken in mere seconds. Don't let password-checking websites give you a false sense of security about your password.

There are two password-checking websites that I use and recommend. The first is https://howsecureismypassword.net. I like this site for its simplicity, its instant feedback, and for allowing me to choose the number of passwords tested per second. The other is www.passfault.com. Passfault does not give instant feedback (you must click "Analyze" each time you want to test a password), and it does not allow you to choose the number of passwords tested per second (though it does allow you to choose between classes of password-cracking machines). The reason I like Passfault is that it does offer much more detailed feedback about what is wrong with an entered password, and it displays dozens of categories of potential password weaknesses.

Online Password Generators: Just as there are online password checkers, there are also online password generators. I do not recommend using any of these; use the one in Password Safe instead. The reason I strongly advise against using online password generators is that you have no idea what the site is doing behind the scenes. Are they recording the password along with your IP address? It is impossible to know, and there are too many other good options out there for creating randomly-generated passwords.

TWO-FACTOR AUTHENTICATION

These days, one does not have to specifically follow security news to know that password compromises happen with shocking regularity. The *Wired* cover story about the hack on Mat Honan in late 2012 fully underscores the weaknesses in passwords. (Mr. Honan is also an excellent case study in the folly of using the same password across multiple accounts—when one of his passwords was hacked it led to the compromise of several of his accounts.) Passwords are becoming a weaker method by the month for securing data. Passwords can be brute-forced, captured during insecure logins, via key-loggers, or lost when sites that do not store passwords securely are hacked.

There is a method of securing many accounts that offers an orders-of-magnitude increase in the security of those accounts: two-factor authentication (TFA). Using TFA, each login requires that you offer something other than *just* a username and password. There are several ways TFA can work, and there are three categories of information that can be used as a second factor. The three possible factors are: something you know (usually a password), something you have (we will discuss these methods more fully below), and something you are (fingerprint, retinal scan, voice print, etc.). A TFA scheme will utilize at least two of these factors, one of which is almost always a password.

Text/SMS: With your cell phone designated as a second factor, you will enter your username and password to login. Before being allowed access to the account, you will be presented with another prompt asking for your one-time code. This code will be sent via text/SMS message to your mobile phone. Upon entering the code, which is typically 6-8 digits, access to the account will be granted.

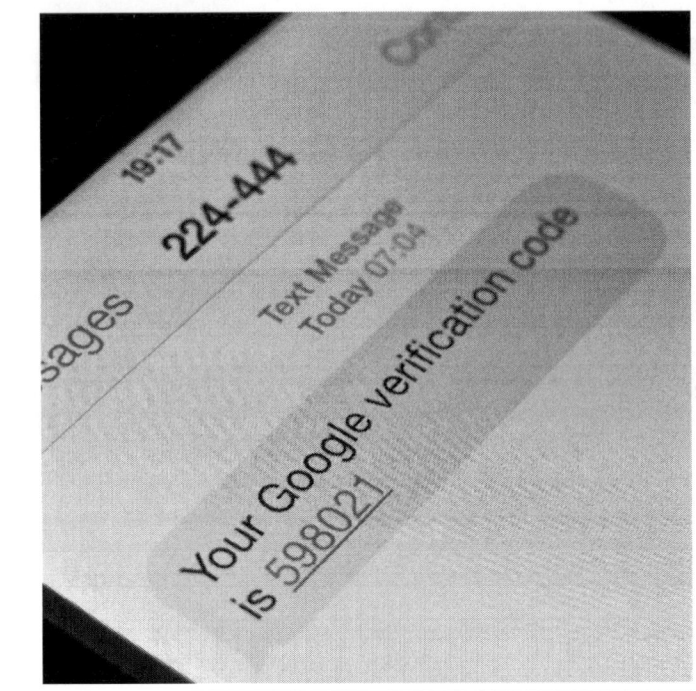

Figure 2.6: A two-factor authentication token sent via SMS.

It is possible with this scheme (and most others) to set up "trusted" computers. For example, you may wish to forego the second factor each time you login on your home computer. In my opinion, this is a convenience that I can live without, even though is a bit onerous to pull out my phone each time I log into my email. If you choose to set up trusted computers, be very selective about which ones you trust. The only computers you should even consider trusting are those that never leave the confines of your home. It should go without saying you should never trust a public computer.

Using the text/SMS scheme of two-factor authentication is a major security upgrade, but it is not as good as the next option we will discuss: the dedicated authenticator app. Text/SMS two-factor can be defeated if your phone's account is hacked and your texts are forwarded. The text/SMS system can also fail if you do not have phone service and cannot receive texts.

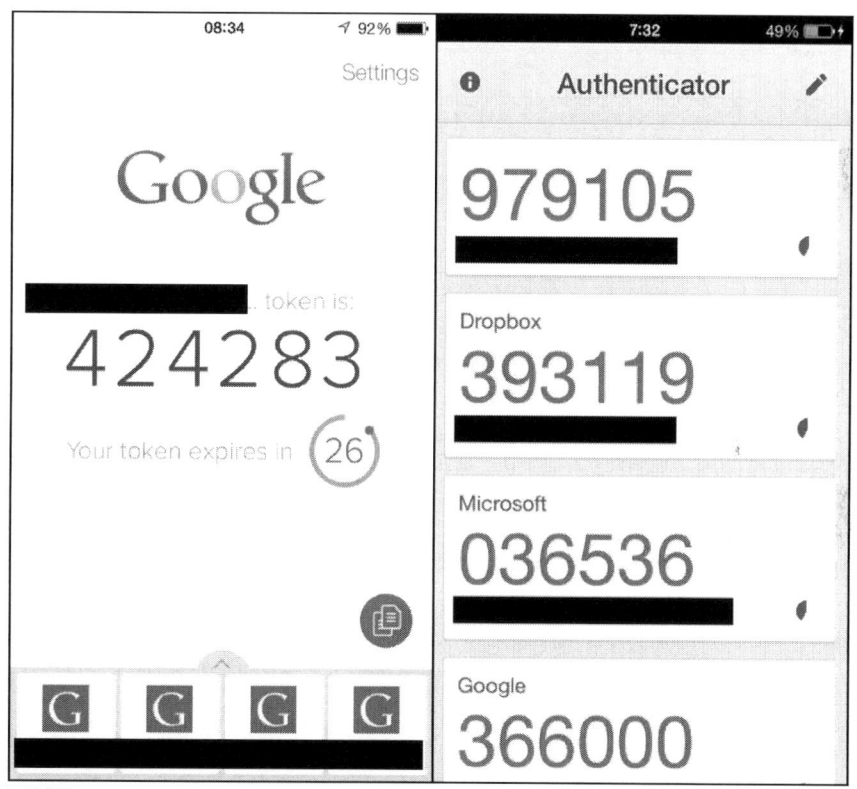

Figure 2.7: Two-factor authentication tokens displayed on Authy (left) and Google Authenticator. Both of these applications are excellent implementations but I prefer Authy because of the ability to passcode protect it.

App: Another option for smartphone owners is a dedicated two-factor authentication app. One such app is the Google Authenticator (available for Android and iPhone). With the app installed on your phone, you will visit the site and enter your username and password. Next, you will open the app, which will display a six-digit, one-time code for that account (this code changes every 30 seconds). You will enter the one-time code to login. Setup for the app is slightly more complicated than setting up text/SMS, but is not terribly difficult.

Once the app is installed on your phone, you visit the site for which you wish to setup TFA. The site will present a QR code (a modernized bar code) that you scan within the app, which links your phone to the account, and adds an entry for the account into the app. Google Authenticator works for a number of sites, including Amazon Web Services, Dropbox, Gmail, Facebook, Microsoft, Wordpress, and more. Another smartphone application that can be used in lieu of Google Authenticator is called Authy. Authy is very similar to Google Authenticator, but I prefer it largely because it can be passcode protected and has a slightly more user-friendly interface.

Though I generally consider app-based tokens more secure than text/SMS systems, it is important to be aware that they are not invulnerable. While an attack on your phone or account could get some of your login tokens, the capture of the token that is transmitted to your app could allow an attacker unlimited access to all your two-factor codes indefinitely. I consider this unlikely, unless you are being targeted by a very sophisticated attacker.

Paper-based TFA: The LastPass password manager has a very original and very effective system of two-factor authentication (of the several methods they offer). It is called "The Grid" and I have yet to see it offered elsewhere. When you set up TFA on the LastPass account using this method, you are given a grid (see Figure 2.8) which you can download in .pdf format. The grid consists of letters across the top, 0-9 down each side, with a random character at each coordinate. After logging in, you are presented with a pop-up dialogue that requires you to enter four characters from prescribed coordinates on the grid. In addition to The Grid, LastPass offers a number of other TFA schemes including Google Authenticator, Yubikey, and more.

Hardware-based TFA: Some very specialized devices exist specifically to provide a second factor. One such device is the Yubikey. The Yubikey is a small device that resembles a USB flash drive (see Figure 2.9). When using the Yubikey for authentication you simply plug it into the computer, and when prompted, press a touch-sensitive button on the top. There are no moving parts to the Yubikey and it is a fairly robust device. Be aware, however, that loss or damage to the device can lock you permanently out of whatever it protected.

There are a great many websites and applications that support the Yubikey. Gmail, LastPass, Password Safe, Paypal, Wordpress, and even full-disk encryption for TrueCrypt-encrypted devices are just a few of the implementations supported by Yubikey. The biggest drawback of the Yubikey is that each device is only good for one account. Another drawback of the Yubikey is that it cannot be backed up; if you lose your Yubikey you are permanently locked out of whatever it protected.

	A	B	C	D	E	F	G	H	I	J	K	L	M	N	O	P	Q	R	S	T	U	V	W	X	Y	Z	
0	d	c	j	3	x	c	3	w	u	n	6	c	r	j	7	6	y	v	5	k	c	k	t	y	w	7	0
1	t	x	j	v	n	s	a	3	j	v	w	z	7	x	5	9	u	c	m	q	9	d	b	2	i	g	1
2	t	r	j	s	u	a	2	2	m	t	w	a	h	9	v	q	x	g	f	3	r	4	6	m	h	3	2
3	n	f	h	7	3	2	q	e	p	2	a	x	c	i	t	t	f	4	n	e	q	j	7	4	d	s	3
4	d	7	t	3	g	5	b	6	n	z	q	y	v	r	2	3	s	n	i	q	n	9	i	r	3	m	4
5	j	z	b	7	x	f	z	e	p	i	x	v	9	i	4	b	7	q	v	5	t	n	s	3	p	h	5
6	j	t	a	m	w	3	z	y	c	s	2	2	u	v	t	v	d	3	g	6	n	d	y	w	7	n	6
7	a	9	d	s	t	s	b	5	i	v	a	g	g	g	h	u	z	v	m	s	b	3	f	v	9	6	7
8	d	7	q	m	7	5	q	x	u	v	e	b	g	z	7	q	g	w	a	d	b	j	m	b	t	j	8
9	p	u	s	p	k	i	b	k	n	2	5	g	z	k	f	m	7	7	u	h	y	t	4	q	7	5	9
	A	B	C	D	E	F	G	H	I	J	K	L	M	N	O	P	Q	R	S	T	U	V	W	X	Y	Z	

Figure 2.8: The very novel yet highly effective LastPass Grid. Upon logging in the user is required to enter the characters found at four random coordinates.

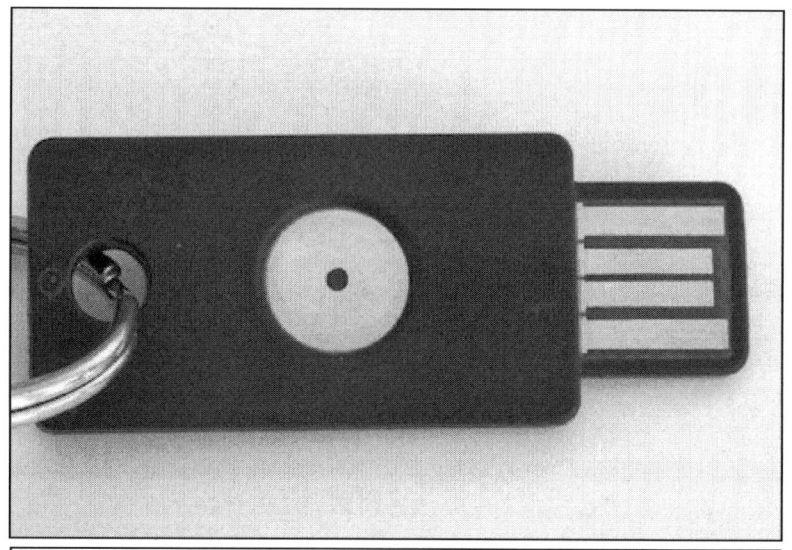

Figure 2.9: The incredibly secure Yubikey two-factor authentication token. Using the Yubikey requires physically touching the metallic circle on the back of the device when it is recognized.

Bad Example: An example of poorly implemented two-factor authentication was the scheme that was used by a popular free email provider (this system has recently been changed, thankfully). After entering your username and password, you had the option to receive a code by SMS or email, or to answer a security question. Answering the security question bypasses the second factor (something you have) and replaces it with an additional "something you know" token. The problem here is that an attacker has the ability to compromise (indeed, he or she already *has* compromised) the password. If an attacker can compromise the password it is fairly reasonable to assume he or she could also compromise the answers to the security questions. By implementing a faulty scheme like this, the email provider made only an incremental upgrade and, in my opinion, gave its customers a false sense of security.

This chapter is by no means inclusive of all methods of two-factor authentication. There are numerous other methods for implementing two-factor, including fingerprint readers, smart cards, and even USB retinal scanners. Implementing two-factor makes you a great deal more secure than a password alone can (even a good password), and you should enable it everywhere it is supported.

CHECKSUM CALCULATORS

Verifying the integrity of a computer program before installing and using it is incredibly important, especially for security software. Verifying the program ensures that it has not been modified. While a modified or look-alike version of more conventional software is almost certainly an attack vector for malware, modified versions of security applications are typically more insidious. A security application that has been modified will probably have no immediately obvious indicators that it has been tampered with. The program will function normally, and appear to do all of the things it was designed to do. The changes made to it will be visible only to someone closely examining the source code. The purpose for such a modification would be to weaken the security it offers or insert a backdoor. This is unacceptable if you are truly relying on a security program to keep your data safe.

The simplest way to ensure you are getting the original, unmodified version of the application is to verify its checksum. Every file created in Windows (or any other operating system) has a checksum. A checksum is simply the product of all the 1s and 0s of a program when hashed through a cryptographic algorithm. Hashing produces a reliable output code that will be of a consistent length, and will not change, no matter how many times the program is copied, moved, renamed, etc., as long as its underlying source code remains the same. If even the slightest modification has been made to the code, the checksum will also change drastically. If you download a program and the checksum is not what it should be, you should not rely on that software.

To verify a checksum, you must have access to a known good checksum to compare it with. This checksum should not come from the same website from which you downloaded the program. If you have been redirected to a look-alike site from which you are tricked into downloading a modified version of the program, it is reasonable to assume that the checksum on that site reflects their version of the software. A better option would be to get the checksum from a trusted, unaffiliated, third-party site. For this reason, checksums for most of the applications mentioned in this book are available at my website: https://yourultimatesecurity.guide/checksums.

.

CHECKSUM PRODUCTS

As an example the following words have been calculated into hashes using the MD5 hashing algorithm. Even though only one letter has been changed in each word, notice how different the resulting products are:

hello: 5d41402abc4b2a76b9719d911017c592
Hello: 8b1a9953c4611296a827abf8c47804d7
hellO: 06612c0d9c73d47a7042afd7024d7c82

The program I recommend for verifying checksums is the CHK Checksum Utility. This program runs in portable mode and does not need to be installed. To verify a program using CHK, open the application and simply drag the .exe or .msi file to be verified into CHK's interface. It will appear in a list view in the interface, and display the name of the file, the file type, the file's size, the checksum (SHA1 by default), and a path to the file.

CHK supports fourteen different hash functions including MD5, SHA-1, SHA-224, SHA-256, and SHA-512. If you wish to change the hash function, open the "Options" pull down menu and select the function you prefer (I recommend SHA-256 or SHA-512). Once the program has been imported and calculated by CHK, retrieve a verifiably good checksum to compare it with (again, preferably from a disinterested third-party site). In CHK, right-click on the file and select "Verify." This will bring up a new window into which you can paste the checksum and click "OK." If the two checksums match, a green check mark will appear beside the application in the CHK interface. If there is a conflict and the two checksums do not match, a red "X" will appear.

If this happens and the two checksums do not match, double-check your work. Ensure that the checksum you are using is from the same hash that CHK is set to use (for example, ensure you did not copy the MD5 hash, but set CHK to test SHA-1 hashes). If the two hashes are not from the same algorithm, go to "Options" and change the algorithm. If the algorithms are the same, ensure that you copied the entire checksum. If you still get an error, something is wrong with the application and you absolutely should not trust it (especially if it is a security application).

The CHK Checksum Utility is free and available at: http://compressme.net/

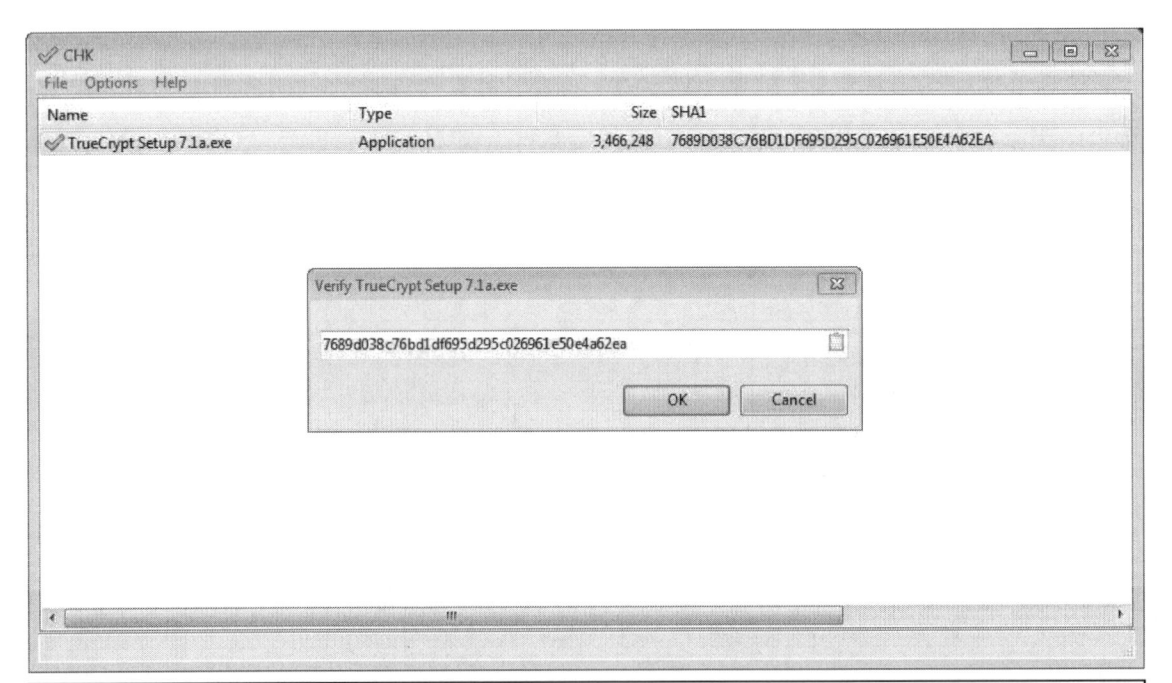

Figure 2.10: The CHK Checksum Utility verifying the authenticity of a TrueCrypt download using a SHA-1 checksum.

cc

SUMMARY

Authentication is a baseline skill for computer and online security. Though it is one that is frequently discussed I am still shocked by the number of people I know who use the same three or four weak passwords on all of their accounts, from their banking institution accounts to semi-reputable online services, and who have little or no awareness of two-factor authentication. Like Chapter 1, the techniques here should be mastered before moving on. No matter how good your encryption may be, it is effectively worthless if you don't protect it with a good password. After using this chapter you should:

- Use a password manager (preferably a host-based manager)
- Use randomly-generated usernames where possible to protect your true email address and reduce your online signature
- Use very strong, difficult to guess or crack passwords
- Enable two-factor authentication everywhere you can
- Verify the authenticity of programs using checksums before trusting them with your security

PART TWO: DATA-AT-REST

JUSTIN CARROLL

CHAPTER 3:
SECURING DATA-AT-REST

This chapter will detail the protection of data-at-rest. Data-at-rest is the information that is stored on your computer's hard drive (or on removable media) when it is not being used or transmitted, which is most of the time. In the event your computer is lost or stolen, accessed by an unauthorized person, or malware is scraping your personal files, encryption will prevent any information from being compromised. This chapter will cover some basics of encryption, encryption programs, and some best practices for effective employment of encryption.

ENCRYPTION BASICS

Encrypting sensitive data is one of the single most important steps users can take in the interest of securing sensitive personal information. Unfortunately, it is also something that many users seem very hesitant to do. To the uninitiated it seems like a lot of work, and may even seem to be a sign of paranoia. Though encryption does require a shift in how users think about their data, it isn't a great deal of work to set up initially. After it is installed and running it is almost transparent to the user.

Before we move into the specifics of the encryption programs it is important to discuss the two broad categories of encryption that are used to protect data stored on a computer. They are file-level and full-disk encryption. I believe that it is important to understand the benefits and limitations of each.

File-Level Encryption: File level encryption allows you to create a file "container" that encrypts all the files within it. When you "close" the container, all the files within it are encrypted, restricting access to anyone who does not possess the correct password. This is perhaps the most commonly implemented type of encryption employed by the average user. I use file-level encryption, but consider it inferior to full-disk encryption.

Full-disk Encryption: Full-disk encryption offers the ultimate security for the data on a computer's hard drive. Full-disk encryption means that the entire hard drive, including all files, the operating system, applications and programs, and anything else on that hard drive is encrypted when the computer is turned off. The only portion of the hard drive that is left unencrypted is the boot loader, a very small portion that allows the computer to accept the entered password and begin the boot process upon startup.

Most users assume that file-level encryption is sufficient as long as all versions of sensitive files are encrypted. Unfortunately, this is fairly inaccurate. While using your computer, it stores various versions of files such as saved recovery versions, records of filenames that you have accessed, internet browsing history, and a great deal of other sensitive information, the majority of it without your permission or knowledge. If your computer is unencrypted, this information can be exploited to reveal sensitive information about you. This information may even reveal the contents of your encrypted files. For example, if you edit a Microsoft Word document, it will automatically create an AutoSave version in the event your computer crashes or you accidentally close without saving. Unless you specifically change the location to which this file saves, it is written unencrypted to your hard drive in a nebulous location that is not always easy for the average user to locate. Full-disk encryption prevents this kind of leakage from being accessed and exploited.

Encryption of the entire hard drive is beneficial for several other reasons. Full-disk encryption is the most transparent form of encryption. After the user initially enters a password and the computer boots, it functions as it normally would. And if your computer is lost or stolen, no information can be recovered from it. When a thief or attacker turns the device on a password prompt will appear, and the computer will not boot up until the correct password is entered. In fact, the hard drive will not even spin. If the hard drive is removed and plugged into another device as an external hard drive, or if the computer is booted with another operating system like a Linux DVD (two common attack techniques to get around operating system passwords), all of the data on the computer will still be inaccessible to the attacker.

Though many users possessing some familiarity with encryption consider full-disk encryption overkill, I firmly believe it should be the standard. Full-disk encryption is the simplest form of encryption to use. Though setup may be a bit more daunting, the simplicity of its day-to-day use (especially in comparison to file-level encryption) far outweighs the hassle of encrypting it in the first place. Once installed and running, FDE only requires a single password (when booting). It is totally transparent from then on, and offers total protection whenever the device is powered down.

Users should also recognize there are downsides to everything, and FDE is no exception. There is a very slight degradation in system performance when using any form of encryption because the computer must decrypt everything on-the-fly as it uses it. I have found this reduction to be minimal. Power users who depend on their devices for processor-heavy functions like video editing or graphic design may find this slow-down noticeable but the overwhelming majority of users will not.

FULL-DISK ENCRYPTION

Full-disk encryption can apply to system and non-system drives alike. System drives are the hard drives upon which the computer's operating system resides and from which it runs; non-system drives are other disks that are connected to the computer. If you do not enable full-disk encryption for your system drive I highly recommend enabling it for your non-system drives and devices, especially those with which you travel. USB flash drives are notoriously easy to lose, and the loss of one containing sensitive data can be extremely damaging.

Encryption Algorithms: There are three encryption algorithms that are used with the programs that will be discussed in this chapter. They are AES (Advanced Encryption Standard), Serpent, and Twofish. AES is currently the United States Government's only approved algorithm for the protection of classified information. The algorithm that underlies AES was selected by the National Institute for Standards and Technology (NIST), in a contest to transition the US Government to a new, improved algorithm from the elderly and inferior 3DES (Third Generation Data Encryption Standard). After selection by NIST the AES algorithm was further vetted by the National Security Agency (NSA) before being certified for the protection of classified information in 2003. Currently there are no known workable defeats for AES.

Serpent and Twofish were both finalists in the AES competition, and both are very strong algorithms. While some of the programs I will discuss below will allow you to use cascaded algorithms (i.e. AES encrypted by Serpent, which is then encrypted by Twofish), AES is currently susceptible to no known defeats, and is sufficient. While I leave it in the hands of the user to decide which algorithm he or she trusts, I will just add a morsel of food for thought: cryptanalysts are probably much busier *working* on defeats for AES than they are for Serpent or Twofish because of the ubiquity and popularity of AES. For this reason, I consider using all of the algorithms for different things: AES for full-disk encryption, Serpent for my file-level encrypted volumes, and Twofish for my Password Safe databases. If a vulnerability is discovered in any one of these algorithms, I still have some level of protection provided by the others.

TRUECRYPT

Until May of 2014 (just a few short months before this writing) TrueCrypt was the de facto encryption program *du jour* for individual and home users. TrueCrypt offered a very robust encryption, was exceptionally feature-rich, and was fairly user-friendly. TrueCrypt could be used for both full-disk and file level encryption, could support various two-factor authentication schemes, was available for Linux, Mac, and Windows, and was totally free. Unfortunately, the developers of TrueCrypt decided that they would no longer support the program and dropped it in a rather public and alarming manner. The TrueCrypt homepage (truecrypt.org) was redirected to a warning page that advised, "WARNING: TrueCrypt is not secure as it may contain unfixed security issues." The site then went on to detail the procedure to migrate data to a different encryption program. In conjunction with this warning, one final version of TrueCrypt, version 7.2 was (and still is) offered. This version is not useful for encryption purposes as it only allows users who had previously used TrueCrypt to decrypt their files if need be.

So does that mean TrueCrypt is no longer a viable encryption option and is insecure? No, it does not. In fact, TrueCrypt is one of the few, free encryption programs that has been independently audited. In October of 2013, a crowd-funded audit was undertaken that found no serious vulnerabilities or "backdoors" in TrueCrypt version 7.1a. (The full cryptographic audit is still ongoing at the time of this writing.) The last stable, trusted, usable release of TrueCrypt, version 7.1a, is still available through many download sites. (For more information on the status and findings of the audit visit: www.istruecryptauditedyet.com.) The TrueCrypt download site I recommend is:

https://github.com/AuditProject/truecrypt-verified-mirror

TRUST, BUT VERIFY

Before fully trusting a download of any security software (regardless of the site from which it is downloaded) I strongly recommend verifying the checksum retrieved from a separate, reputable website. This verification process is discussed more fully in Chapter 2.

TrueCrypt can be used on Linux, OSX, and Windows. Once you have downloaded, verified, and installed TrueCrypt, you will find that it is an incredibly feature-rich encryption program. TrueCrypt offers the ability to create file-level encrypted containers (called "volumes"), hidden volumes (which are built inside standard volumes and offer a layer of plausible deniability), and full-disk encryption for the system drive and non-system drives. It is also capable of encrypting a partition or entirety of a USB flash drive or hard drive. Further, with TrueCrypt you can use two-factor authentication for volumes (using keyfiles), choose any of three very strong encryption algorithms or use them in combination, and even create a hidden operating system on your computer.

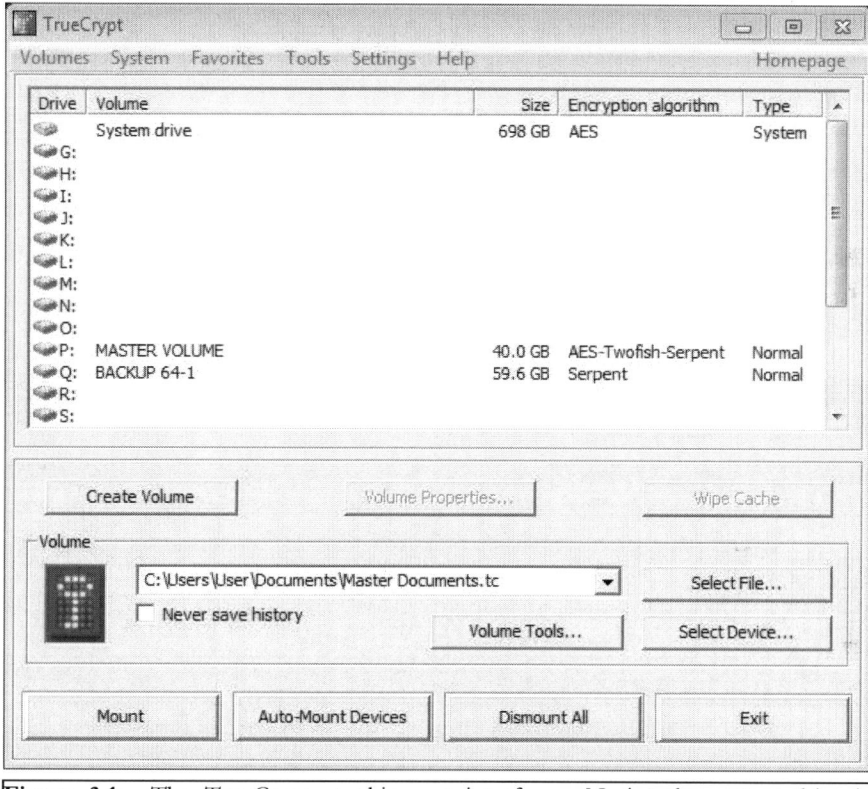

Figure 3.1: The TrueCrypt graphic user interface. Notice the system drive is encrypted, as well as file volumes.

TrueCrypt is incredibly well documented, and the 150-page TrueCrypt User's Guide that is included in the download of the program does a very thorough job of explaining how to use most of the functions available in the program. For this reason, I will not duplicate this effort here. To access the TrueCrypt User's Guide, open TrueCrypt, click the Help drop-down menu, and click the first option: User's Guide.

How I Use TrueCrypt: My preferred method of using TrueCrypt is to use both file-level encrypted volumes and full-disk encryption. This belt-and-suspenders approach gives me peace of mind that my data is secure no matter what. Here is my recommendation for how to do it:

First, full-disk encrypt your computer using the "Encrypt the system partition or entire system drive" option in the TrueCrypt Volume Creation Wizard. Consult the TrueCrypt User's Guide for exact instructions on how to do this. As previously discussed, this will protect all of the contents of your entire device if it is lost or stolen. Be aware that in order to fully encrypt your hard drive, TrueCrypt will prompt you to burn a "TrueCrypt Rescue Disk" onto a CD. Though there are ways to bypass the requirement to burn an actual disk, I highly recommend completing this step.

This rescue disk contains volume header information for emergency use. In the event your encryption becomes corrupted, you can boot from the disk, enter the correct password, and the encryption can be repaired, once more allowing you access to your files. It is a common misconception that this disk contains the password. It does not, so be under no misconceptions: if you forget your password the TrueCrypt rescue disk will not let you back into your device.

Next, build an encrypted volume (or series of encrypted volumes if you desire compartmentalization) that is large enough to store all of your sensitive documents. I would recommend storing not only credit reports, work documents, résumés, and other obviously sensitive information, but family photographs and other seemingly innocuous files as well. Though typically not considered "sensitive," these items can reveal a great deal of information about you and your family including your interests and hobbies, your patterns of life, valuables that you possess in your home, etc. (In my house, *everything* gets stored in a TrueCrypt volume.) This volume may be quite large, but this won't be an isue as long as you have space on the hard drive. Once all of these items are secured in a TrueCrypt volume, verify the contents, ensure you didn't miss anything, and delete the unencrypted versions (see the section on secure file deletion later in this chapter).

Using two layers of encryption like this may seem like overkill to some. This method offers two advantages, though. First, it allows me to dismount the TrueCrypt volumes that contain my sensitive documents and walk away from my device for a short time (i.e. to run to the restroom if I am in a [secured] space I share with co-workers). Second, if multiple users have access to the device (a family using a common computer, for instance), it allows you to store items privately that you do not want the other users to access. Finally, by using very strong, very different passwords on the boot loader and volumes, you have the peace of mind of knowing that to recover all your sensitive files, an attacker will be forced to break two passwords which will require twice the work and consume twice the time.

TrueCrypt Favorites: One extremely useful feature of TrueCrypt is its ability to designate volumes as "Favorites." Favorites allow you to mount all your favorite volumes at once (if they share a password), will consistently assign them to the same drive letter each time they are mounted, and allow you to give them a custom name. I find all of these features extremely helpful. I always mount two TrueCrypt volumes at a time (my primary and a backup), and giving them custom names helps me quickly discern which is which. Another plus of being able to mount all favorites at once means I only have to enter one password to mount them.

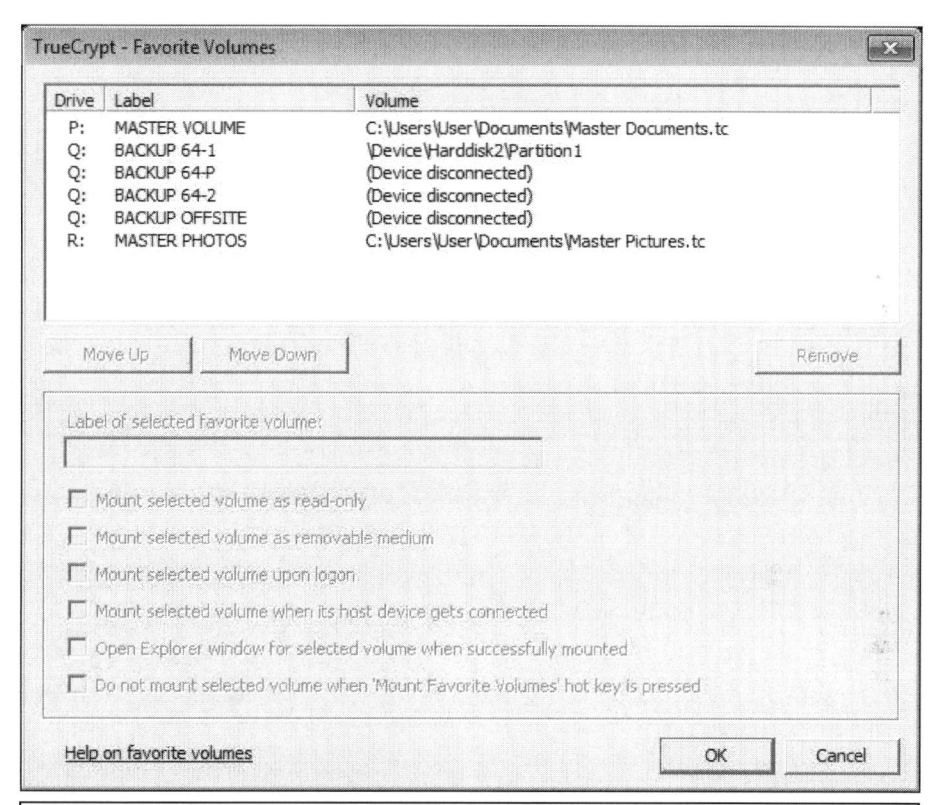

Figure 3.2: TrueCrypt volume favorites. In addition to the ability to assign custom names, Favorites also allows you to consistently mount volumes to the same drive letter.

Being able to consistently and easily mount volumes to the same drive letter each time is extremely helpful as well. This helps in setting up a number of other features on your computer. Even though they are independently encrypted, I store my Password Safe databases inside a TrueCrypt volume because of the disproportionate amount of damage that would be done if they were compromised. When I open Password Safe it attempts to open the database from the last location from which it was opened. If I mount to a different drive letter each time, I would then have to manually navigate to the database. This is inconvenient and time consuming, and I can completely avoid this by mounting my volume(s) as Favorites. I also set up Microsoft Office to store auto-saved versions inside a TrueCrypt volume, which is mapped according to a drive letter. If this drive letter changes the program will force me to manually choose the save location. The most important reason I use Favorites, though, is for my backup system. The program I use for backups (which will be discussed later in this chapter) will not back up my data correctly if I mount my original and duplicate volumes to incorrect drive letters.

One final useful feature of TrueCrypt Favorites is the ability to assign a consistent set of behaviors to mounted Volumes. These behaviors can be customized to meet your needs. Figure 3 displays the list of behaviors that can be assigned to each Favorite volume, including mounting as read-only or removable medium, opening Windows Explorer when the volume is mounted, etc. As is the case with all other features of TrueCrypt, more thorough explanation is contained in the TrueCrypt User's Guide. To access the Favorites menu in TrueCrypt, click the "Favorites" drop-down menu and click "Organize Favorite Volumes…."

Keyfiles: The ability to use keyfiles is an often overlooked feature of TrueCrypt. Keyfiles serve as a second authentication factor for volumes and can increase the security of encrypted volumes significantly. When mounting a volume that uses keyfiles, the user must enter the correct password and select the correct keyfile(s) that are associated with that volume. Keyfiles are simply files: photos, videos, executable programs, text documents, .PDFs, or any other type of file can be a keyfile. If you have difficulty selecting a keyfile, TrueCrypt has a built-in keyfile generator. When creating a volume or changing a volume password, you can elect to use keyfiles by checking the "Use Keyfiles" checkbox. From now on you will have to add these keyfiles each time you mount the volume.

KEYFILE SAFETY

Though any file type can be used as a keyfile, I recommend exercising care when selecting one. I prefer to use a file type that cannot easily be modified (such as a .jpeg or .mp4) rather than ones that can easily and thoughtlessly be altered (such as .docx or .txt). If the file is modified in any way there is a very good chance that it will no longer be recognized as the required keyfile and you will subsequently be unable to get back into your TrueCrypt volume. I much prefer to use image or video files that are not easily changed. Further, I strongly recommend backing up keyfiles. Backup keyfiles can be stored on a USB flash drive, in the cloud, on another machine, or in your email inbox, but if so they should probably be concealed among a number of other innocuous files.

Keyfiles increase security by requiring both the correct password and the correct keyfiles to mount the volume. You can add as many keyfiles as you want (I have successfully added as many fifty keyfiles). An attacker attempting to open your volume would have to know the password, as well as two other pieces of information: the fact that the volume requires keyfiles, and what those keyfiles are. Further, the attacker would require access to these files. If you store them in the cloud or on a USB flash drive that you carry in your pocket access to them could be very difficult to acquire.

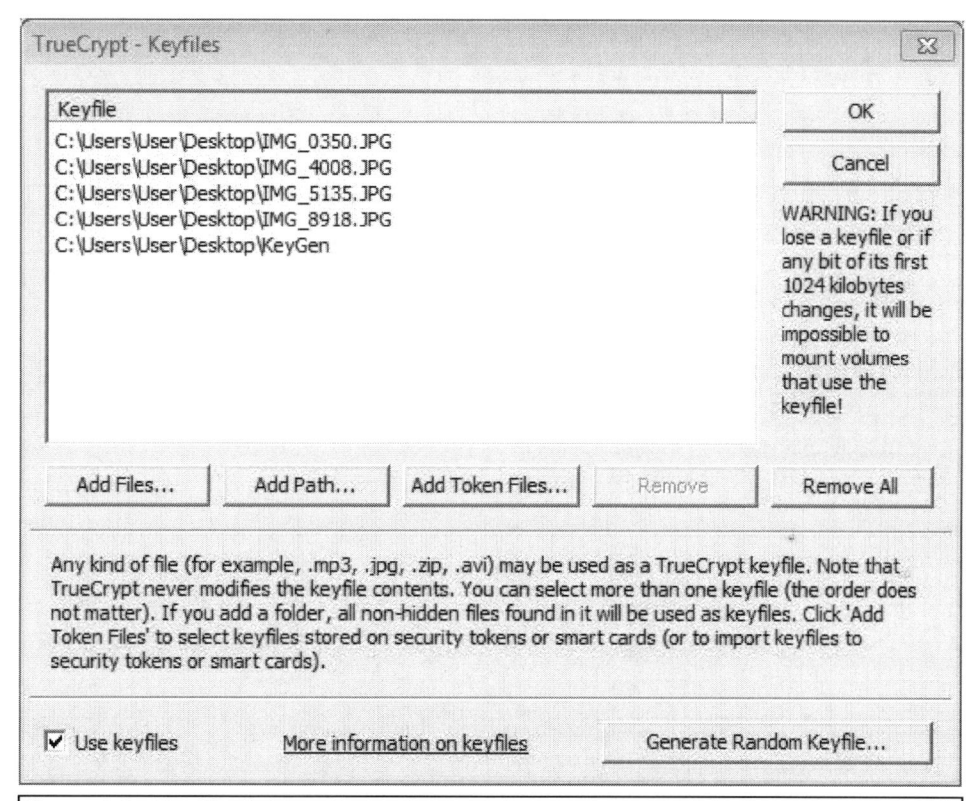

Figure 3.3: Keyfiles being added before opening a volume. Obviously storing keyfiles on your desktop as indicated in this example is a bad idea; they should be hidden among thousands of other innocuous files if possible.

Below we will discuss some other encryption options. This is not because of any uncertainty around TrueCrypt; indeed, TrueCrypt is one of the few independently audited encryption options out there, and I still trust it as fully as anything else despite the lack of future support.

DISKCRYPTOR

One program that is touted as an alternative to TrueCrypt is DiskCryptor. It offers some, but certainly not all, of the functionality of TrueCrypt. DiskCryptor is a free and fully open-source program that offers full-disk encryption for system and non-system devices and partitions. DiskCryptor does not offer file-level encryption but does support the use of keyfiles and the AES, Serpent, and Twofish algorithms. For what it is worth, I have worked with DiskCryptor and feel comfortable considering it my full-disk backup solution in the event a serious vulnerability is discovered in TrueCrypt.

DiskCryptor is incredibly easy to implement. After downloading and installing it, open the simple interface which shows a list of drives attached to your computer. To encrypt a non-system drive, select the drive you would like to encrypt by clicking on it. Click "Encrypt" and a new dialogue will appear. The first option in this new dialogue is to select the encryption algorithm. The same options that are available in TrueCrypt are available in DiskCryptor: AES, Twofish, and Serpent, as well as cascaded versions of the three. The next option is the wipe mode. This will overwrite any data on the drive to permanently delete it before encrypting (for more information on overwriting, see the next chapter). The three overwrite options are the DOD 3- and 7-pass methods, and the Gutmann method. There is also the option to skip an overwrite altogether by selecting "None."

Clicking "Next" will advance the dialogue to the next screen where you will be prompted to input a password. Here DiskCryptor offers a very cool feature: a built-in password checker. The password checker lets you know what character types are used in your password and gives you an indication of its strength with a vertical bar graph that rates your password as "Trivially Breakable," Low, Medium, High, and Unbreakable. I don't know that I would consider any password unbreakable, but this is a nice feature that is based on the length and complexity of the password. Like TrueCrypt DiskCryptor also supports the use of keyfiles as a second authentication factor.

After selecting the encryption algorithm, wipe method, and password, clicking "OK" will begin encrypting the disk. This may take some time depending on the size of the disk and the speed of your processor. Selecting a wipe method will add significantly more time (up to several hours), as well.

Once your drive is encrypted using it is a simple matter. Plug it into your PC and open DiskCryptor. When the drive is recognized by DiskCryptor click "Mount," enter the password, and add any necessary keyfiles. The drive is now mounted as a virtual drive and will appear as a hard drive in My Computer in the same way mounted TrueCrypt volumes are mounted as virtual drives. When you are finished working with the files on the drive dismount it by clicking "Unmount."

There are several additional options that can be selected In DiskCryptor's "Tools" menu, such as backing up the header for a volume, changing a volume's password, benchmarking, and encrypting a CD to name a few. There are also several options under "Settings" that let you customize some of the functions of the application including whether it begins at startup, how volumes are unmounted, etc. DiskCryptor also allows you to set hotkeys for several functions: Mount All, Force Unmount All, Wipe Passwords, and Blue Screen.

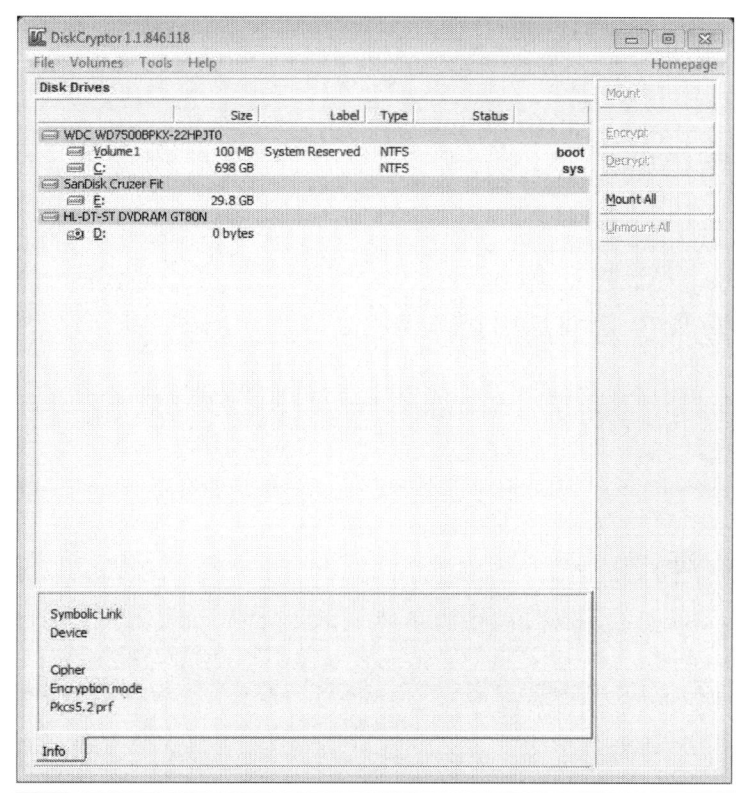

Figure 3.4: The DiskCryptor graphic user interface. DiskCryptor is incredibly simple to use and has four basic functions: Encrypt, Decrypt, Mount, and Unmount.

Though not a full-fledged replacement for TrueCrypt because of its inability to conduct volume-level encryption, DiskCryptor does offer an uncomplicated interface, simple volume creation, and some good encryption options. It is also important to note that when full-disk encrypting your system drive DiskCryptor places severe limits on your password (0-9, a-z, and A-Z only).

DiskCryptor is free and open source and available at: https://diskcryptor.net/wiki/Downloads

> **VERACRYPT**
>
> In the last few months a number of friends and colleagues have migrated to VeraCrypt, a slightly updated version of TrueCrypt that is being touted as the "new" TrueCrypt. Personally, I am very hesitant to do this just yet. Although TrueCrypt is no longer supported and no new versions will be offered by the TrueCrypt Foundation (the consortium of individuals who made TrueCrypt), there is nothing to indicate that it is in some way compromised. Further, TrueCrypt is one of a very few independently vetted encryption programs available and is, in my opinion, the best option currently offered. Once VeraCrypt has been around for a while and gained some endorsement from some prominent cryptographers and others in the security community I will consider migrating to it but for now I trust TrueCrypt far more because of its long-established reputation.
>
> On the upside, the learning curve for VeraCrypt should be a relatively gentle one. With an interface and functions that mirror those in TrueCrypt nearly perfectly it should be a painless transition if and when the day comes.

7-ZIP

Though typically considered a compression program that allows you to "zip" files into the much smaller .zip file format, 7-Zip also offers the ability to encrypt individual files. If you have a small number of files that you would like encrypted without having to create an encryption volume 7-Zip is a good solution. Additionally the ability to encrypt files individually allows you to create layers of encryption. You can encrypt the file, place it within an encrypted volume, and assuming you have used different passwords on each layer of encryption, have a double-layer of encryption over your most sensitive files.

7-Zip uses AES-256 encryption. In addition to encrypting the files, it also offers the ability to encrypt the filenames. This is a very important feature as filenames can reveal information about the contents of the files themselves, making 7-Zip a great tool for use when uploading to the cloud or anywhere else the files may be visible to a third-party.

To use 7-Zip download and install the application. Once installed 7-Zip can be used to encrypt individual files via the right-click context menu. Select the file you wish to encrypt and right-click on it. From the context menu select "Add to Archive." This will bring up an additional dialogue which will give you a number of compression protocols. This dialogue will also allow you to enter a password. Entering a password will automatically create an encrypted copy of the file. If this is the only version of the file you wish to retain it is important to delete the original securely as described in the next chapter.

To open a file that has been encrypted using 7-Zip right click on the file. From the right-click context menu select 7-Zip. In the context menu a fly-out menu will appear. Select "Extract Here." You will be prompted to enter a password. When you enter the password an unencrypted version of the file will be extracted. If you modify the file the encryption process must be repeated. This is not the most convenient solution but automated processes like CryptSync (discussed below) make 7-Zip much more user-friendly.

7-Zip is free and open source and available at: http://www.7-zip.org/

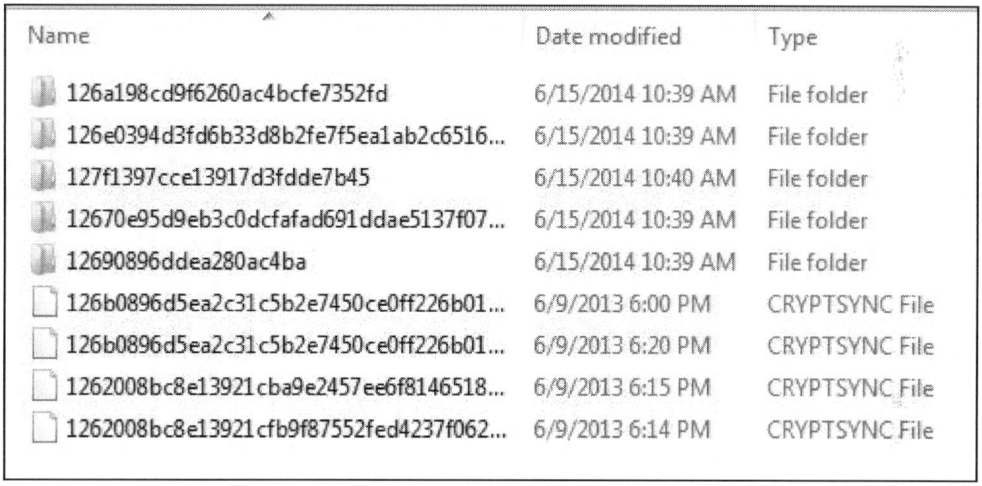

Name	Date modified	Type
126a198cd9f6260ac4bcfe7352fd	6/15/2014 10:39 AM	File folder
126e0394d3fd6b33d8b2fe7f5ea1ab2c6516...	6/15/2014 10:39 AM	File folder
127f1397cce13917d3fdde7b45	6/15/2014 10:40 AM	File folder
12670e95d9eb3c0dcfafad691ddae5137f07...	6/15/2014 10:39 AM	File folder
12690896ddea280ac4ba	6/15/2014 10:39 AM	File folder
126b0896d5ea2c31c5b2e7450ce0ff226b01...	6/9/2013 6:00 PM	CRYPTSYNC File
126b0896d5ea2c31c5b2e7450ce0ff226b01...	6/9/2013 6:20 PM	CRYPTSYNC File
1262008bc8e13921cba9e2457ee6f8146518...	6/9/2013 6:15 PM	CRYPTSYNC File
1262008bc8e13921cfb9f87552fed4237f062...	6/9/2013 6:14 PM	CRYPTSYNC File

Figure 3.5: File- and folder names encrypted with 7-Zip. Encrypting filenames is often overlooked but is an important step because filenames can reveal information about the contents of the file.

BITLOCKER/EFS

Microsoft offers full-disk and file-level encryption options with some versions the Windows 7 operating system. These are known as Bitlocker and the file-level Encrypting File System (EFS). Both of these programs use the AES algorithm to encrypt data, and both are easily implemented from the right-click context menu. BitLocker supports full-disk encryption and offers the ability to encrypt removable disks. Unfortunately, Microsoft does not package these products with all versions of Windows, nor is it available separately. BitLocker is only packaged with Windows 7 (and Vista) Ultimate and Enterprise editions, and in the Pro and Enterprise editions of Windows 8.1. These are the top-tiered versions of the operating system, a needless expense for most home users. For this reason, I will not go into great detail explaining their implementation here. If you do have one of these versions of Windows and wish to use the applications, visit http://windows.microsoft.com/en-US/windows7/products/features/bitlocker. This Windows site will guide your through the setup and use of Bitlocker. For more information on the Encrypting File System visit: http://windows.microsoft.com/en-us/windows/what-is-encrypting-file-system#1TC=windows-7

Any and all of the above encryption applications could be used in tandem with each other. Personally I find using more than one or two programs on a daily basis to be tedious and unnecessary, but it may have its advantages. For example, one may wish to use DiskCryptor for full-disk encryption, TrueCrypt for file-level encryption, and 7-Zip for encrypting files individually. This would ensure that if there was an as-of-yet undiscovered vulnerability in one of the applications some protection would still be afforded by the others.

BACKUPS

Anyone reading this book should already understand that backups are a critical component of a thorough information security posture, and in the event a hard drive fails (as has happened to me twice), your computer is lost, stolen, or irreparably damaged. It should also go without saying that backups should be encrypted *at least* to the level of the original data being backed up. In my opinion, if it's worth backing up, it's worth backing up twice.

I do not use traditional full-image backups that record all the settings and applications on my computer. Though it would take some time and effort, if my computer crashes I can easily restore all of the programs on it. All I am truly concerned with when backing up are the documents and photographs that cannot easily be replaced. The program I use for these backups is CryptSync.

Intended primarily for use with cloud storage, CryptSync is free and allows you to make copies of pairs of folders. For example, if I want a copy of My Documents to go to a DropBox account, I open CryptSync and choose "My Documents" as the original folder and my DropBox folder as the destination folder. CryptSync will create a copy of My Documents in my Dropbox folder, and keep it updated as I make changes to files in My Documents. Another major benefit, and the main reason I choose CryptSync is that it will also encrypt the copy that is sent to the destination folder using 7-Zip or GnuPG, both of which utilize the AES-256 encryption algorithm (7-Zip offers the advantage of compressing files). If you are storing data in the cloud, I highly recommend you encrypt it first. CryptSync is an excellent tool for such encryption. CryptSync will even encrypt your file names if you so choose, because the names themselves can reveal information about the contents of the file.

This is not quite how I employ CryptSync, though (because as you well know by now I do not use cloud storage). I employ CryptSync to synchronize the master TrueCrypt volume on my hard drive not with a cloud storage provider, but instead with a full-disk encrypted USB flash drive. To some, encrypting twice like this may seem heavy-handed, but I do not consider it to be. These backups are stored on USB flash drives which, as I have previously pointed out, are extremely easy to lose (I have lost several). I like knowing that my most sensitive, personal files are doubly encrypted with drastically different passwords for each layer of encryption so that if the USB drive is lost, I can sleep peacefully with the knowledge that no one has access to my files. Further, not all of these backups are in my physical control.

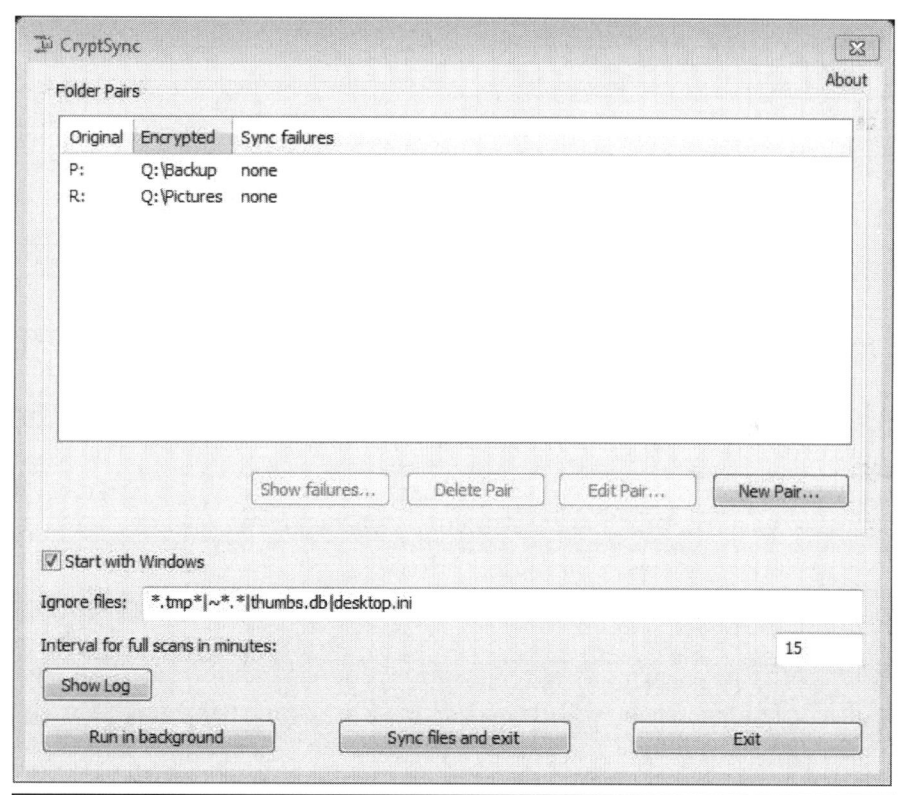

Figure 3.6: The CryptSync user interface. The "P:" and "R:" drives listed under "Orignial indicate that these are the drives to be backed up to Q:\Backup and Q:\Picutres, respectively.

I make three backups, one on each of three 64 Gb USB flash drives. One of these is carried on my keychain at all times, one is stored in my home, and one is stored offsite in a safe deposit box. Each of these backups serves a distinct purpose. The one in my house is always plugged into my computer, is always up to date, and is primarily in place to restore my files if my computer's hard drive fails. The one on my keychain is updated weekly so it is reasonably up-to-date should my house burn down or my computer be stolen while I am away. The third one is stored offsite, is updated monthly, and is available in the event a serious calamity befalls my entire geographic region, or some other reason prevents me from salvaging one of the other copies. Though it may be out-of-date by a month (at most) it is still a good starting point, and most of my data can be salvaged.

To set this system up I open CryptSync and choose the drive letter to which I have my TrueCrypt volume mounted and designate it as my original folder. This necessitates that I always mount the volume to the same drive letter. This being the case, in TrueCrypt I have assigned this volume as a system favorite so it will always mount to the same "P" drive. I then mount one of the fully-encrypted USB flash drives and mount it as driver letter "Q," again making it a favorite so it will consistently mount to the same drive letter and will function correctly with CryptSync.

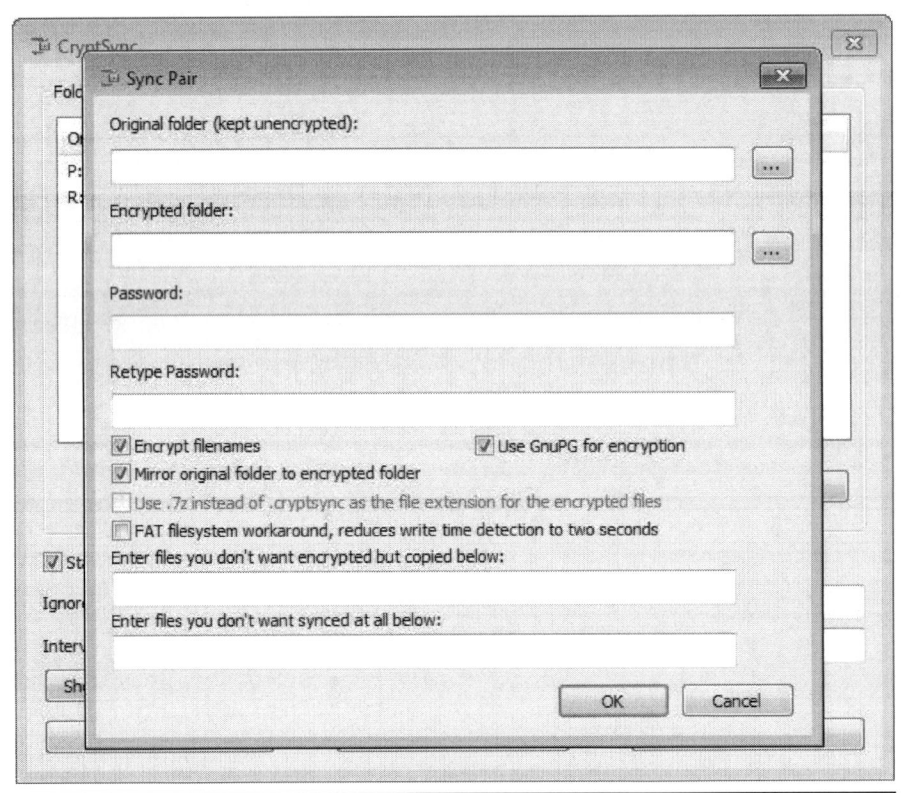

Figure 3.7: The setup menu for building a new CryptSync pair. CryptSync is incredibly feature rich and works wonderfully as a backup utility.

CryptSync is free and available at: http://stefanstools.sourceforge.net/CryptSync.html

OTHER BACKUP UTILITIES

There are numerous other backup utilities out there that will do full system image backups. Most of them require a paid subscription and I do not find them necessary. Full disk image backups offer you the ability to restore your computer (or a new one) to its condition at the time of the last backup but they take a long time to run and slow your system down while doing so. I find I do not need this level of protection, but if you do I would recommend you choose one that encrypts the backup with AES, Serpent, or Twofish encryption. If your backup utility does not allow you to encrypt the backup natively, ensure that it will allow you to create backups to a hard drive that is encrypted with a separate encryption utility like TrueCrypt or DiskCryptor. Regardless of which backup utility you use, use something. The loss of precious data is not something I would wish on anyone.

SUMMARY

Regardless of which encryption program you choose, use something. Though I prefer the applications mentioned here, they are far from the only ones available. Even the poorest encryption programs out there will provide *some* level of protection. To paraphrase Bruce Schneier, there are two types of encryption: encryption that keeps your sister from reading your diary and encryption that protects you from governments. Though I prefer the latter, the first would still be better than nothing. If you do nothing other than this, please full-disk encrypt your device. This should be the standard. In addition you should also:

- o Set up file-level encryption using TrueCrypt or EFS (if you have it)
- o Fully encrypt USB flash drives, hard drives, CDs and DVDs, and other external media with an encryption program like TrueCrypt or DiskCryptor
- o Encrypt individual files, as needed, with an application like 7-Zip
- o Use a backup utility that supports encryption (I like CryptSync)

CHAPTER 4:
SECURE FILE DELETION

Being able to securely delete files that are no longer wanted or needed is an important aspect of computer security. If your device is fully encrypted this is less of concern as no files, deleted or otherwise, will be recovered from your device. You may, however, still desire to sanitize a computer prior to reselling, donating, or gifting it, and if you do not have full-disk encryption thorough deletion is especially important. Or, you may just prefer to know everything is gone once it has been deleted, as I do. To do this I use several secure erasure programs.

First, it is important to understand that there are two types of memory in a computer. The first and most commonly referenced is non-volatile and is technically referred to as "storage." This is the computer's hard drive and it contains data that is intended to be saved permanently. The other type of memory (which is correctly called "memory") is Random Access Memory (RAM). RAM is considered volatile memory, or memory that dissipates and is lost when the computer is shut down.

A computer's RAM is used to store temporary files, open programs, open files for use in on-the-fly encryption applications like TrueCrypt, and a host of other things for which some short-term storage is needed. Fortunately the data contained in RAM is typically unrecoverable within a few moments of the computer being shut down. Under certain conditions (typically very cold conditions) the information in RAM can be recovered hours later but this requires a very sophisticated (and expensive) attack. Because of this, I worry very little about what is stored temporarily in RAM.

I am much more concerned, however, with the security of the information that is stored on my computer's hard drive. The storage in a hard disk drive (HDD) is persistent by design. Unfortunately this information can also be difficult to get rid of when it is no longer needed or wanted. When using Windows 7 the most common way of deleting a file is to select it and hit the

Delete or Backspace key which sends the file to the Recycle Bin. When the Recycle Bin is emptied the file is presumed to be gone forever.

Unfortunately this does not actually remove the file from the hard drive. Deleting a file in this manner simply removes the information that the operating system uses to locate it. The operating system then allocates the space on the hard drive where the file resides as "free space." The file is still almost totally intact on the hard drive until it is overwritten with new information. Though it would not seem like it, it can take an extremely long time for the entire file to actually be overwritten. In the meantime, as long as the file remains intact it is easily recovered from your hard drive, even by a novice.

Recuva: Recuva is a freeware program that allows you to recover deleted files from your computer. Recuva is a very simple, user-friendly application that does a remarkably good job considering its cost. I recommend running Recuva before running a secure file deletion software for two reasons. First, if you have been using your machine for a while you will likely be surprised to find all the previously deleted files that still reside on your hard drive. Second, running Recuva can occasionally give you an indication as to whether or not you need to perform some of the steps listed below.

WARNING!!!

Only run Recuva on a computer that you personally own and on which you are the sole adult user. Running this program on a computer that you share with roommates, romantic partners, or co-workers may reveal information that they do not desire you to see, and that you almost certainly do not want you to see. I have personally witnessed (and experienced) some embarrassment as a user who lost one file looked on and reddened as many others (typically .jpegs) surfaced after asking me to help. On the flip side of that coin, during my tour in Iraq Recuva was used to recover hundreds of compromising photos on public computers on military bases, underscoring the need for good file deletion practices.

To use Recuva install the application or download the portable version. Recuva must be run with Administrator privileges so if you are working from a Standard User account (which you should be) you will have to right-click the application and select "Run as Administrator." After entering your Administrator password you will be presented with the Recuva Wizard. Click Next, then select the radio buttons for the file types for which you wish to search. The most comprehensive of these, and the one I typically choose, is "All Files." This is the most exhaustive search and will net the most results. Click Next again, then you will select a location to search. I recommend choosing the "In a specific location" option and selecting an entire hard drive. If you are doing a pre-assessment on your own computer this will most likely be your C drive. Click Next once more, and on the following screen check the "Enable deep scan" box, then click Start. This will begin the scan.

Recuva will now scan the selected location for files. This may take some time depending on how much free space is on your hard drive. Once the program finishes its work the results will be displayed and you will have the option to restore or delete each file. This should give you a good idea of your need (or lack thereof) to wipe free space with the programs discussed below.

Recuva is free and available at: http://www.piriform.com/recuva

If your computer is subject to a true forensic attack the tools used will be much more sophisticated and capable than Recuva. First, a bit-by-bit copy of your entire hard drive will be made to preserve the original. With the fresh copy, each file will be carved from the hard drive and examined at the bit level. Even small fragments of files may reveal sensitive information under these conditions. If this attack fails to reveal any information more sophisticated techniques may be used, such as a laboratory attack, under which your hard drive will be disassembled and examined under a forced electron microscope. At this point it is important to make clear the following: If you are subject to such a forensic examination, you have probably made some very serious and very well-financed enemies who may be able to retrieve the desired information through other avenues and secure deletion may not save you. I still like to take a redundant approach to security, though, and feel much safer knowing that I have increased the difficulty of extracting files from my machine.

ENCRYPTION AS ERASURE

As awareness of full disk encryption becomes more pervasive the corporate world is taking notice. More and more companies are full-disk encrypting computers and FDE is being considered by some as form of data erasure. If a computer is lost, the reasoning goes, it is fully encrypted and nothing can be recovered from it, even under sophisticated attacks. This logic is correct and another reason I am such a strong advocate of full-disk encryption. I do take great pains to erase files securely, though, on the off chance my encryption is compromised or my password is broken.

SECURE FILE DELETION BASICS

The surest way to get rid of unwanted files is known as "secure file deletion" or "data erasure." When a file is written to your hard drive, it is written as a series of ones and zeros. These ones and zeros are transcribed to the disk by flipping magnetic switches; one direction for "1," the other for

"0." A secure deletion program will overwrite these files with a random series of ones and zeros, obscuring the original information.

Name	Passes	Description
Single	1	One pass of pseudorandom data
DOD 5220.22-M (8-306. /E)	3	All 0s, all 1s, one pass pseudorandom data
RCMP TSSIT OPS-II	7	All 0s, all 1s, all 0s, all 1s, all 0s, all 1s, pseudorandom data
Schneier Method	7	All 1s, all 0s, five passes pseudorandom data
Gutmann Method	35	Passes 1 – 4: Pseudorandom data Pass 5: 01010101 Pass 6: 10101010 Pass 7: 10010010 Pass 8: 01001001 Pass 9: 00100100 Pass 10: 00000000 Pass 11: 00010001 Pass 12: 00100010 Pass 13: 00110011 Pass 14: 01000100 Pass 15: 01010101 Pass 16: 01100110 Pass 17: 01110111 Pass 18: 10001000 Pass 19: 10011001 Pass 20: 10101010 Pass 21: 10111011 Pass 22: 11001100 Pass 23: 11011101 Pass 24: 11101110 Pass 25: 11111111 Pass 26: 10010010 Pass 27: 01001001 Pass 28: 00100100 Pass 29: 01101101 Pass 30: 10110110 Pass 31: 11011011 Passes 32-35: Pseudorandom data

Just as there are numerous encryption algorithms, there are also numerous overwrite algorithms. Most of the programs I will discuss offer the ability to do a single pass of pseudorandom data, or one pass of randomly generated ones and zeros. They will also offer much more complex algorithms, including a 3-pass, 7-pass, and the infamous Gutmann 35-pass. These more complex algorithms do not merely write 3, 7, or 35 passes of pseudorandom data. Rather, they work in intricate, well-defined patterns as shown in the chart on the facing page.

For most purposes a single overwrite should be sufficient to make your data unrecoverable to all but the most sophisticated attacks, and it is debatable whether more passes really make much of a difference. What is not debatable is the time they take. For each pass the computer has to generate that same amount of data. For example, if you are overwriting one gigabyte of data with a 7-pass overwrite, the computer has to write 7 gigabytes of data to the hard drive. Not only does this take time, it also exerts wear and tear on the hard drive (which has a finite life cycle). For the vast majority of overwriting purposes I rely on three passes. Only when something extremely sensitive must be destroyed will I resort to the more complex, and more time-consuming overwrite algorithms.

There are two other factors to consider when discussing file deletion and data remanence. They are alternate data streams (ADS) and cluster tips. Alternate data streams are small "sidecar" files that accompany some original files. They frequently contain metadata about the file. For example, in Internet Explorer ADSs are used to store favicons in website shortcut files. Because of the information they have the potential to contain, ADSs should be deleted along with the original file. All of the deletion programs we will discuss below offer the ability to delete alternate data streams.

Cluster tips refer to small, unused sections of a cluster. Files are stored on the hard drive in clusters and a file will usually take up more than one cluster. If a file takes up 5.3 clusters, the sixth cluster will have .7 (or 70%) free. This last .7 of a cluster is the cluster tip. This cluster tip may contain some sensitive, recoverable information and should be overwritten along with the rest of the file. The erasure programs presented in this chapter allow the overwrite of cluster tips.

It is also important to note at this point that erasure techniques do not work as well when permanently removing *individual* files on solid-state drives (SSDs), though a *full wipe* of SSDs will work as well as one conducted on a HDD. SSDs store data in an entirely different manner than HDDs, and in one that does not lend itself to easy and effective overwriting of individual files. If you have a device with an SSD, full-disk encryption is your primary means of data erasure (see sidebar on page 87). Though I do not wish to downplay the importance of FDE for *all* computer users, it is especially important for SSD users.

File-level encryption offers some defense against data recovery, too. Unfortunately, there are numerous data leaks in the Windows operating system. Anyone gaining access to your machine would very likely be able to recover scads of metadata, partial file fragments, registry entries, and other information that could be used to piece together your sensitive information. This is another reason I am so adamant about full-disk encryption.

ERASER

Eraser is my preferred program for the targeted, secure deletion of selected files. Every file that gets deleted on my computer gets permanently deleted with this application. Eraser is incredibly easy to use, offers a number of features, and does an excellent job of permanently deleting files. The first step after installation is opening Eraser and modifying the basic settings.

To modify the basic settings in Eraser open the application. The interface is very streamlined, with only three options: Erase Schedule, Settings, and Help. Click the Settings icon. The first item in the settings is the checkbox allowing Eraser to be integrated into Windows Explorer. This will ensure Eraser is available via the right-click context menu. The next section concerns the secure deletion settings. The dropdown menus for "Default file erasure method" and "Default drive erasure method" contain a comprehensive list of options, depending upon your desired overwrite method. By default, Eraser makes the default file erasure method the most secure option (Gutmann's 35-pass), while the default drive erasure method is a single pass (due to the length of time taken to wipe free space). Select the method of your choice.

> **THINK BEFORE YOU DELETE**
>
> I should note at this point that you should exercise caution when using secure deletion software, especially when deleting multiple files at once. Once a file is gone it is gone for good and there is no recovering it. During the writing of this book I had each chapter in a separate Microsoft Word document. After I transferred them all to a single document I used Eraser to get rid of the individual files. Unfortunately there was one chapter that I had overlooked when copying the text over, forcing me to rewrite the entire chapter from scratch. Somewhat ironically, it was this chapter.

Scrolling down Eraser will offer a number of other options. First ensure "Force lock files to be unlocked for erasure" is checked. This will reduce the incidence of errors when you attempt to erase a file that is locked. Eraser also allows you the option to replace deleted files with pre-selected files for the sake of "plausible deniability." Were anyone to forensically examine your computer there would be a file where the deleted file had previously been, making it less obvious that a file had ever been deleted from that location.

The Erase Schedule option allows you to plan erases at specific times: immediately, on restart, or recurring. A recurring erase would be an excellent means of cleaning your machine if you generate a large number of files in the same location(s) on a daily basis that all need to be deleted at the end of the day. You can designate a target (targets may be files, files in a folder, the recycle bin, unused disk space, or a drive or partition) that gets cleaned automatically. The task can be set to run at a specific time daily, weekly, or monthly, or only on certain days of the week. I only use this function to wipe my free disk space monthly. Even though I use this function infrequently, I see its utility in everyday use. If allowed to run in the background on startup, Eraser's most useful functions can be accessed directly from the right-click context menu. This is incredibly convenient and the three functions I use most commonly are:

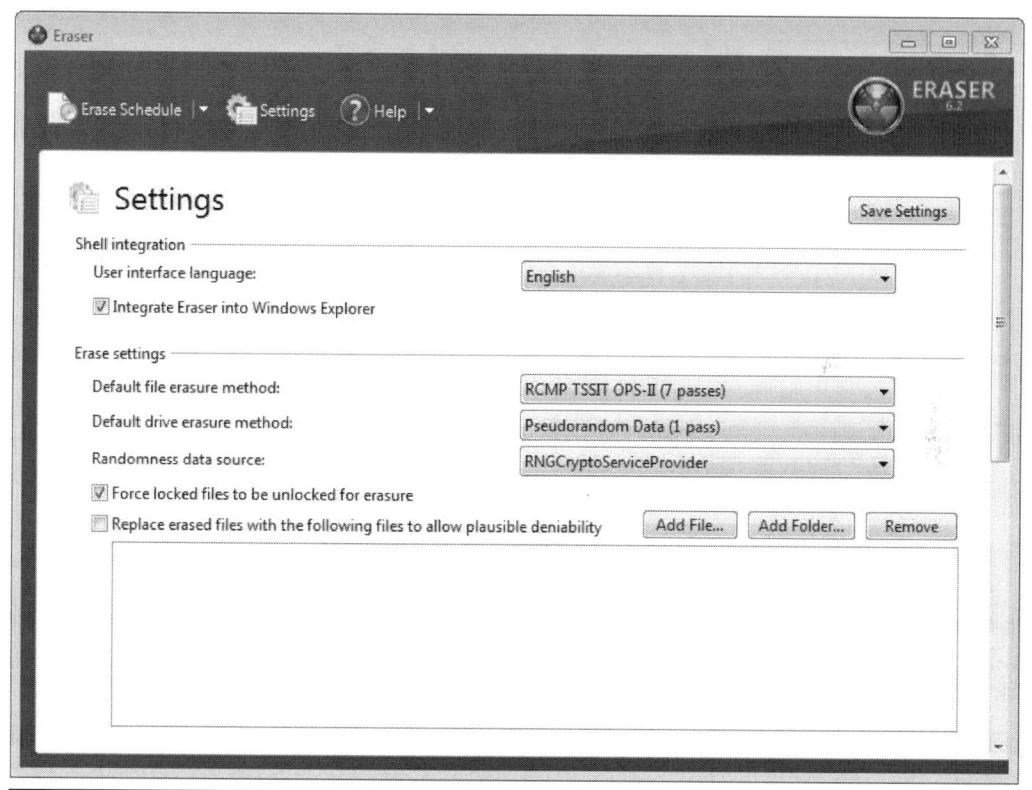

Figure 4.1: The setup menu Eraser 6.0.2. If you use Eraser primarily through the right-click context menu you will only rarely see this.

Erase: This is the simplest yet most useful function in the application. The Erase function allows you to quickly delete a file. To access this function simply select the file, right click on it, and select "Eraser." Two options will appear: Erase and Secure Move. Select "Erase" and the file will be securely deleted with the overwrite algorithm you chose when setting up the program's settings.

Secure Move: Another useful feature of Eraser, Secure Move, allows you to copy a file to a new location and get rid of the original in a single function. When you select a file and choose "Secure Move," Eraser will ask you where you would like to put the new file. Navigate to that location, and click "OK." Eraser will then make a copy of the file in the new location and delete the old copy using the default overwrite algorithm.

Erase Unused Space: Eraser offers the option to erase the unused space on a drive. This ensures that if files have previously been deleted insecurely they will not remain recoverable. Cleaning unused space can take a very long time if you have a lot of it and depending on what overwrite algorithm you use, and each additional overwrite puts wear on your hard drive. I recommend doing this only occasionally. I will use this option once a month with a single pass just to ensure I haven't accidentally allowed something to be deleted insecurely. If you are consistently deleting files securely with Eraser this is probably unnecessary.

Eraser is free and available at: http://eraser.heidi.ie/

CCLEANER

This is one of my absolute favorite applications and one that I use several times a day. CCleaner is not designed to be used for deleting an individual, targeted file, but it can be used in that manner. The other, official features of CCleaner are what make it so attractive to me. With over a billion downloads CCleaner is extremely popular as a user-friendly general cleanup software.

CCleaner (formerly known as "Crap Cleaner") cleans up all the accumulated detritus of your operating system. As you use your Windows PC numerous files are created by the OS, recording what files you open, what programs you use, and other data. Obviously, this information would be of large benefit to anyone conducting a forensic analysis of your machine and it is a good idea to keep these files to a minimum. CCleaner will securely erase these files but there is also a more practical reason to use CCleaner.

Many of these useless files that accumulate are created by the OS in an attempt to speed up your system. Pre-fetch data, for instance, is designed to help the computer "remember" which files you access frequently so it can bring them up quickly. While this works well in theory, over time the accumulation of all this data ends up slowing the system down (I have seen CCleaner remove as many as 8 gigabytes of data from an exceptionally "dirty" system). Because of the large volume of junk CCleaner removes running it regularly may also improve your system performance drastically, especially on aging machines or machines that have never been cleaned.

CCleaner is exceptionally easy to use. First, download and install the program. Once the program is installed open it, and on the left-hand side of the GUI there are several icons: Cleaner, Registry, Tools, and Options. Before actually cleaning your system click the Options icon. This will present a list of selections, the first of which is Settings. Click Settings next. The settings menu will contain the basic settings you can manipulate in CCleaner. Since this chapter is dedicated to data erasure we will focus on the Secure Deletion settings.

First, select the "Secure file deletion (slower)" radio button. This will open up some new options that are unavailable by default. They are Wipe Alternate Data Streams and Wipe Cluster Tips; both should be selected. Just above these options is a drop-down menu allowing you to select the number of desired overwrite passes. For CCleaner I typically select a single pass, or the Simple Overwrite option. If you desire a more thorough cleaning you may select from any other the other options, keeping in mind that more passes increases the time taken to run the cleaning process of this application. Finally, at the bottom of these settings select "Wipe MFT Free Space." The Master File Table (MFT) is a list of all the files on a Windows system. As files are deleted, space in the MFT becomes free. That space can contain information about files that were previously on the system, which will ensure these filenames are not recoverable from the MFT.

After changing these settings return to the main screen by clicking the Cleaner icon in the left-hand pane. Just to the right of this pane there will be two tabs containing options that can be selected. These are the items that CCleaner will delete when it is run. The 35 Windows options are standard, and I recommend selecting all of them except Wipe Free Space. Be forewarned that this will take an extraordinary amount of time (up to several hours depending on the size of your free space, the overwrite algorithm selected, and your processor speed). I prefer wiping free space with Eraser as outline above. The second tab contains options that are specific to applications installed on your machine. Again, I recommend selecting all of these options.

After modifying the erasure settings and selecting the items to be cleaned CCleaner is now ready to go. In the lower right-hand corner of the interface select "Run Cleaner." CCleaner will warn you that you are about to permanently delete files from your system. Check the "Don't show this message again" box and click "OK." If you have never run CCleaner before this may take a significant amount of time. I recommend running CCleaner daily and do so just before shutting my computer down each time, ensuring my system is cleaned at least once every day. If I am working on certain tasks on the Internet and do not wished to be tracked from one activity to the other, I will run CCleaner between sessions to ensure that no cookies were left behind from the previous session.

By running CCleaner so frequently it never takes more than a few seconds to finish, and is totally worth the security and privacy it offers.

The other option CCleaner offers that I recommend running occasionally is the registry cleaner. Each time you install, uninstall, or modify a program, random bits of that program are left behind in the registry. Not only does this create a trail of the programs that were once installed on your machine, over time it can slow your computer down, too. The registry cleaner is very simple and requires no changes in any settings. To use it click the "Registry" icon in the left-hand pane. On the bottom of the interface click the "Scan for issues" button. This will scan the registry for stray bits of data. When this process has completed click the "Fix selected issues" button at lower right.

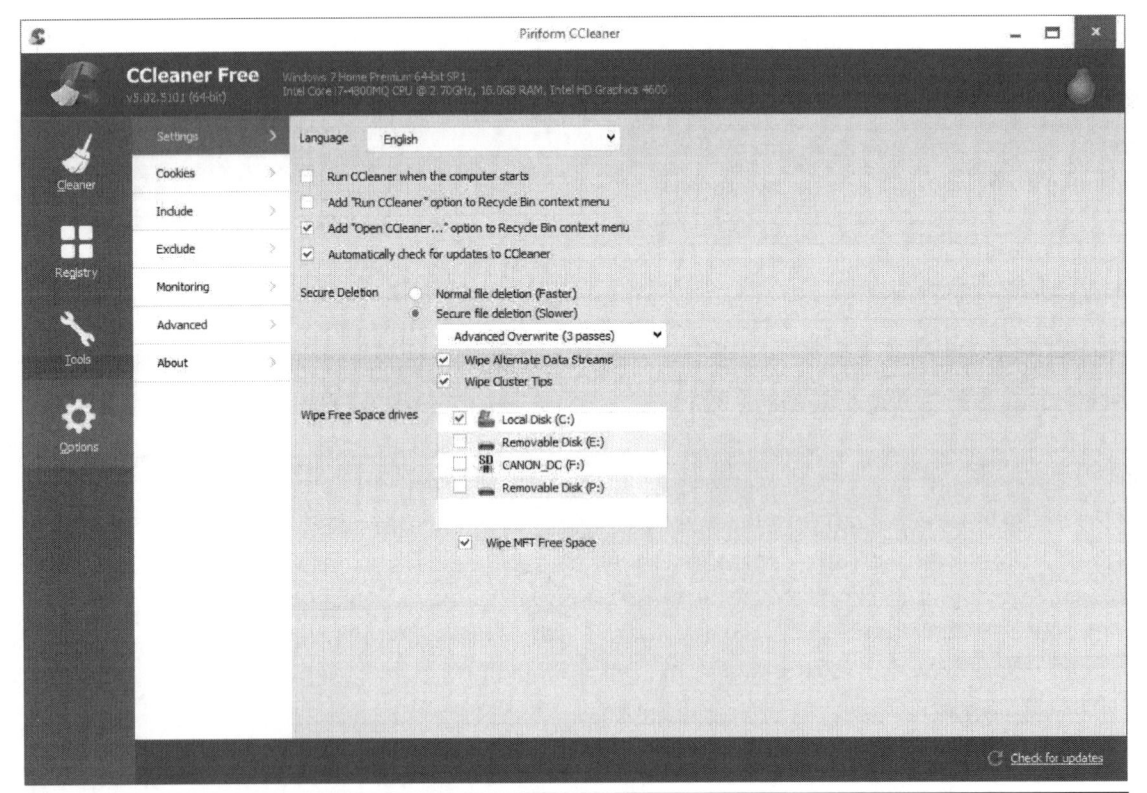

Figure 4.2: The settings in CCleaner. The important options to change are "Secure file deletion" (use the number of passes you are comfortable with), Wipe Alternate Data Streams, Wipe Cluster Tips, and Wipe MFT Free Space.

Before actually fixing the issues, CCleaner will as you if you want to back up changes to the registry.

If this is the first time you have used this feature and have hundreds of issues to be fixed, backing up the registry in its current configuration is probably not a bad idea. If the cleaning creates instability in your system you can revert back to the pre-cleaning copy of the registry (I have been using CCleaner since 2005 and have never had an issue like this but I always backup the registry when working on a a friend's computer, just in case). Create this copy and save it in a location where it won't be forgotten (like your desktop or your primary encrypted volume). Next, click "Fix all selected issues". You may have to run this several times, as fixing the first set of issues may reveal others. Keep running this until there are no more issues to resolve. The CCleaner registry cleaner only needs to be run every month or after installing, uninstalling, updating, or otherwise modifying a program.

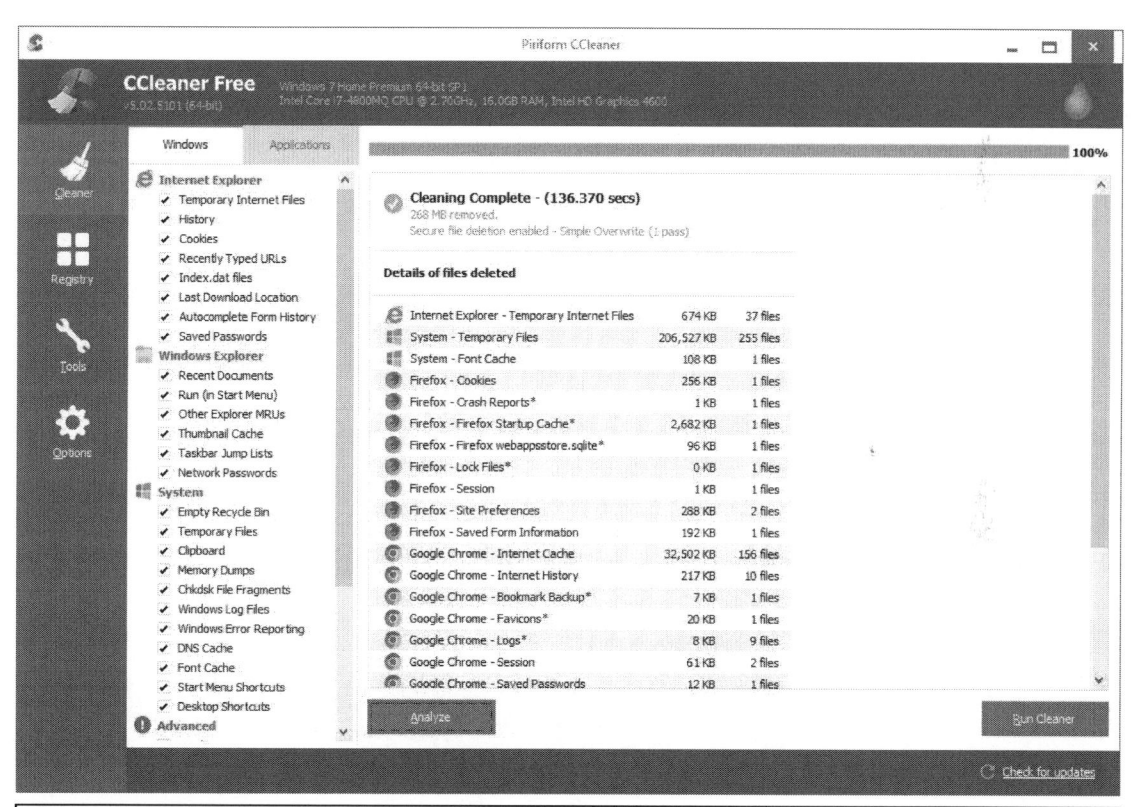

Figure 4.3: The CCleaner interface immediately after cleaning. I recommend cleaning with CCleaner once a day or immediately before shutting down your computer.

Not only will CCleaner keep your system clean, it will also keep your system running smoothly. I run it on a daily basis and it is one of only five applications pinned to my taskbar. As mentioned in Chapter 1, CCleaner can also be used to remove programs from startup and has a very capable uninstaller through which you can uninstall unwanted programs.

CCleaner is free and available at: http://www.piriform.com/ccleaner

CCENHANCER

Though CCleaner is a very thorough program, CCEnhancer can greatly increase its abilities. Produced by a third party, CCEnhancer is a portable application (it does not need to be installed to work) that downloads a small file that it then imports to CCleaner. This file contains data needed for CCleaner to clean hundreds of other programs and adds scores of options to programs cleaned natively by CCleaner.

To use CCEnhancer, download the application. When working in a Standard User account, right-click the CCEnhancer.exe file and select "Run as Administrator." Upon entering your Administrator password, the application will open. Click "Download Latest" and CCEnhancer will begin downloading the most updated .ini file. When it is finished you will be asked if you want to open CCleaner. When CCleaner opens, it will take a moment to "think" as it imports the options available in the .ini file. When CCleaner imports these options you will have hundreds of new application items that may be cleaned by CCleaner, as well as options to clean applications that are not cleaned by CCleaner alone.

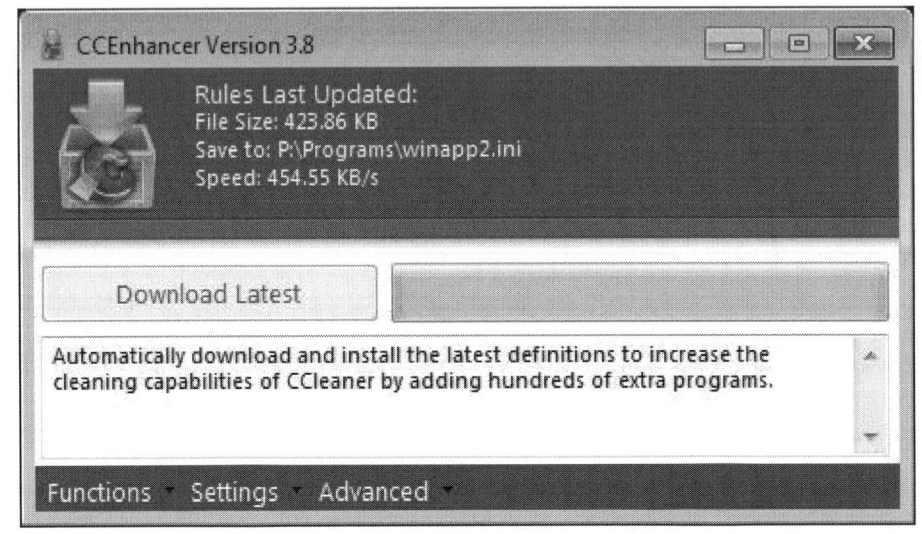

Figure 4.4: The very simple interface for CCEnhancer. Run this small application as an Administrator, download the latest .ini file, and let it open CCleaner.

CCEnhancer only has to be run occasionally. After you have run it once, the expanded cleaning options will always be present in CCleaner. I do run it once a month in case there are any new additions to the .ini file.

CCEnhancer is free and available at: https://singularlabs.com/software/ccenhancer/

DARIK'S BOOT AND NUKE

If you have reached the end of your relationship with a computer or its hard drive and wish to ensure that nothing will be recovered from it whatsoever, I recommend using Darik's Boot and Nuke (DBAN). DBAN is a bootable application that, upon startup, will wipe your entire hard drive completely. It is truly the "nuclear option," and one that should be used sparingly, as <u>nothing</u> will be left behind on your hard drive. No files, no applications, no operating system—nothing. To use DBAN, download the .iso (bootable) file and burn it to a disk. You must burn it as a bootable disk. To do so in Windows 7, insert a CD or DVD into your optical drive, right-click it, and select "Burn disk image."

When the disk has finished burning, insert it into the optical drive of the target machine and boot from the disk. Upon booting the disk, you will be presented with several choices as shown in Figure 4.5. Typing F2 will tell you more about DBAN, typing F3 will give you a list of quick commands, and typing F4 will show you the DBAN RAID disclaimer. Pressing the Enter key will allow you to run DBAN in the "interactive mode," which allows you to select certain options. Typing "autonuke" into the command prompt will begin the autonuke process, which is fully automated. The program will begin wiping your hard drive with default settings and show you a progress bar.

At this option menu I recommend pressing Enter, the option to customize the wipe. This will allow you to choose drives and erasure methods. DBAN supports single passes (a choice of all 0s or pseudorandom data), the DOD 5220.22-M three pass method, the RCMP 7-pass method (first six passes alternating between all 0s and all 1, seventh pass pseudorandom data), and of course, the Gutmann 35-pass method.

If you have first full-disk encrypted your hard drive, kept it clean with Eraser and CCleaner, and then wipe it completely using DBAN you can sleep soundly in the knowledge that no data will ever be recovered from it.

DBAN is free and available at: http://www.dban.org/

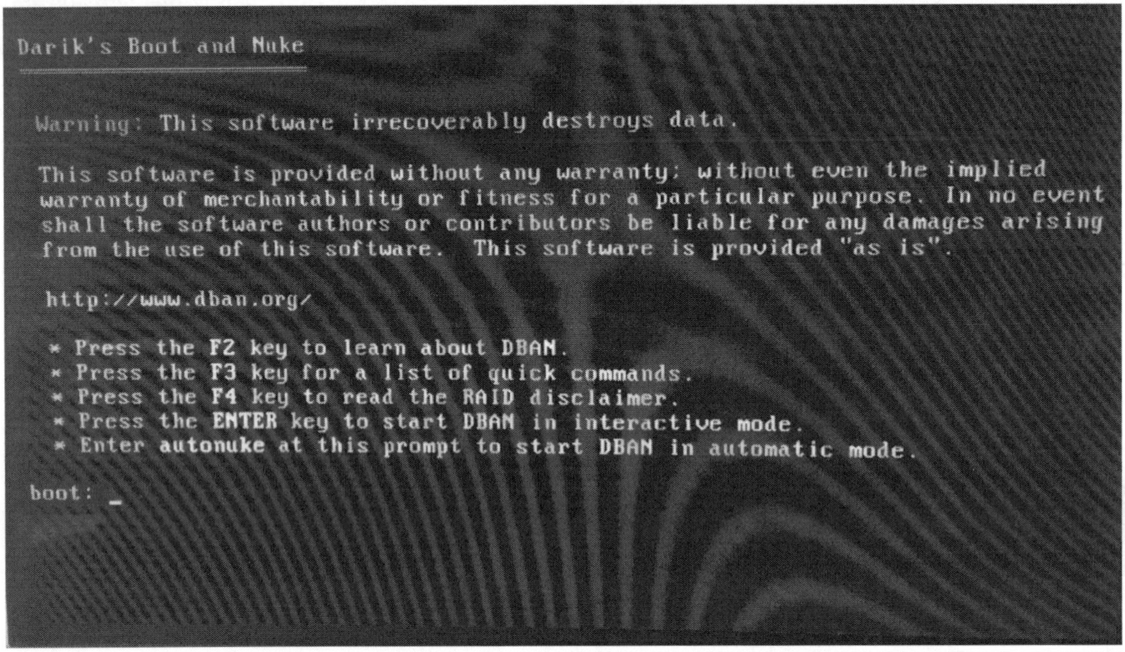

Figure 4.5: Darik's Boot and Nuke, immediately before being run on a Windows computer.

DEFRAGMENTING

Though defragmenting your hard drive is a basic function of maintaining a Windows machine and would seemingly be more appropriate in Chapter 1, I mention it here for a reason: defragmenting before wiping your machine can leave residual bits of sensitive data behind. Because of this I recommend doing a secure overwrite of free space before you defragment.

When files are saved to your computer's hard drive, they are rarely saved in perfectly linear order. As files are added, moved, and deleted on the hard drive new slots for data open up in random places across your hard drive. When a new file is added to, or created on the computer, it will often become fragmented to fill smaller open clusters on the hard drive. This can slow your computer down because it takes time to retrieve bits of the file from these various locations. Defragmenting is a process that attempts to make the files contiguous by reorganizing them and putting each one together, in its entirety, in one location.

There are numerous benefits to defragmenting (more commonly called "defragging"), the most obvious of which is that your computer performs faster when retrieving files. Defragmenting can have an adverse effect upon secure file deletion, however. If you have insecurely deleted sensitive files and then defragment, bits of these files may be overwritten with other files as they are shuffled around. This can potentially leave bits of them behind (especially in cluster tips). This may not be a security concern for most, but for those of you who are exceptionally worried about forensic analysis, wipe before defragging.

Windows has a built-in defragmenting function, but I recommend a third-party application. If you choose to use the built-in application, you can access it by navigating to **Start >> Control Panel >> System and Security >> Administrative Tools >> Defragment your hard drive**.

Defraggler: Though the Windows option works I find that Defraggler typically does a better job and has a more user-friendly GUI. To run Defraggler, download and install the application. If you are working from a Standard User account, right-click the icon and select "Run as Administrator." After entering your Administrator password the application will open. Clicking Analyze will begin an analysis of the selected disk and let you know whether a defrag is needed or not, as well as displaying a comprehensive, color-coded drive map that will show your contiguous files, fragmented files, and free space. Clicking "Defrag" will begin the process of defragmenting your drive which may take several hours depending on its size, the percentage of used space, and the state of fragmentation.

Defraggler is free and available at: http://www.piriform.com/defraggler

MANAGING DATA LEAKAGE

Windows 7 stores an incredible amount of information and information about your computer usage. Productivity software stores copies of files in seemingly random locations. Windows tracks the programs you use and how often you use them. Documents are pinned to the task bar to make them easier to retrieve. All of this information and much, much more makes up what I refer to as "leakage" and can paint a fairly accurate picture of what you do on your computer and the files contained in its hard drive to anyone who is successfully attempting to exploit your computer. Though the surest method of protecting this data is a good combination of full-disk encryption and secure file deletion, there are steps you can take to (somewhat) control how much of this information is saved in the first place. The steps mentioned here are by no means exhaustive; the applications you need to modify will vary greatly depending on what is running on your machine. There are a few settings we can modify in Windows that will be universal, however.

With the security measures already in place (full-disk encryption and a comprehensive system of secure file deletion) these steps may seem redundant. I like redundancy, especially where security is concerned. If someone manages to access my computer in an unencrypted state, I would prefer less information be available to them. And if my secure deletion applications are not working properly for some reason (I have done something wrong, the program has been compromised or has a bug, etc.), I still like to know I have done everything I can to limit the information stored on my machine.

The first of these steps is the list of recently used programs and documents that is pinned temporarily in the Windows Start menu. By default your most recently used applications and files are kept on top in the Start menu so you can access them quickly and easily. Anyone seeing these can probably make assumptions about the type of work you do on your machine, as well as seeing file names if they have enough visual access. To limit this information, open the Start menu and right-click inside it. Select Properties, and click "Start Menu" on the ensuing window. In the middle of the window is a box labeled "Privacy." Uncheck both of the options in this box: "Store and display recently opened programs in the Start menu" and "Store and display recently opened items in the Start menu and the taskbar." These items will no longer be displayed.

Figure 4.6: The privacy settings for the Windows Start menu.

A suite of applications in Windows that leaks data purposefully is the Microsoft Office Suite. This is done through the AutoRecover functions that are intended to save a copy of your work in the event your computer's power is interrupted. This is great for productivity—I have had this happen and was glad to have an automatically saved copy of my work to which I could revert. However, this is a problem for the security of my documents. Even though I have only stored these documents in encrypted volumes, the unencrypted AutoSave versions are still here and recoverable in plaintext.

To avoid this, I choose the location where these versions are saved rather than relying on the default location provided by Windows. To do this, open Microsoft Word and select the "File" tab on the ribbon. From the menu on the left-hand side of the application, select "Options." This will bring up the Options dialogue. Within this dialogue click "Save" to display the options for automatically saving the document.

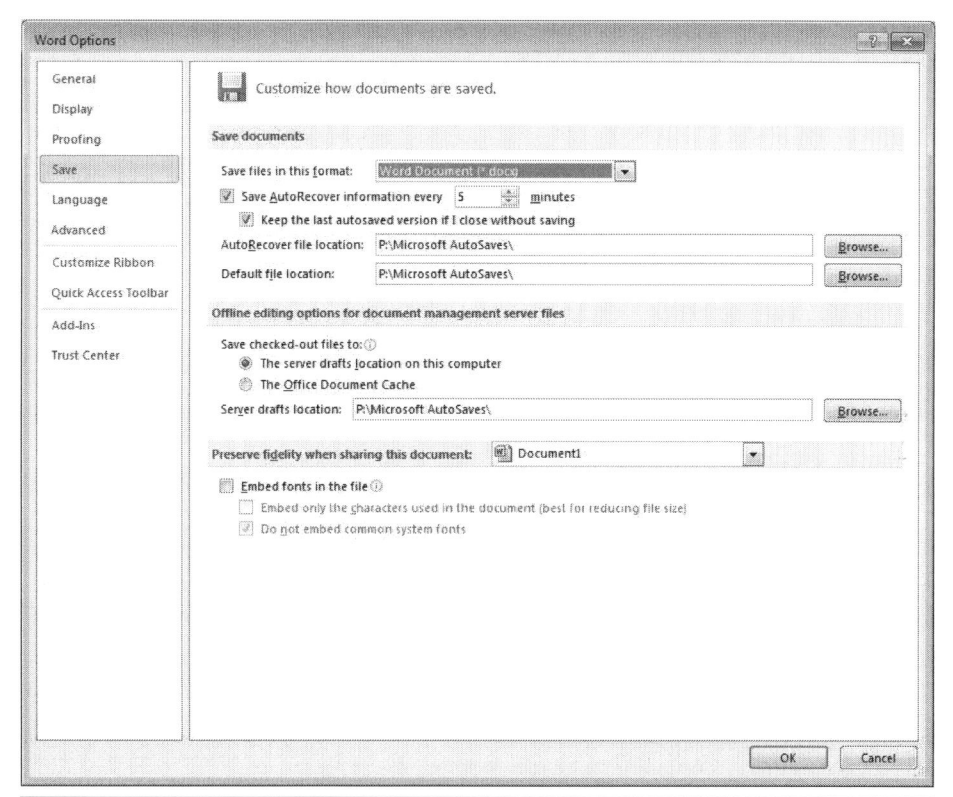

Figure 4.7: The Save options for Microsoft Word 2010. Many applications save information like this and you should be aware of where it is going and how it is being saved.

You have the option to choose how often the file is saved. The more often you save it, the less work you will lose if you lose power, but this can also slow your machine down by overtaxing RAM. I go with a middle-of-the-road five minutes for my saving frequency. I enabled the "Keep the last auto-saved version if I close without saving" during the writing of this book because of the large amounts of information being changed on a daily basis, but for more casual use I would not enable this. Next, and most importantly, are the "AutoRecover file location" and "Default file location" options. For both of these, I use a custom location: a folder named "Microsoft AutoSaves" that is located inside my encrypted volume. This ensures that all of my AutoRecover versions and documents I save to the default location are encrypted.

Again, this list is not comprehensive, but it should get you thinking about the applications you run and what they save in the background. If at all possible, make your default and automatic save locations an encrypted volume to prevent sensitive files from being written to the hard drive in plaintext. Think similarly about data-in-motion. If you use a mail client, you may want to look in the settings too see what connections are being made, what information is being sent automatically, and whether these settings can be changed.

SUMMARY

Secure file deletion may seem like an overly paranoid step but I contend it is necessary. If a file is no longer needed there is no reason it should reside on the hard drive for months or years. This is especially true if you intend to gift, donate, or even trash the device. Before I began working on this book I worked on a very secure military installation. One day while walking by a dumpster, I happened to notice a desktop PC had been thrown away. Naturally I pulled it out. Upon further inspection, I realized it was a personal computer that someone had brought to work to throw away.

I took the computer home, found a power cable for it, and powered it up. I was shocked at what I found on the machine. The individual who trashed his computer in a dumpster had not deleted anything off the hard drive, nor was anything encrypted. The information still on the machine included his scanned military ID, thousands of family photographs, and other personal information. He was fortunate that the computer was found by me and not someone with more malicious designs. I did him a favor and ran DBAN on the machine before disposing of it properly.

This story should serve to underscore the importance of this chapter and the need to delete files properly. Deleting a file (insecurely) through the Recycle Bin does not make the file go away any more than throwing a computer in a dumpster makes it disappear. It is still there and you are relying only on the hope that no one will go looking for it. By attempting to limit the amount of information that is saved without your knowledge or consent and deleting securely on a regular basis you can have the peace of mind that little (if anything) could be recovered off of your device. In addition to removing files securely, programs like CCleaner and Defraggler will also help keep your machine running in top form.

This chapter covered:
- o Erasing targeted files, secure moving files, and wiping free disk space with Eraser
- o Performing general cleanup functions with CCleaner and improving CCleaner's capabilities with CCEnhancer
- o Using DBAN to "nuke" an entire hard drive, operating system and all
- o Defragmenting and the Defraggler application

PART THREE:
DATA-IN-MOTION

JUSTIN CARROLL

CHAPTER 5:
SECURING DATA-IN-MOTION

Data-in-motion is information that is in transit from one device to another. This data is vulnerable to a number of exploits. Your traffic may be intercepted by legitimate entities to serve you advertising information, ensure you are complying with the Digital Millennium Copyright Act, or for other reasons. On the other end of the spectrum, data may be intercepted by an attacker. A malicious actor may sniff (intercept) your packets, set up a man-in-the-middle attack, or launch an evil-twin attack, depending on what you are most vulnerable to.

One of the most important steps you can take to protect yourself is to encrypt all of your data-in-motion to the extent possible. This is possible through a number of methods including Secure Sockets Layer (SSL) and Transport Layer Security (TLS), high quality, modern Wi-Fi encryption protocols, and the use of Virtual Private Networks and the Tor network. These factors working together can protect that data while it is in motion from one place to another.

SSL AND TLS

Two protocols, Secure Sockets Layer (SSL) and Transport Layer Security (TLS), are the first line of defense in securing your data-in-motion. These two encryption protocols rely on asymmetric encryption. This is a form of encryption where the site to which you are connecting and your computer negotiate an encryption key for the information they will exchange. Websites encrypted with SSL or TLS are "HTTPS" sites, and are considered secure. In addition to websites, connections to mail clients, online calendars, data transferred between devices, and other services like Voice Over Internet Protocol (VoIP) and instant messaging applications are frequently encrypted with one these protocols.

Transport Layer Security is an upgraded version of the aging SSL protocol and provides very robust encryption for data-in-motion. Most reputable sites should employ TLS, though some sites still rely on SSL 3.0. Despite the differences in the two protocols, many still refer to both generically as "SSL," making things somewhat confusing. (In order to simplify here, I will refer to all such connections as SSL/TLS). Until early 2014, I considered SSL/TLS to be fairly secure if implemented properly, but a litany of vulnerabilities was revealed in these protocols over the last year.

One of these vulnerabilities was known as "gotofail," and was specific to Apple's products. The vulnerability was patched in iOS 7.0.6, then a few days later in OS X Mavericks 10.9.2. Shortly thereafter, the Heartbleed bug was discovered twice within two weeks by independent researchers. In very early 2015 it was revealed that a Wi-Fi provider on airlines was intentionally issuing fake SSL certificates. Though these connections were initially encrypted, they could be decrypted by the Wi-Fi provider. More recently, the Superfish adware was discovered being installed as OEM software with a certain brand of laptops. Much like the in-flight Wi-Fi provider, Superfish used a self-signed certificate to tamper with the encryption on supposedly secure connections for the purpose of sending customized advertisements to users.

When using a site that is encrypted with SSL/TLS, it is a good idea to check the certificate of the site if you have any question whatsoever about its authenticity (or maybe even if you don't). Clicking on the padlock icon (shown on encrypted connections) just to the left of the address bar of Firefox (see the next chapter on internet browser setup) will display a small amount of information about the site you are visiting. Clicking the "More Information…" button will bring up an additional dialogue. The "Security" tab in this dialogue will display some technical details about the connection, including whether or not the connection is secure, whether or not the site is leaving a cookie on your computer, and if you have visited the site previously today. In the bottom portion of this view are some technical details about the security of the connection.

Clicking on the "View Certificate" button will open an additional window that will provide very detailed information about the certificate. There are a couple of things you should look for here. First, the "Issued To" information should match the name of the organization that owns the website you are visiting. For example, if you visit https://bankofamerica.com, the Issued To Common Name should be Bank of America (see Figure 5.2). Next, the expiration date of the certificate should be for one year. Most certificates are only issued for one year and you should proceed with caution if a certificate is valid for longer than one year.

Finally, the certificate should be issued by a reputable certificate authority (CA). There are a limited number of CAs, and while this list is not comprehensive, some of the most popular CAs are Symantec (which includes VeriSign, Thawte, and GeoTrust), Comodo, GoDaddy, avast! Web/Mail Shield, GlobalSign, and DigiCert. Be aware that some very large organizations (Google, for example) may have internal certificate authorities. Though it takes a lot of time and patience, checking the authenticity of a certificate before you input your authentication credentials on any website is a good idea. If you do not do so on all sites, you should definitely consider going to the trouble when you are connected to an untrusted internet connection like public Wi-Fi, since SSL/TLS connections still offer a decent layer of security despite the highly publicized exploits against it.

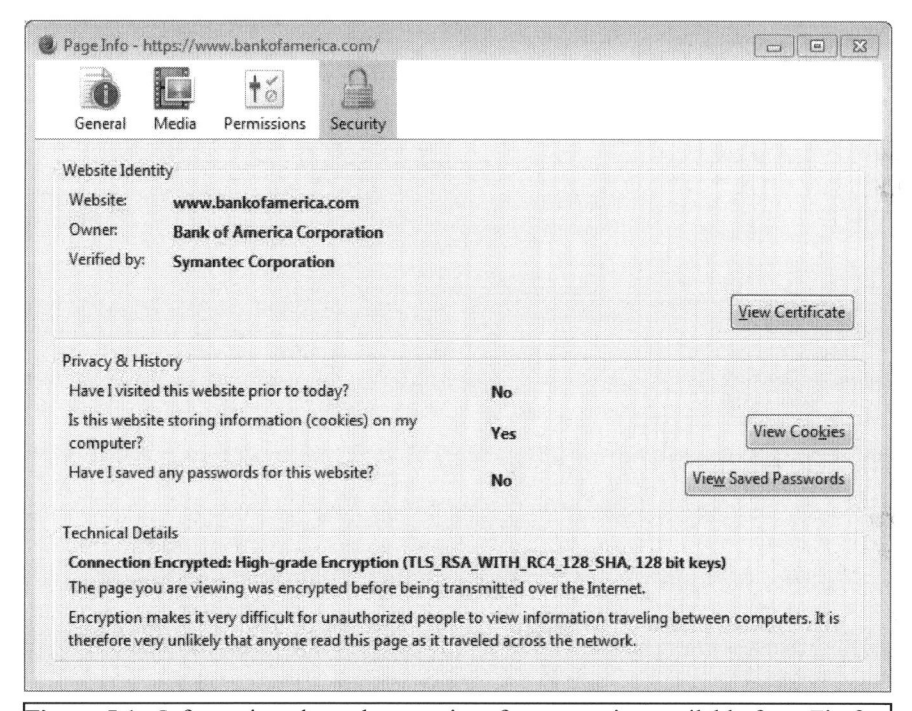

Figure 5.1: Information about the security of a connection available from Firefox. This information is accessed by clicking the padlock icon during a secure connection, and then clicking "More Information...".

The vulnerabilities and exploits discovered in SSL/TLS are demonstrative of the need to be cautious about relying on a single point of failure in a security system. SSL and TLS encryptions are a good first layer but should not be relied on totally. A good defense-in-depth will have multiple, strong, overlapping layers of security. If one of these layers fails (as has been the case with SSL and TLS many times, across various platforms, and in various implementations in the year prior to this writing) the other layer(s) will still provide some security. One of the strongest layers you can add to your defense to protect your data-in-motion is to use a Virtual Private Network.

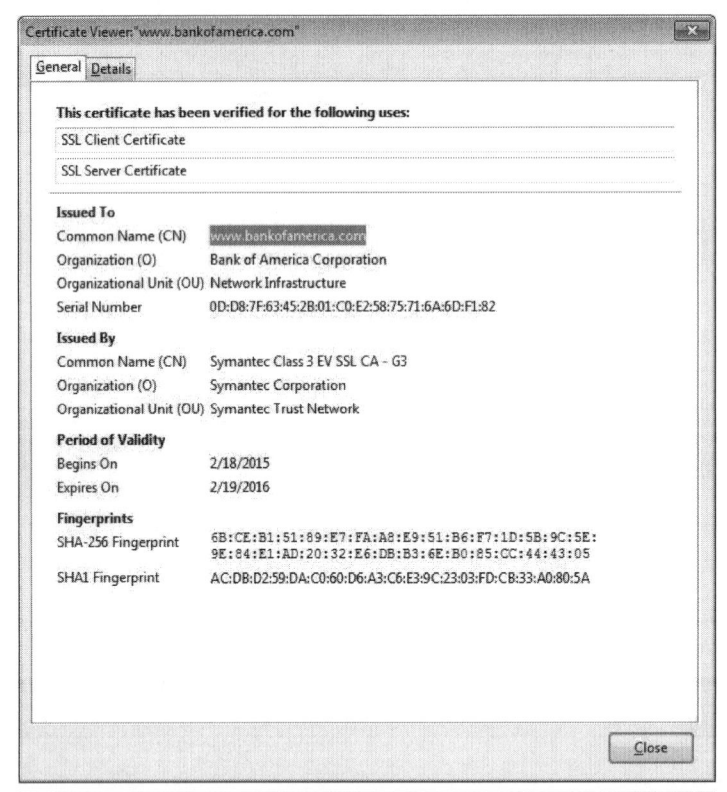

Figure 5.2: Certificate information available through Firefox. Be especially careful to check the "Issued To" information, expiration date, and "Issued By" information.

VIRTUAL PRIVATE NETWORKS

Virtual Private Networks (VPN) provide a good mix of both security and privacy by routing your internet traffic through a secure tunnel. The secure tunnel goes to the VPN's server and encrypts all the data between your device and that server. This ensures that anyone monitoring your traffic before it reaches the distant server will not find usable, unencrypted data. Privacy is also afforded through the use of a distant server. Your traffic that exits the VPN's server does so in plain text (or ideally, still encrypted with HTTPS if you are visiting an SSL/TLS capable site) en route to the destination site, but it is mixed in with the traffic of scores or hundreds of other users, making it much more difficult to distinguish your traffic from all the rest. Also, because your traffic appears to be originating from the VPN's server websites will have a more difficult time tracking you, aggregating data on you, and pinpointing your geographic location.

Virtual Private Networks are not a perfect anonymity solution. The best VPNs for privacy purposes are paid subscriptions with reputable providers. Though some providers take anonymous payment in the form of Bitcoin or prepaid gift cards, it is difficult (though not impossible) to create an account with one of these providers without associating yourself in some manner. Additionally, if you use the VPN from your home's internet connect, the VPN provider will have your IP on record, which can be used to identify you.

There are several excellent paid VPN providers out there and I strongly recommend them over free providers. Free providers may monetize through somewhat questionable means, such as data aggregation (which compromises one crucial benefit of a VPN: privacy). Paid VPN providers will generally offer a number of options that will increase your privacy and security. The first option you should pay attention to is the number of servers they have.

Exit servers: Most reputable VPN service providers will have a number of geographically remote servers from which your traffic will exit and appear to websites to be originating from. This allows you a number of servers to choose from when connecting prior to each browsing session giving you the ability to distribute your usage over a number of servers. It also gives you the ability to switch servers if one is exceptionally slow (as may be the case depending on the number of users on the server and your distance from it). Further, if you are traveling to a country that has internet restrictions and you cannot access certain sites, connecting to a VPN server in another country can allow you to bypass these geographic restrictions. When using a VPN, ensure that you patch the WebRTC vulnerability in your browser (discussed in Chapter 6). This vulnerability allows websites that you visit to capture your true IP address despite the use of a VPN.

Encryption: Another set of options a good VPN provider will offer is the ability to choose between a variety of encryption and tunneling options. These will typically include OpenVPN, IPSEC, L2TP, and PPTP. This versatility is desirable because although most VPN services will work well cross-platform (Windows, Linux, OSX, Android, iOS, etc.) some devices may not work with certain protocols. Further, some VPN providers will even sell routers (or allow you to set up your own) with their VPN software built-in, allowing all of your home's traffic to be protected with a VPN connection. This is helpful, as not all devices (such as smart TVs and gaming systems) have the ability to have VPN software installed.

Two other factors that are definitely worth considering when choosing a VPN are bandwidth restrictions and speed limitations, both of which can be annoying. It is also possible to build your own VPN. If you have a computer at your home that can be left on and used for little else, you can create your own, free VPN with software that is native to Windows 7. However, this is not my preferred option. Though it encrypts all traffic from your computer to the VPN portal at your house, it does not protect anything leaving your home, which would still be vulnerable to Wi-Fi sniffing, packet inspection by your internet service provider, location tracking, and other forms of monitoring. If you are only concerned with protecting your signal when using public Wi-Fi hotspots or for securely accessing files on your home computer or server remotely this may be sufficient for your needs.

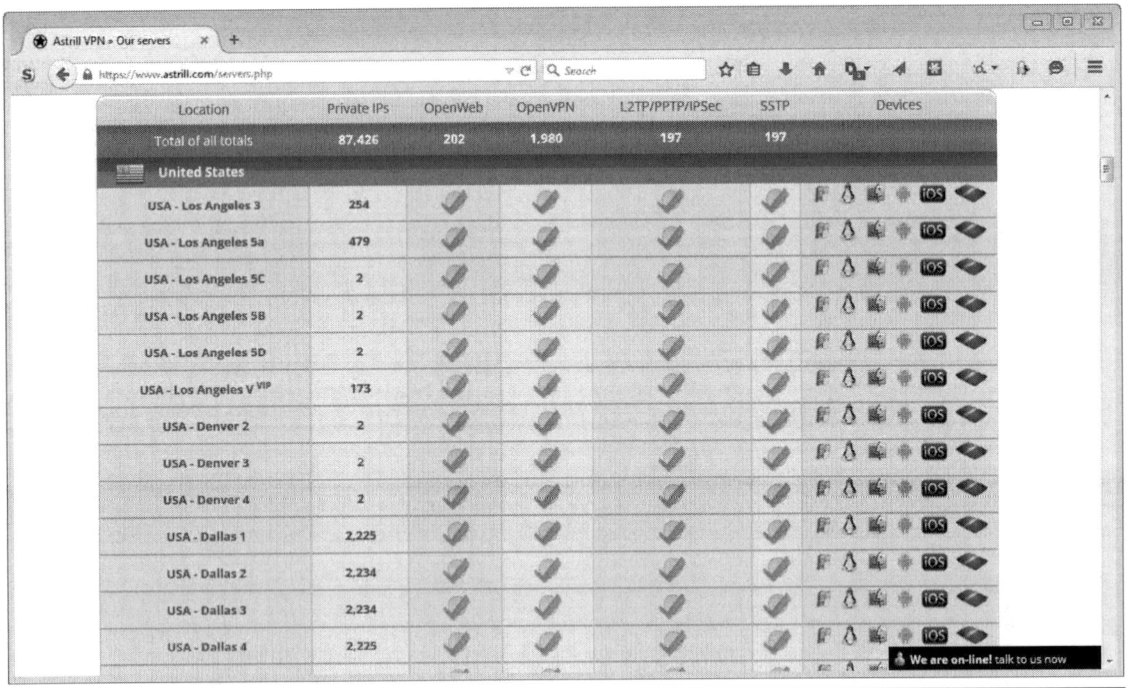

Location	Private IPs	OpenWeb	OpenVPN	L2TP/PPTP/IPSec	SSTP	Devices
Total of all totals	87,426	202	1,980	197	197	
United States						
USA - Los Angeles 3	254	✓	✓	✓	✓	iOS
USA - Los Angeles 5a	479	✓	✓	✓	✓	iOS
USA - Los Angeles 5C	2	✓	✓	✓	✓	iOS
USA - Los Angeles 5B	2	✓	✓	✓	✓	iOS
USA - Los Angeles 5D	2	✓	✓	✓	✓	iOS
USA - Los Angeles V VIP	173	✓	✓	✓	✓	iOS
USA - Denver 2	2	✓	✓	✓	✓	iOS
USA - Denver 3	2	✓	✓	✓	✓	iOS
USA - Denver 4	2	✓	✓	✓	✓	iOS
USA - Dallas 1	2,225	✓	✓	✓	✓	iOS
USA - Dallas 2	2,234	✓	✓	✓	✓	iOS
USA - Dallas 3	2,234	✓	✓	✓	✓	iOS
USA - Dallas 4	2,225	✓	✓	✓	✓	iOS

Figure 5.3: A partial list of VPN servers available to Astrill VPN users. A good variety of server locations is important when considering a paid VPN service.

A good VPN service provider will offer a totally transparent privacy policy about the information they collect on your usage. The best ones will retain only minimal records, and although bound by law to cooperate with warrants and other legal instruments, if they do not store the information in the first place, they cannot turn it over. It is important to realize that paid providers are also vulnerable to financial and legal pressure from their host-nation governments to cooperate with measures that may compromise security for all users.

There are several VPN providers that I have used and recommend. I also fully recommend that you, as the user, conduct your own research and find the provider that works best for your situation.

Some VPN providers that meet all of the criteria list above, and that I personally recommend are (in alphabetical order):

Astrill VPN	https://www.astrill.com/
Private Internet Access	https://www.privateinternetaccess.com/
Witopia	https://www.witopia.net/

VPN ENCRYPTION PROTOCOLS

Most VPN providers will offer a number of encryption algorithms including PPTP, L2TP/IPSEC, and OpenVPN, so which one do you choose? I rule out PPTP automatically as it offers only minimal security. IPSEC is generally considered the strongest encryption available, though it has recently been alleged that this protocol has been deliberately weakened by the U.S. National Security Agency. That leaves OpenVPN which is based on open-source code. OpenVPN offers very strong encryption and is generally regarded as faster than IPSEC, but unfortunately it is not available on all platforms. I will leave it up to the reader to choose between IPSEC and OpenVPN, with the caveat that I most frequently use IPSEC on most of my devices.

Though I consider VPNs important enough to pay for and do not prefer free VPN services, there are two that I would recommend if your personal situation necessitates a free solution:

CyberGhost VPN: CyberGhost has two tiers, a free service and a paid service. The only differences between the free and paid versions is that when using the free version, your VPN session will terminate after three hours and you have only a limited list of exit servers from which to choose. Aside from this inconvenience it still offers the protection of the paid version.

CyberGhost VPN is available at: https://www.cyberghostvpn.com/en_us

Spotflux: This is a relatively new service by a small company in Brooklyn, New York. Like CyberGhost, Spotflux monetizes through a tiered, direct pay system and offers free VPN service to desktop users.

Spotflux is available at: https://www.spotflux.com/

Using a paid VPN service is a part of my daily digital routine and the minimum level of security that is acceptable to me when my computer is connected to the internet. It is the absolute minimum when accessing the internet via a public Wi-Fi hotspot (whether it is unsecured or not). Though most VPN services require a paid subscription I am happy to pay this for the peace of mind that is provided in return. By monetizing directly paid VPN providers have a distinct financial stake in not being caught collecting user information.

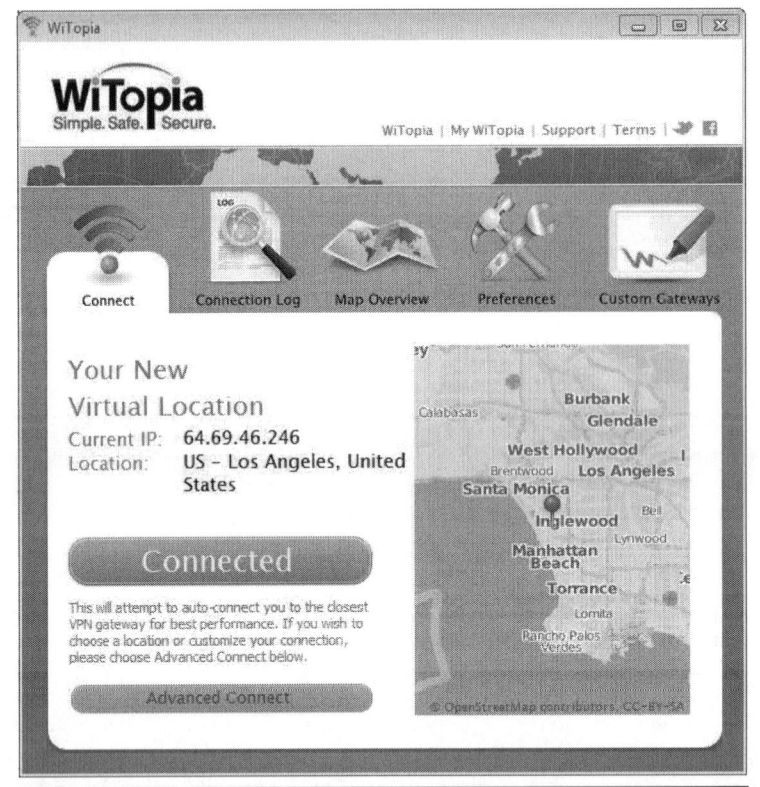

Figure 5.4: The WiTopia VPN interface. The Current IP and Location are the user's virtual location. Regardless of where he or she is physically located all traffic will appear to originate from the virtual IP in Los Angeles.

WI-FI SECURITY

As was pointed out in the introduction to this book, security and convenience are inversely related. Wi-Fi is an undeniable convenience. Negating the need for a physical cable, Wi-Fi allows us to access the internet from just about anywhere at just about any time. Intrinsic to this convenience, however, is a great deal of insecurity, especially when compared with wired internet connections.

Wi-Fi is nothing more than a radio transmission that carries data packets between your computer's Wi-Fi card and the wireless router. Because of this anyone with a capable radio can "listen" in on your traffic. Simply listening in by capturing your packets as they travel to and from your computer is called sniffing. Sniffing requires some specialized (but free) software, a Wi-Fi card that can be placed in promiscuous mode (the ability to "listen" to all Wi-Fi traffic while not broadcasting), USB Wi-Fi antennas that can be purchased very inexpensively, and only very little technical know-how.

While some of the techniques we will discuss below are changes made to your operating system, the majority of this chapter will deal with securing your wireless signal and best practices when using Wi-Fi.

WI-FI SNIFFING TOOLS

While I do not recommend sniffing strangers' Wi-Fi traffic, capturing packets is not terribly technically demanding and can even be beneficial. Seeing first-hand how Wi-Fi is exploited can underscore the point of how insecure Wi-Fi truly is and help you understand the importance of good encryption. Sniffing your home network is also a good way to see what vulnerabilities it has. If you are interested you will need the following:

Software: There are various Wi-Fi sniffing programs and many of them are free. Using them typically requires using a Linux operating system. Backtrack is a penetration-testing specific Linux OS and comes with Wi-Fi exploitation tools built in.

Hardware: The only specialized hardware you need is a promiscuous-capable Wi-Fi card. These are available online for as little as $30. And since Backtrack can be booted and ran from a DVD, you can use your existing PC.

Technical know-how: Though hacking Wi-Fi is relatively simple it does require some specific knowledge. The graphic user interfaces for most of the programs consist mostly of a command prompt, so good working knowledge of Linux command line is necessary, though most of these commands can be found online.

WI-FI SETTINGS IN WINDOWS 7

Wi-Fi should be turned off when your computer is not actively connected to a network, and the computer should not be set to connect automatically to networks. When your computer is not connected to your network (e.g. when you are traveling), it will actively search for networks it is set to automatically connect to. This searching is not passive. Other computers can detect this searching, and see the name of the network(s) with free, openly-available software. If your networks are all being broadcast, it is trivially easy for an attacker to set up an "evil twin" attack. To execute this form of a man-in-the-middle attack, an attacker will set up a network that has the same name as one of your trusted networks. When your device recognizes this name, it will connect to the rogue network automatically (unless you have disabled automatic connections) allowing your traffic to be routed through his or her device and potentially compromising it. Even SSL/TLS-encrypted traffic is vulnerable to a technique called "SSL Stripping." If, on the other hand, you have disabled automatic connections, the names of your stored networks will not be available to the hacker. Be aware that these network names also leak details about you.

To set your Wi-Fi networks to manually connect, navigate to **Control Panel >> Network and Internet >> Network and Sharing Center**, then select **Manage Wireless Networks**. You should see a list of all the networks your computer "remembers."

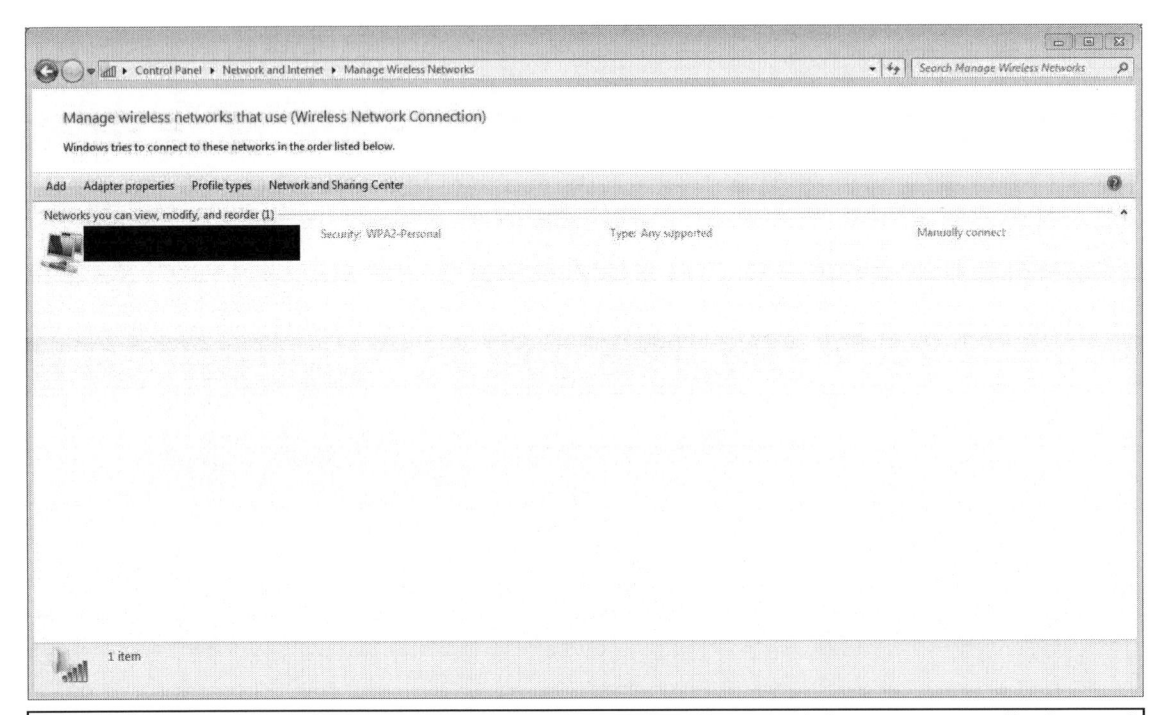

Figure 5.5: The Windows list of Wi-Fi networks. Note that this network is set to "Manually Connect". Also note that this is a very clean list of one, single trusted network. The fewer networks you have saved the better.

Next, right-click on each network that you need to change from an automatic connection to "Manually Connect," and select "Properties." In the Properties dialog, uncheck the following boxes: "Connect automatically when this network is in range," "Connect to a more preferred network if it is available," and "Connect even if the network is not broadcasting its name (SSID)." This will ensure that your computer is not broadcasting requests for known networks and protects you against several types of Wi-Fi exploits.

BASIC ROUTER SETUP

When setting up your home's network there are some basic steps you can take to make your account much more secure than the average account. Some of these settings will require that you be physically connected to the router via an Ethernet cable.

Change management account credentials. The first step you should take when setting up your home's network is to change the management account credentials. This account is the account you log into to change the router's settings. Anyone having access to it can turn off your encryption, view your usage logs, or take other malicious actions. The default credentials that are preset on the router are openly available information and could allow anyone connecting to your network to make changes to your router.

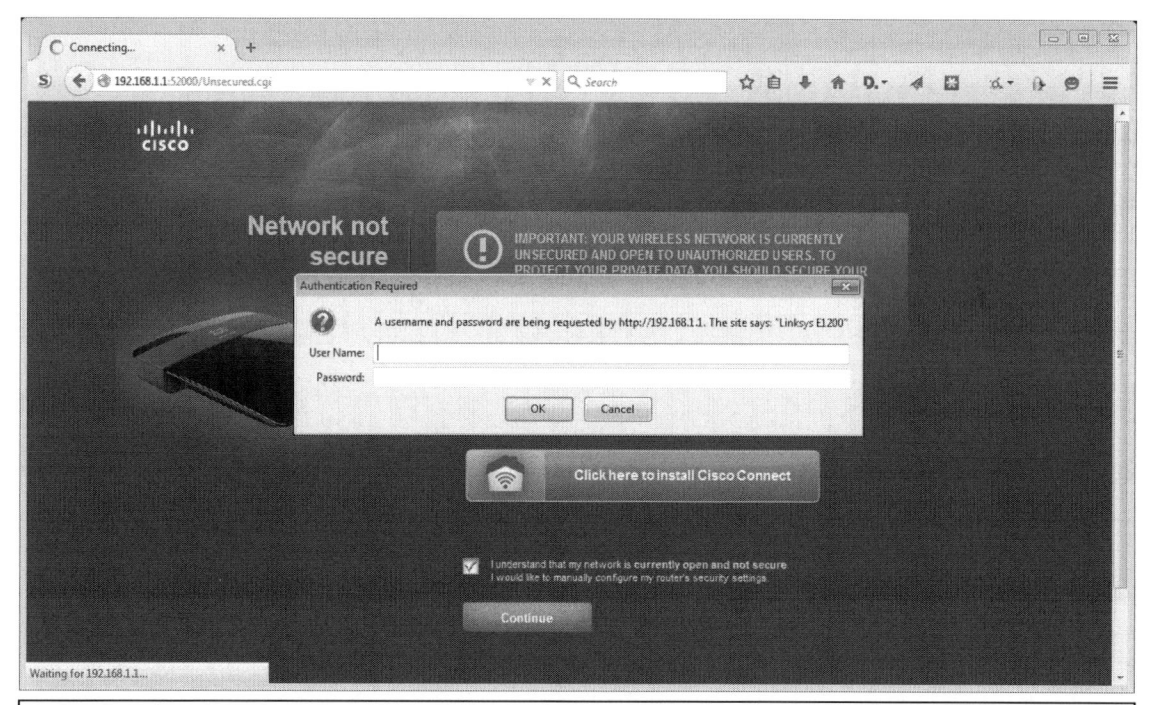

Figure 5.6: The account management login for a LinkSys wireless router. The default credentials are admin (username) and admin (password) and should be changed immediately.

To change these settings, log into your router by typing the router's internal Internet Protocol (IP) address into the address bar while connected (via a wired or wireless connection to the router). The internal IP address for most Linksys routers is 192.168.1.1, while most D-Link and NetGear routers use an IP of 192.168.01. This will bring you to the administrator login page. If you have never changed your router's login credentials they are probably set to the default. Conduct an Internet search for the default username and password, then change these credentials immediately using a randomly generated username and a good, strong password (as discussed in Chapter 2).

You can also make it more difficult to change the settings on your router by changing the IP address used to log into it. Login credentials can be defeated, so this step makes it more difficult for an attacker to connect to the router. The IP address can be changed to anything between 192.168.0.0 and 192.168.255.255, but ensure you remember what you change it to. As soon as this change is saved and takes effect, you will need the new IP to log back into the router to make additional changes.

Disable remote management. Remote management gives you the ability to log into and change the router's management system without physically accessing the router or being connected to the router's network. When this function is disabled you may be required to physically connect to the router with an Ethernet cable to log into the management account. Though slightly inconvenient, you shouldn't have to make changes to the router very often and the security upgrade is well worth it.

Encrypt the signal. Next, encrypt the wireless signal using WPA2 encryption. There are several options on many routers for encryption, including WEP (Wired Equivalent Privacy), WPA (Wi-Fi Protected Access), and WPA2, but the only one you should consider using is WPA2. WEP has been broken for years and is extremely easily defeated (even with a very good password) through an attack known as a "statistical attack." WPA has serious vulnerabilities, especially with its Temporary Key Integrity Protocol (TKIP). WPA2 is a re-engineered version of WPA offering AES encryption and the greatest security for wireless networks currently available. If your router does not offer WPA2-PSK (Pre-Shared Key) (802.11n) upgrade your router as soon as possible. Do not neglect to assign a good password to your network. Though it may take some time and effort to enter the password on your devices, it only has to be done once.

Change your SSID. You should also change the SSID, the name of your network that is broadcast to your devices. Though it is possible to (and some recommend this) hide the SSID, this is a fairly ineffective technique. Wi-Fi sniffers (programs designed to detect and exploit Wi-Fi networks) can easily find hidden networks. Finding a hidden network may simply make a random attacker curious. Instead, rename the network with a name that does not leak information about you.

Renaming your network is an excellent opportunity to provide some disinformation about your home. There are websites that map every known wireless network (https://wigle.net is a good example). Anyone seeing your true name attached to a network can make a reasonable assumption about the location of your residence. Instead of naming your network something personally relatable to you like "Carroll Family" or "Carroll Wi-Fi," use some false information or use a name similar to that of one of your neighbors. If anyone is looking for your house based on Wi-Fi networks, this will make it more difficult to locate.

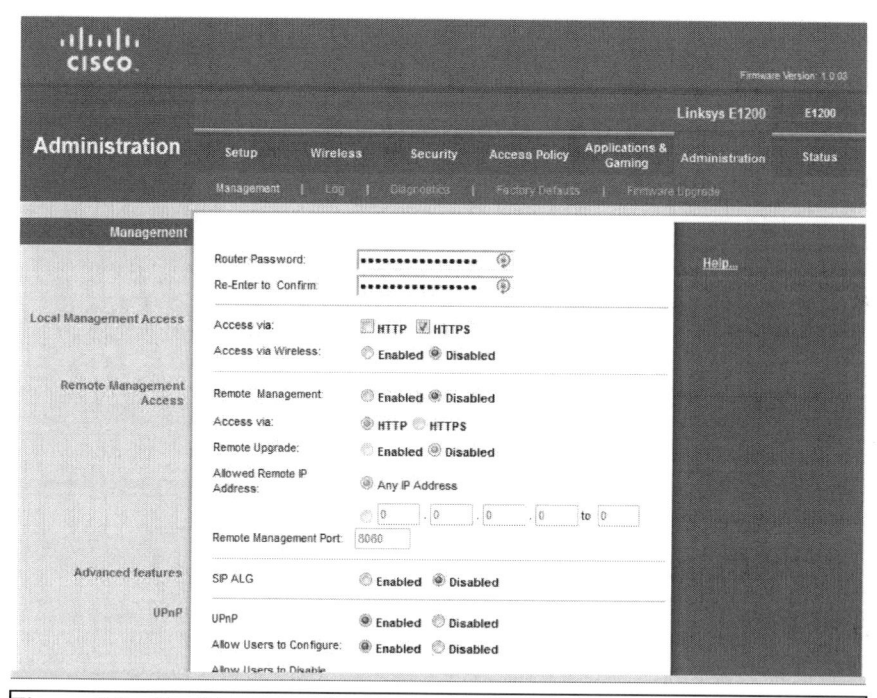

Figure 5.7: On this screen the user many disable Remote Management of the router. It is also recommended that all management sessions be conducted over an HTTPS connection.

Opt-out of Wi-Fi mapping. Wi-Fi networks are now mapped in tandem with other mapping efforts. This means that if your network name is collected, it can be looked up as an overlay on a map. This allows anyone to map your location, based on your Wi-Fi networks, by capturing the SSID that your computer broadcasts when searching for a network to connect to. To prevent your home network from being mapped (at least by Google), an option you can take is to terminate your router's SSID with the suffix "_nomap" (for example: SmithFamilywifi_nomap). This is the opt-out for Google's Wi-Fi network mapping. Any router SSID containing this suffix will not be included on

Google map overlays that display Wi-Fi networks.

Disable Wi-Fi Protected Setup (WPS). Wi-Fi Protected Setup is a convenience feature that is intended to make it easier to connect to a wireless device. Rather than entering the password when connecting to an encrypted network the user can physically push the WPS button on the router when connecting for the first time or enter a six-digit WPS code. Unfortunately, the WPS protocol is broken. No matter how strong the password on your network is, cracking the simple six-digit WPS code can grant access to the network. Disable WPS completely, even though it makes logging into your network more time consuming (though again, you only have to do this on your home network on initial setup and when you change the password).

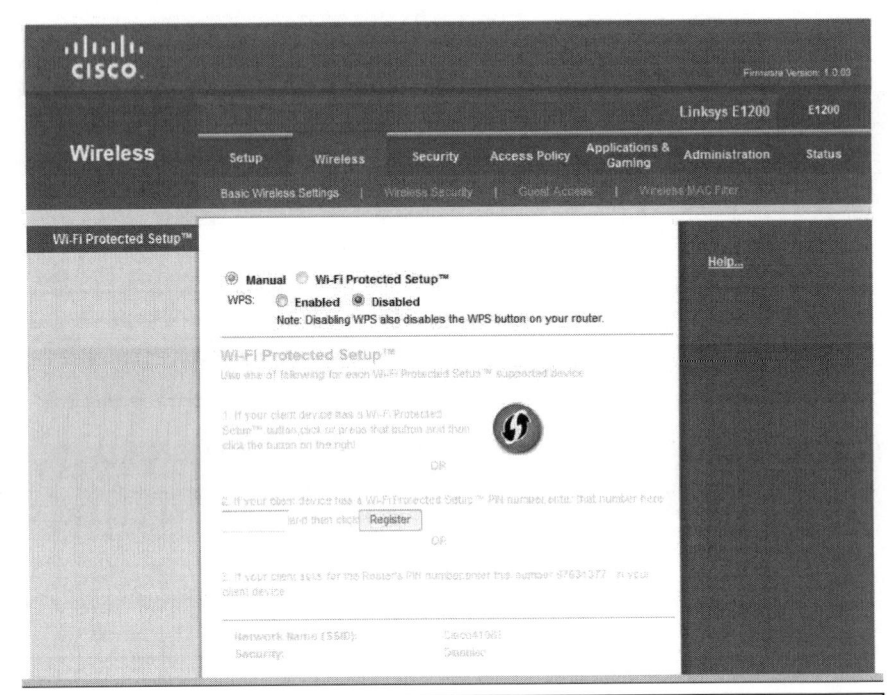

Figure 5.8: The configuration screen to disable Wi-Fi Protected Setup (WPS). This protocol is broken and should not be used.

Turn off the signal when not in use. In the setup menu for most routers, you can elect to turn the router's signal off between certain hours and on certain days, at times when everyone in your home is typically asleep or everyone is gone, for example. Unless you rely on wireless IP cameras or other Wi-Fi devices as part of your physical security system, there is no need to leave your router on when you are going out of town; simply unplug it. Powering the router off lowers its profile; the less time it is on and broadcasting, the smaller its attack surface.

Scan your home network: Though this does not pertain to router setup specifically, it is a good step to take after setting up your home router. My antivirus application of choice (Avast Free Antivirus) can conduct a home network scan. It will test to see if your devices are visible from the internet, check router security configurations, and ensure that your wireless signal is encrypted. You can run this scan on any network to which you are connected to give you an idea of the security of the network before you use it to transmit potentially sensitive information.

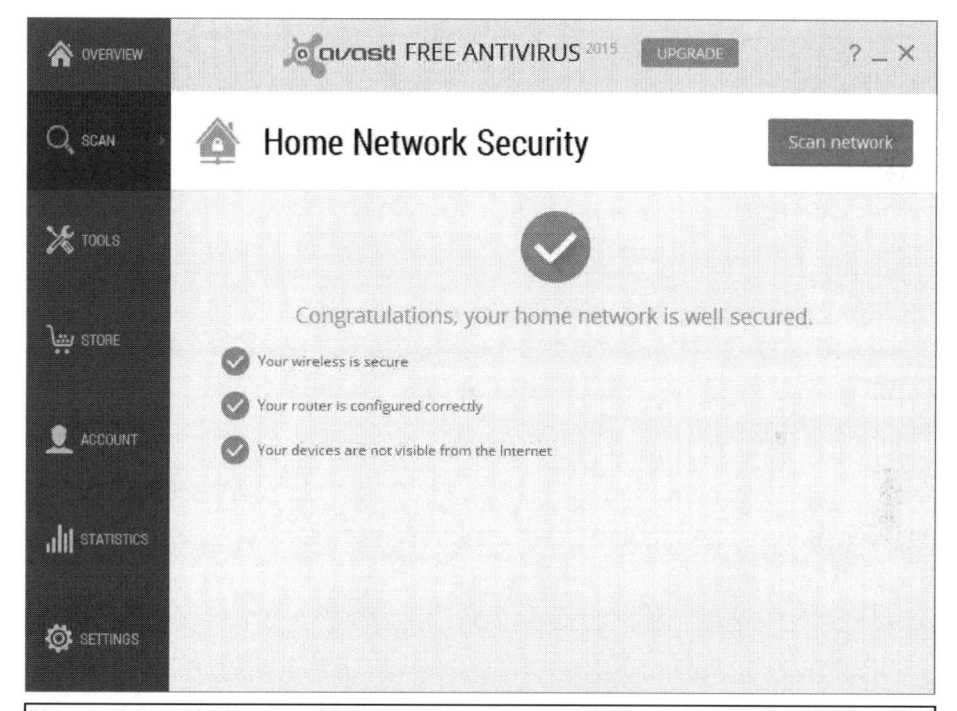

Figure 5.9: The successful results of a Home Network Scan using Avast Free Antivirus. This scan is a good indicator of the security of any network to which you connect.

MAC filtering. One security measure that is sometimes touted but is largely ineffective is MAC filtering. A MAC address (Media Access Control) is a number unique to your device, analogous to its electronic ID. Filtering MAC addresses allows connections only from devices on a "whitelist" (a preapproved list of trusted devices). While MAC filtering is good in theory it is very easily defeated through MAC spoofing, a technique used by attackers to capture your MAC and assign it temporarily to their device. This technique is not especially difficult, especially by anyone with the ability to crack your (WPA2) encryption. Additionally, MAC filtering requires you to log into the router and update the whitelist each time you need to connect a new device.

A technique that is allowed on many routers similar to MAC filtering (though slightly less onerous and certainly even less effective as a security feature) is to limit the number of devices that may connect at a given time. Long ago, when I had a single Wi-Fi capable device, I capped this number at one single device that could be connected to my router at a given time. If you have only one device that should ever be connected this may be somewhat effective. This is intended to keep networks uncrowded to manage bandwidth, though I occasionally hear it listed as a security measure.

BEST PRACTICES FOR UNTRUSTED/UNENCRYPTED NETWORKS

There are times when it is expedient to use an untrusted, unencrypted wireless network. While ideally you would never use such a network, the convenience of such networks make them hard to resist. Some basic best practices when using these networks (if you must use them) can make your browsing much more secure.

Absolute Best Practice: Don't use them. Again, Wi-Fi is terribly convenient and it can be hard to resist the urge to connect and watch YouTube, download your podcasts, or log in and get some work done while you wait to board your flight. The risks of using untrusted networks are very high though, and it is extremely rare that I will use one.

If you can wait to use the internet until you get home (or at least to your hotel, where you can use a wired connection), do so. If not, do not enter any sensitive information (like login credentials) on that network, and follow the steps listed below.

Connect to the right network. Every day criminals and hackers set up fake wireless access points to lure the unsuspecting into connecting to them. This is often done in public spaces where dozens of Wi-Fi networks exist and a free hotspot does not raise much suspicion. With names like "Free Wi-Fi" or "Public Hotspot," these insecure connections are used naïvely by many who treat them no differently than their home network. Unfortunately, many of these are merely traps to capture login, banking/credit card, and other sensitive information.

When you check into a hotel, visit a coffee shop or bookstore, or use Wi-Fi at a public library, ask someone who works there which network you should use. If two or more networks have very similar names, take a closer look and ask for clarification if you need to. It is worth the hassle to ensure you are on a legitimate network.

Use a wired connection if available. Many hotels offer in-room, hard-wired connections. Some coffee shops offer wired connections, too. Using a wired connection will not make you invincible, but because of the switching involved in transmitting and receiving packets it does make intercepting and exploiting your traffic much more difficult. It also reduces the likelihood of you connecting to a phony network to almost nil.

Capturing Wi-Fi packets is notoriously easy and can be pulled off by even unskilled attackers, but attacking wired networks is much, much more difficult. There are still many exploits against wired connections, but they are far fewer in number and require far more technical know-how. Also, be aware that even if the traffic over a wired network is not being maliciously attacked, your packets are still vulnerable to inspection on the router to which you are connected, and by the internet service provider.

Use a VPN or Tor. Using a virtual private network or Tor (see the section concerning Tor in the next chapter) is one of the best security measures you can take if you must connect to any untrusted network, wireless or wired. While it does not prevent your packets from being captured, it will ensure your traffic is encrypted from your device to the exit server. Any packets that are captured on the local wireless network will be encrypted and therefore unusable. Using one of these measures will protect you against inspection by both the owner of the router (i.e., the coffee shop or hotel) and the internet service provider.

If you have a VPN for work that you must log into to access your office's server, you can probably connect to it before accessing the internet from an unsecured Wi-Fi. Even though it will not protect your traffic from your office's IT department, it will secure your connection and prevent the packets from being captured in plaintext locally.

Define the network as Public: When connecting to a Wi-Fi network, Windows will ask you if you would like to define the network as Home, Work, or Public (see Figure 5.10). Each of these settings gives the network different privilege sets, with the most secure being Public and the least secure (but the one with the most accessibility) being Home. A "Home" network in Windows is one with a great many sharing permissions enabled, allowing other devices on the network to access any shared folders on your machine. To prevent this, always define the network as "Public" (even my home Wi-Fi network is considered Public on my machine).

Do not open files. Running more applications means presenting more attack surface. When using an untrusted network you should be exceedingly cautious about opening any attachments you download, or running any applications other than the web browser you are using on the network. This will lessen the chances of information being automatically sent by these applications over an unsecure connection.

Remove the network or set to manually connect: If the network is one that you will probably not use again in the future (or not use frequently), you should remove it from the list of networks Windows "remembers." To do so, navigate to **Control Panel >> Network and Internet >> Network and Sharing Center**, then select **Manage Wireless Networks** from the menu bar on the left. Right-click on the network you wish to delete and select "Remove network."

If you will be using a certain network frequently in the future and would like to leave it as a known network, change the settings so that you must manually connect to it. To change this, navigate to Manage Wireless Networks as described in the previous paragraph. Right click on the network and open the properties. Uncheck "Connect automatically when this network is in range." Either of these options, removing the network or setting it for a manual connection, will prevent Windows from actively searching for that network in the future, eliminating your attack surface for evil twin attacks, and reducing information leaked about your Wi-Fi networks.

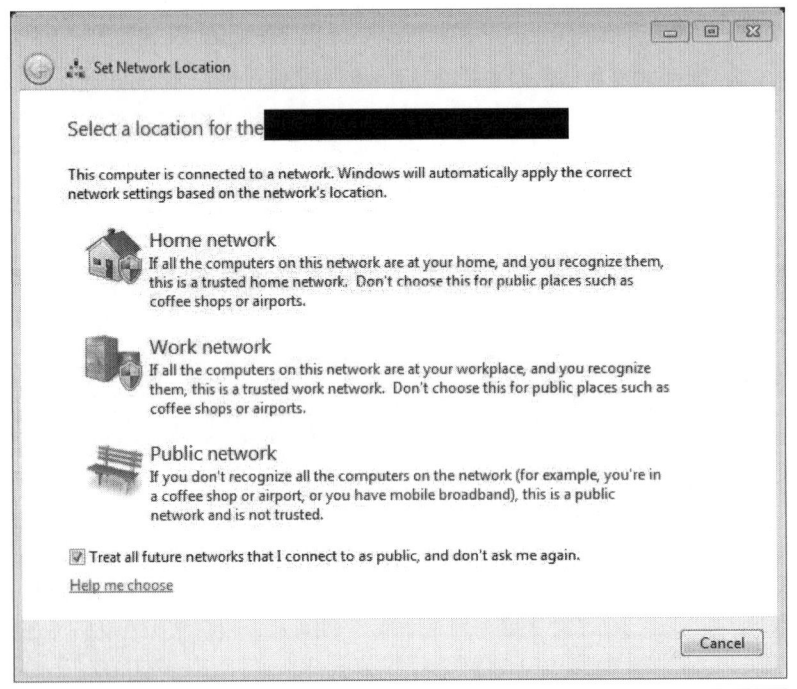

Figure 5.10: The option to define a network as Home, Work, or Public. My recommendation is to define all networks as public. Note that the "Treat all future networks that I connect to as public and don't ask again" box is checked.

CONSIDERATIONS FOR AIR GAPS

Though it does not concern data-in-motion (in fact, it is the very antithesis of data-in-motion), the end of this chapter is a good time to address some considerations for running an air-gap. There is not enough information here to merit a dedicated chapter, but this information should be addressed and it should be addressed before moving on to the data-in-motion considerations we will begin discussing in the following chapter.

What is an air gap? The concept of running an air-gapped computer is relatively simple: Keep a literal air gap between the computer and an internet connection (the term "air gap" was coined before the advent of Wi-Fi). The machine should never be connected to the internet, greatly reducing chances of being infected, hacked, or otherwise exploited. In practice, maintaining an air gap is extremely difficult. Running one does not make a computer completely invulnerable to attack, but it does make a computer significantly safer than one connected to the internet, all other things being equal.

The first consideration and question you should ask yourself is, "Do I need an air gap?" Though I do not discourage air gaps at all (I run one), they are extremely tedious to do correctly and obviously require the expense of a second machine (one that can access the internet, and the other one that cannot). For journalists, high-profile executives, individuals entrusted with trade secrets, and the extremely security conscious the answer to the question above may be "yes." If you require extraordinary security, an air gap affords it. There are several best practices that must be followed when using an air-gapped computer, which will allow it to provide the full measure of security necessary to warrant the inherent inconvenience and expense of having one.

Purchase anonymously. Maintaining an air-gap is serious business, and if you really need one you need it to work correctly. If you have examined your personal circumstances and determined that an air-gap is a necessity for you, you should make the purchase as anonymously as possible. If the device is not associated with you because no one knows you purchased the machine, there is far less risk of it being targeted personally.

When you purchase the computer, pay cash at a big-box store. There is privacy in the large numbers of devices they sell, and you won't be remembered. (Though there are certainly security cameras in the store to record you being there. If you are truly worried about that, have someone make the purchase for you. Again, I will indulge any level of paranoia.) If you connect the computer to the internet during the initial setup process and/or to download your software load, don't do so from your home Wi-Fi connection or a VPN that is already associated with you.

Install minimal programs: The fewest possible number of programs should be installed on an air-gapped machine. As mentioned in Chapter 1, more applications on a machine represent more potential attack vectors and more potential risk. I recommend an encryption program, a general cleanup tool (like CCleaner or Bleachbit), and the absolute minimum number of utilities you can get by with (e.g. a PDF reader, word processing application, etc.). These programs may need occasional updates. When they do, do not connect the machine to the internet to update them as this totally defeats the air gap. Rather, burn the necessary update files to a disk as described below.

Use optical media to transfer files: An air-gapped machine is not very useful if files cannot be transferred to and from it. Unfortunately, it is difficult to safely transfer these files with anything other than optical media. Flash drives and USB hard drives are not a secure method of transferring files to or from your air-gapped machine. The primary insecurity stems from the fact that it is impossible to tell when they are being read from or written to. Though many USB flash drives have an LED that lights up or blinks when reading or writing is occurring, they don't distinguish between the two. If you are reading a file from a USB flash drive the light will be on, but you have no idea if malware is, at the same time, writing a file secretly that will be transmitted when you connect that same USB device to a computer with an internet connection. Though this may seem far-fetched, if you are someone who *really* needs an air gap, it is a real threat. Air gaps are not impenetrable, and jumping the air gap with media is one way they are defeated.

"AIR GAP JUMPERS"

As I have mentioned earlier, an air gap does not mean a system is impenetrable. There are still malware programs that can "jump" the air gap and either insert destructive malware onto, or exfiltrate data off of, an air-gapped computer. Two such examples are Stuxnet, a joint U.S./Israeli application used to successfully attack an Iranian nuclear facility and "agent.btz", a program that jumped U.S. military air gaps and was suspected to be Chinese in origin. Fortunately such attacks are extremely sophisticated and are extremely unlikely to be employed against the average home user. If you have been targeted or are in a high-risk occupation that necessitates the use of an air gap you should be aware of these threats and not take best practices lightly.

Instead of using USB devices to transfer data to an air gap, burn a CD/R or DVD/R, preferably of the smallest capacity you can find that will hold the files you need to transfer. It would be difficult for files to be written secretly to an optical disk, as you will hear the disk drive spin up when a read or write occurs. It is possible that files being exfiltrated by malware from an air-gapped device (or malware being infiltrated to it) could be written at the same time as the files you are burning, but if you use a disk that is just big enough for what you need to move, you leave little space for the hazardous files. If you are not moving enough data to fill up a disk, move some random data to fill the disk to capacity, regardless of which way your data is moving across the air gap.

Encrypt, encrypt, encrypt: When using optical media to transfer files across the air gap, you will be unable to delete the files when finished. However, if the disks and the files on them are encrypted with good, strong passwords you shouldn't need to. (If you are still worried about it, destroy the disks by microwaving or shredding them. Or if you are extremely paranoid, do both.)

Physically disable connectivity: Connecting an air-gapped computer to the internet (via wired or wireless connection) can negate the entire purpose of maintaining an air gap. You should also strongly consider physically disconnecting the Wi-Fi card. Wi-Fi may be turned on by accident, or it may be turned on as part of a malicious attack. Should your machine become infected, malware may silently turn on Wi-Fi selectively to exfiltrate files off of the machine or insert additional malware. If your computer is equipped with Bluetooth, it too should be disabled.

If you are concerned about your air-gapped computer being physically connected to the internet (perhaps by your teenager in search of a device on which to watch a video, or perhaps by you, by mistake) you can tape over the Ethernet port or fill it with a non-conductive epoxy. If this sounds like an extreme measure, it is. My air-gapped computer will never be connected to the internet, even when it is retired, so I am unconcerned about permanently removing its connectivity capabilities.

Setting up and maintaining an air gap is not a simple affair, nor it is an extremely inexpensive one. While I do not discourage anyone from attempting to achieve the highest level of security he or she may desire, air gaps aren't for everyone. But if you are seriously concerned with the protection of your sensitive data, a well-maintained air gap is perhaps the most secure option available to you.

SUMMARY

Protecting data-in-motion is difficult and requires a great deal of trust in the systems you employ. Using overlapping security measures is the best approach. This chapter covered a number of security measures including:

- o The SSL/TLS encryption protocols, and how to verify certificates and the authenticity of a website before trusting it
- o Virtual Private Networks and their importance to a strong digital security footprint
- o Factors to look for when selecting a VPN service provider, including exit servers and available encryption protocols

- o Wi-Fi Security settings for Windows 7 and basic Wi-Fi router setup for security
- o Best practices for using untrusted or insecure wireless networks
- o Considerations for setting up and maintaining an air gap

CHAPTER 6:
INTERNET BROWSER SECURITY

Your internet browser serves as your computer's ambassador to the internet. How it presents itself to the websites you visit (and their third-party advertisers) will, to some extent, influence how they behave in return. Additionally and perhaps more importantly, it will certainly dictate what browsing information your computer stores. Setting up your browser is an important step in controlling your virtual perimeter and protecting your personal privacy. I will not equivocate on choice of browser: I use Firefox for maximum security. This is not to suggest that Firefox is inherently more secure or that it is an inherently security- or privacy-focused browser. However, Firefox offers the user the greatest control over security and privacy settings, and there are numerous add-ons for Firefox that can harden the security of the browser.

Firefox is free and available at: https://www.mozilla.org/en-US/firefox/new/

The first and most basic step you should take is to ensure your browser is up-to-date. Outdated browsers with security holes are an extremely common attack vector. Browser updates are issued frequently to patch these vulnerabilities as they are discovered. You can check your version of Firefox by clicking on the "Menu" button (three horizontal lines stacked on top of each other, aka "the hamburger") located on the top right of the Firefox interface. This will open the menu options. Go all the way to the bottom of this menu, click on the Help button (indicated by a question mark), then choose the very last option, About Firefox. This will open a new window that will display the version of Firefox you are running, or a warning that the version you have is out-of-date. (Version 35.0.1 was current at the time of this writing.) If yours is an older version, update it immediately.

Once you have ensured your browser is the latest stable version, some settings must be modified to ensure the greatest possible privacy and security. To access the settings again go the Menu button, open the menu, and select "Options" (the gear icon). The Options dialogue consists of eight categories: General, Tabs, Search, Content, Applications, Privacy, Security, Sync, and Advanced. We will discuss several of these tabs in much greater detail below.

Figure 6.1: The Firefox web browser. Though there are many browser options I prefer Firefox because of its extreme ability to be customized for security and privacy.

General (see Figure 6.3): Under the general category there are two options that can be changed. The first is the Home Page. You may pick any homepage you like, or use a blank page. I personally prefer to use https://duckduckgo.com as my homepage (see Search Engines below), though you may choose a blank page or any website to which you wish your browser to automatically open.

The next setting that should be modified under this category is Downloads. By default Firefox saves downloaded files to a "Downloads" folder but this is not ideal because files are not immediately visible to the user they may be forgotten, unencrypted, in the Downloads folder. Instead I prefer to have Firefox always ask me where to save files and let me make the decision for each file I download. The alternative is to set the default save location to a TrueCrypt volume; in this case even if you forget about the file it will not be left unencrypted on your hard drive. This process is also greatly assisted by using TrueCrypt Favorites to ensure your preferred volume is always mounted to the same drive letter as described in Chapter 3.

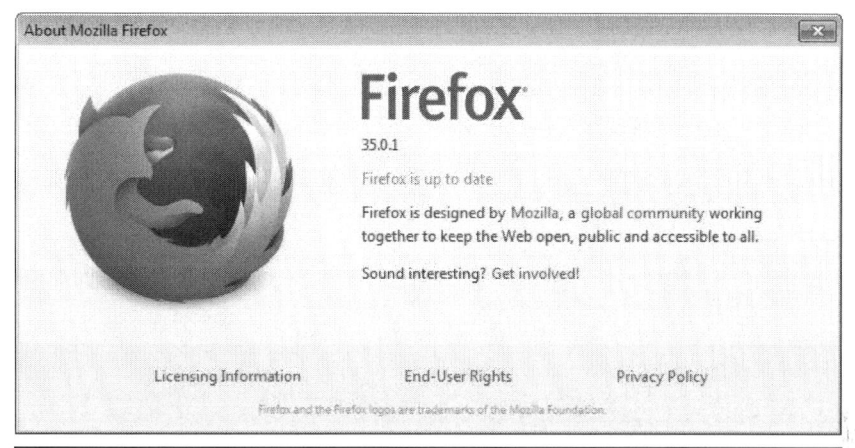

Figure 6.2: Firefox's version number as displayed in the "About Firefox" dialogue. You should check this at least weekly and ensure you are running the most up-to-date version of the browser.

Search: Under the Search tab in the Options menu you have the ability to change your default search engine. My preferred default search engine is DuckDuckGo (https://duckduckgo.com). DuckDuckGo does not track or store any information on its users. While other search providers track, collate, store, and earn tens of millions of dollars annually by selling user information. DuckDuckGo is also full-time HTTPS encrypted, providing an additional layer of security to all of your searches.

There are a number of other search engines available and I generally recommend leaving them all checked. Though by default your searches will be sent to DuckDuckGo, leaving all the other options checked makes them available with a single click. We will modify the default search engine further with the Disconnect Search add-on discussed later in this chapter.

Content: This tab has one security-related option: the ability to block pop-up windows. I recommend checking the "Block pop-up windows" check box. Some pop-ups will still get through but Firefox does a decent job of blocking most of them. I recommend an add-on below that is much more heavy-handed in blocking pop-ups (and a lot of other annoying ad content, as well).

Figure 6.3: The Firefox General options. In this dialogue change the default location to which files are saved an the homepage if you wish.

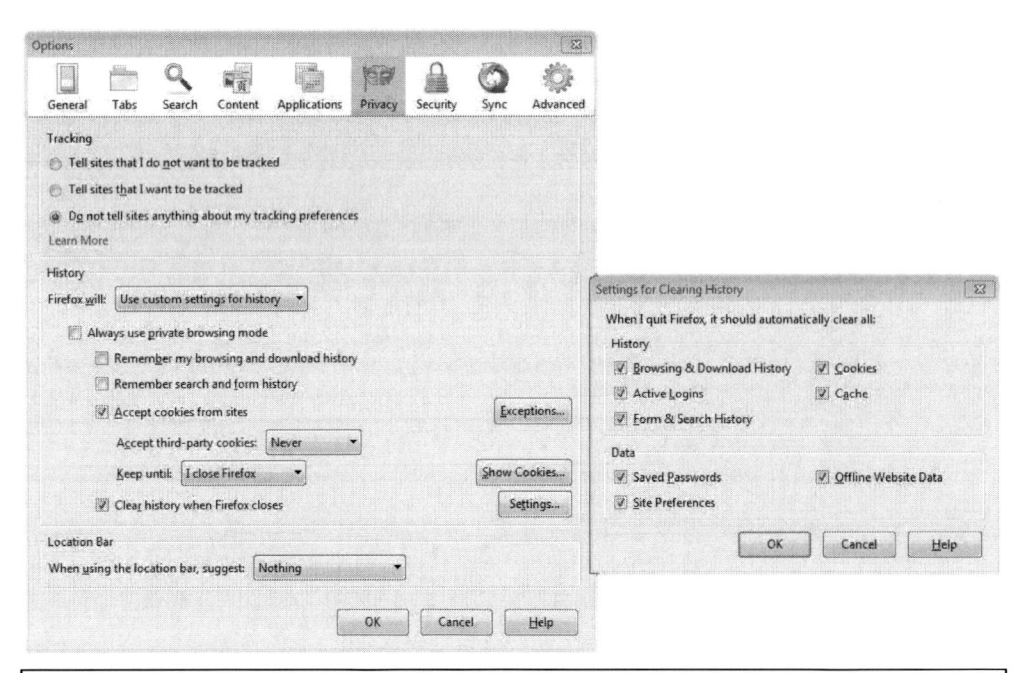

Figure 6.4: The Firefox Privacy options. The dialogue shown at right is an additional dialogue that is presented when the "Settings" button in the Privacy options is clicked.

Privacy (see Figure 6.4): The privacy category is where we will do much of the real work of deciding what information Firefox stores and what it does not. The first section under Privacy is Tracking, which has three options: users can choose to tell sites they do wish to be tracked, do not wish to be tracked, or tell the sites nothing about their tracking preferences. Because sites have no obligation to honor your requests not to be tracked (and because I will take other, more aggressive steps to limit online tracking) I leave this site at the default, "Do not tell sites anything about my tracking preferences" though you may elect to tell sites that you do not wish to be tracked.

The next section within Privacy is History. Under the "Firefox will:" pull-down, select "Use custom settings for history." This will allow you to choose everything that is stored or forgotten when you close your browser. Next, uncheck "Always use private browsing mode." Though "Always use private browsing mode" *probably* removes everything, I like the granularity and control of choosing these settings and seeing for myself exactly what items Firefox will delete. Next, uncheck "Remember my browsing and download history," and "Remember search and form history." This will prevent Firefox from remembering any history through your browsing session.

Next, check the box that says, "Accept cookies from sites." This will allow cookies from the sites you visit. Without cookies, it is very difficult to make purchases, use online streaming services, or enjoy many of the other potential benefits of the internet. Though accepting cookies is not ideal, we will take steps to get rid of them upon closing Firefox. Next, under the "Accept cookies from third party sites" drop-down, select "Never." Third-party sites are sites that I have not visited but that are still attempting to track my internet usage for marketing purposes. I have no need to accept their cookies. Under "Keep until" (which refers to how long cookies are retained), select "I close Firefox." By default, cookies may last 30, 60, or as long as 90 days, and may track your browsing sessions throughout that entire period.

"PRIVATE" BROWSING MODES

Do not rely on Firefox's native "Private Browsing" mode (or on other browsers' analogs like Incognito or InPrivate modes). Though these modes are designed to prevent any information from your browsing session from being stored on your computer, researchers have proven that they are not always fully effective. Controlling all of these settings manually allows you to define exactly what Firefox does and does not store and gives you confidence that all your browsing sessions are "private".

Finally, check the box that says "Clear history when Firefox closes." This will delete remnants of your session that Firefox has retained. Before moving on click the "Settings" box to the right. This will bring up an entirely new dialogue that will allow you to select exactly what is cleared (see Figure 6.4). These items are: Browsing and Download History, Active Logins, Form & Search History, Cookies, Cache, Saved Passwords, Site Preferences, and Offline Website Data. Select all of them. Finally, under the location bar suggestion option select "Nothing."

Security: Under Security check the "Warn me when sites try to install add-ons" box. This will require you to approve or deny a site when an add-on attempts to execute. This affords you some level of protection against annoying add-ons or semi-malicious add-ons that would track your browsing history. Next deselect both the "Block reported attack sites" and "Block reported web forgeries" options. Both of these options *could* allow Firefox to track your web activity by sending the sites you visit to Mozilla for vetting against a whitelist. Though I don't distrust Mozilla or Firefox, I still prefer to send them as little information about my browsing sessions as possible.

Finally deselect the "Remember passwords for sites" and "Use a master password" options. When Firefox stores a password, it does not do so in the most secure manner. Additionally, when you visit a website for which Firefox has a stored password, your credentials may be automatically transmitted to that site. This is not ideal if you are working on an insecure or untrusted internet connection. If you have saved passwords within Firefox in the past, transfer them to your password manager (to see them click the "Saved Passwords" button). Once you have transferred the passwords, delete them all from Firefox by clicking "Remove All" in the Save Passwords dialogue.

Advanced: Under the Advanced tab there are five additional tabs: General, Data Choices, Network, Update, and Certificates. Under the Data Choices Tab I recommend unchecking all three of these options. Telemetry, the Firefox Health Reporter, and the Crash Reporter all collect data about your usage of Firefox. While most of this data should be anonymized and only consist of metadata about your browsing, I still prefer not to transmit it.

The most important option in the Advanced options is the Update tab. This will choose when and how Firefox is updated, and keeping your browser up-to-date is incredibly important for security reasons. I recommend choosing "Check for updates but let me choose whether to install them." This option makes me aware that an update is available, but lets me choose the time and place that I install it, and gives me time to research the update and understand how it will impact my security and privacy. If you choose this option do not ignore the notifications that an update is available.

WebRTC vulnerability fix. There is one final setting we will adjust in Firefox. During the writing this chapter, a new vulnerability was discovered in Firefox and Chrome that allows websites to see your true IP address despite the use of a VPN (discussed in Chapter 5). When using a VPN any site you visit should only see the IP address of the VPN's exit server preventing them from correlating you with your visit with your geographic location and building profiles based on your IP address.

Thankfully this vulnerability is very easy to correct but it cannot be corrected through Firefox's Options dialogue. To correct it go to your URL bar in Firefox and type "about:config." This will open a menu where power-users can make many adjustments to the application (many of these adjustments can be made through the Settings, but many cannot). Bypass the warning and scroll down to "media.peerconnection.enabled." This setting is "true" by default. Double-click this line which will toggle the value to "false." This is all that is required to turn off WebRTC and secure this vulnerability.

FIREFOX ADD-ONS

Add-ons are small extensions that can be used to customize Firefox. The add-ons listed here make Firefox more private and more secure, make it more difficult for your browsing history to be tracked, and reduce the possibility of certain types of malicious attacks successfully occurring against you.

Each add-on in this section (with the exception of NoScript) is more or less "fire and forget," meaning that once installed they require no interaction with the user to perform their intended functions. They are also unlikely to "break" (i.e. render inoperable on your machine) websites, a problem that can occur with some of the apps discussed later in this chapter. Because of the low maintenance these add-ons require, they are suitable for beginner or non-security conscious users. If I am asked to "fix" a friend's computer, I will install these add-ons for him or her (again, with the exception of NoScript) and I have yet to receive a complaint. These applications provide a good baseline level of security and hardening for the browser as well as limiting the ability of websites and ISPs to track your browsing habits.

These add-ons are not presented in either an ascending or descending order of importance or utility. They are presented merely in alphabetical order. I feel that each is important and have trouble narrowing this down to a shorter list of just a couple. Some of the functionality of these extensions overlap. If this is the case I will attempt to clarify the need for the redundancy.

All of these add-ons are free, and most are available at https://addons.mozilla.org/en-US/firefox/ unless otherwise indicated.

Better Privacy: Better Privacy is a simple, transparent add-on that performs a very important purpose: deleting resilient "flash" cookies which sometimes referred to as locally stored objects (LSOs). LSOs are not formatted as, and may not be recognized as, cookies. Because they do not look like standard cookies to Firefox, they may not be deleted when Firefox closes and may track your internet browsing from session to session. Better Privacy detects and deletes these cookies and upon closing Firefox will delete them for you. I love Better Privacy because there is no icon in the upper toolbar, it requires no interaction from me, and it consistently performs its function.

> **COOKIES**
>
> Several steps will be taken throughout the process of securing Firefox that deal with cookies, including changes in Firefox's privacy settings and the Better Privacy add-on. For this reason it may be helpful to discuss what cookies are, and the threat they represent.
>
> Cookies are small pieces of data placed on your computer by the websites you visit. They are placed there to be helpful; cookies remember which links you have clicked, they products you have looked at, and sometimes your login information so you are already logged in when you visit the page again. In fact, accepting cookies is often required to complete a purchase on a webpage. If your browser won't accept a cookie, the site you are visiting cannot remember what items are in your cart. For this reason I recommend accepting cookies from the sites that you visit, at least for the duration of your browsing session.
>
> Unfortunately, cookies are capable of doing much more than remembering which videos you have previously viewed on a website; cookies can also be used to spy on you. Third-party cookies are placed on your machine not by each site you visit, but by a third-party that is partnered with the "host" site. These cookies are purely for analytical purposes and track your browsing from site to site. Some popular websites may allow as many as 40(!) third party cookies to be installed when you visit their site. Each one of these can record your username/account name, IP address (which can be resolved to your physical location), and each site that you visit, all of which can be used to create a comprehensive picture detailing your online activity. This is why I recommend never accepting third-party cookies (see Figure 6.4), and why we will take such pains in the future to ensure cookies are deleted upon closing the browser.

Disconnect: Though I have used a number of add-ons over the years in an attempt to defeat tracking, the one I prefer now is Disconnect. Disconnect detects and blocks trackers and shows a graphic display indicating how many advertising, analytics, social, and content requests are made when you visit a site. It also shows how many of these are blocked and which ones are not. Disconnect also saves both bandwidth and time by not allowing advertising content to be served to you.

Though NoScript (discussed below) can help prevent tracking like Disconnect and may be considered redundant by some, Disconnect is a dedicated anti-tracking app. I believe what redundancy *does* exist between these two add-ons is necessary because frequently, NoScript is too heavy-handed and will not allow a site to work properly, in which case I have to allow the page (whether permanently or temporarily). When this occurs and a page is allowed to run I still want some protections in place. Disconnect does not replace NoScript (and vice-versa) but they do complement each other well.

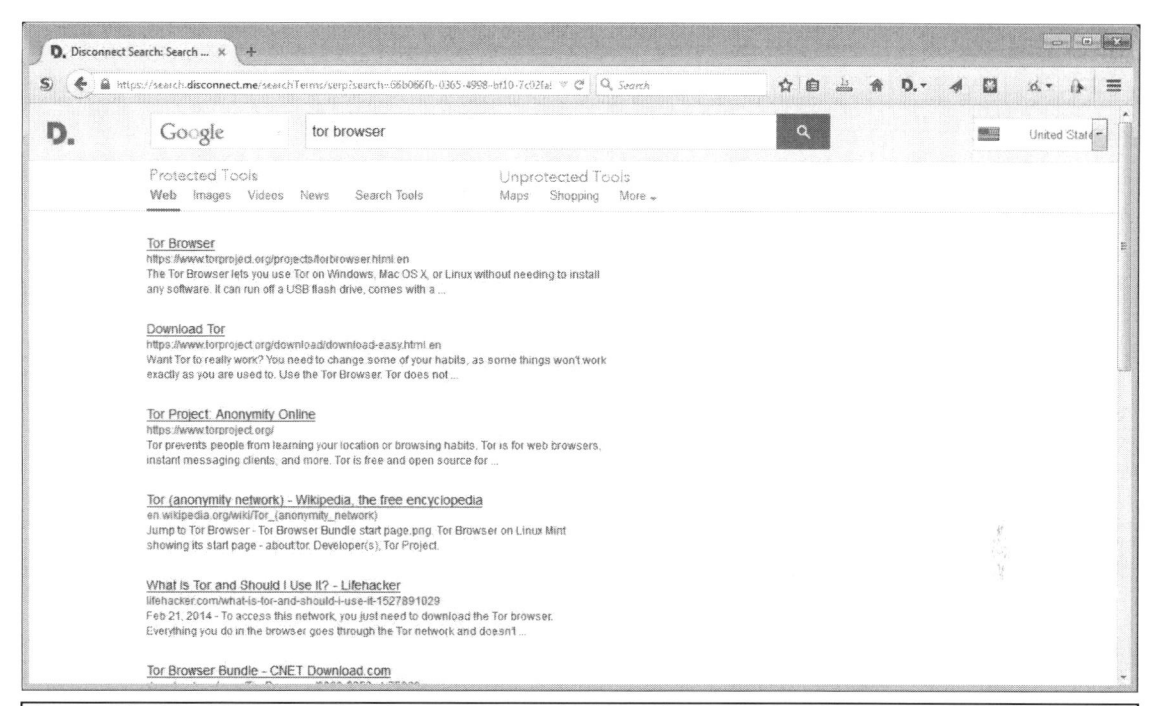

Figure 6.5: The Disconnect Search page. Not only does Disconnect Search protect your searches, it also gives you five search engines at the click of the mouse via the pulldown menu beside the search bar.

Disconnect Search: This is one of my favorite Firefox extensions. Disconnect Search can replace the default search engines in Firefox and route all of your searches through a "light" VPN via a Disconnect server. This allows you to search semi-anonymously because the search provider does not see from whom the search is originating. Additionally, if you set Disconnect Search as your default search engine, all your searches (whether from your homepage, Google.com, the address bar, or the search bar) will be routed through Disconnect Search.

When you search through Disconnect Search your search terms are sent to your preferred search engine and those are the results that are returned. If you don't like those results, there is a dropdown menu right in the search page that allows you to search through any of the other search engines supported by Disconnect Search: Bing, Blekko, DuckDuckGo, Google, and Yahoo!. Disconnect Search will warn you that because they trust DuckDuckGo, search requests are sent directly to that search engine. I like Disconnect Search if for no other reason than the convenience of having five search engines immediately available through a dropdown menu.

HTTPS Everywhere: As discussed earlier in this work, the HTTPS (HyperText Transfer Protocol

– Secure) protocol is intended to encrypt data-in-motion between two devices using the SSL and TLS encryption protocols. Though vulnerabilities exist in HTTPS it should be considered the first line of defense for your data-in-motion. The HTTPS Everywhere add-on can help ensure you establish and maintain HTTPS connections throughout your browsing sessions.

Unfortunately, many sites have the ability to offer HTTPS connections but only do so during "sensitive" portions of the session such as login or financial transactions. During the rest of your session many sites will revert back to plaintext HTTP. The HTTPS Everywhere add-on was designed to force any site with the HTTPS capability to encrypt the entire session, and it works very well. Encrypting your entire session will ensure that anyone sniffing your Wi-Fi, or otherwise inspecting your traffic, will encounter much more unusable, encrypted information. HTTPS Everywhere was developed and is maintained by the Electronic Frontier Foundation (EFF).

HTTPS Everywhere is free and available at: https://www.eff.org/https-everywhere

---

"MALICIOUS" ADD-ONS

There are a myriad of add-ons for Firefox and many of them offer convenience as their primary selling point. They will make websites easier to use, remember information for you, or make shopping on ecommerce sites more convenient. Unfortunately, many of these add-ons can compromise your security and privacy. Some of these add-ons will actively track your browsing sessions, some may insecurely store data, and others may be vectors for malicious code. Further, the more add-ons you have the more unique your browser is making you vulnerable to a technique called browser fingerprinting. Think twice and do your due diligence before installing and trusting an add-on.

NoScript: NoScript is the nuclear option of security-focused browser extensions. NoScript blocks all scripts and plugins (including Java, Javascript, and Flash) from executing except on trusted websites and it performs a number of other browser-related security functions as well. Unfortunately the security of NoScript comes at a cost: NoScript has a very steep learning curve. Because it blocks so many scripts, NoScript tends to "break" many websites. In many cases, this may be desirable as NoScript prevents videos from automatically playing, stops animations, prevents pop-ups and other advertising, and generally makes busy pages much more manageable. For sites that you *need* to work, this can be quite frustrating initially, after installing the add-on. For this reason, the application allows itself to be customized to whitelist certain sites and to allow scripts to run on a case-by-case basis. Clicking the NoScript icon on a page will display all of the scripts that are running on the page, and will present options for dealing with each script individually, as well as settings that apply to all scripts on a page and globally. These options are:

Allow scripts globally (dangerous): This setting basically removes all protections afforded by NoScript and lets all scripts on all pages run. Unfortunately, this option is not reset when you close and reopen your browser. There are some occasions where using this option is desirable. If, for example, I am creating a new account or making an online purchase, and may be redirected to a page where scripts blocking may interfere with password input fields, captchas, etc., I will allow scripts globally, but only for that transaction. As soon as I am finished I will enable script-blocking again.

Allow all of this page: Permanently whitelists the entire page. Be aware that permanently whitelisting a site on NoScript will place the name of the site in a list on your computer. This list is unencrypted and may be viewed by anyone with access to your computer, allowing him or her to see what sites you visit frequently enough to permanently whitelist.

Temporarily allow all of this page (italicized): allows all the scripts on a page to run for the duration of the browsing session. This setting will be reset when you close your browser.

When you no longer wish to allow scripts on a given page NoScript also gives you the ability to revoke permissions. Additionally each script on the page will have an "Allow" or *"Temporarily allow"* option, allowing you to finely tune each page to make the content you desire visible while blocking everything else. Though using NoScript can be frustrating at first, once the sites you primarily use have been whitelisted and are working well, the add-on requires little intervention except when visiting new sites or sites that are not permanently whitelisted.

This section has only covered the tip of the security iceberg that is NoScript. In addition to preventing scripts from executing, NoScript also prevents Cross-Site Scripting attacks, allows you to force sites to use HTTPS connections (where available), prevents clickjacking attempts, and provides automatic boundaries enforcement (ABE). For more information on the incredible capabilities of NoScript visit https://noscript.net/

NoScript is free and available through the Firefox Add-Ons menu.

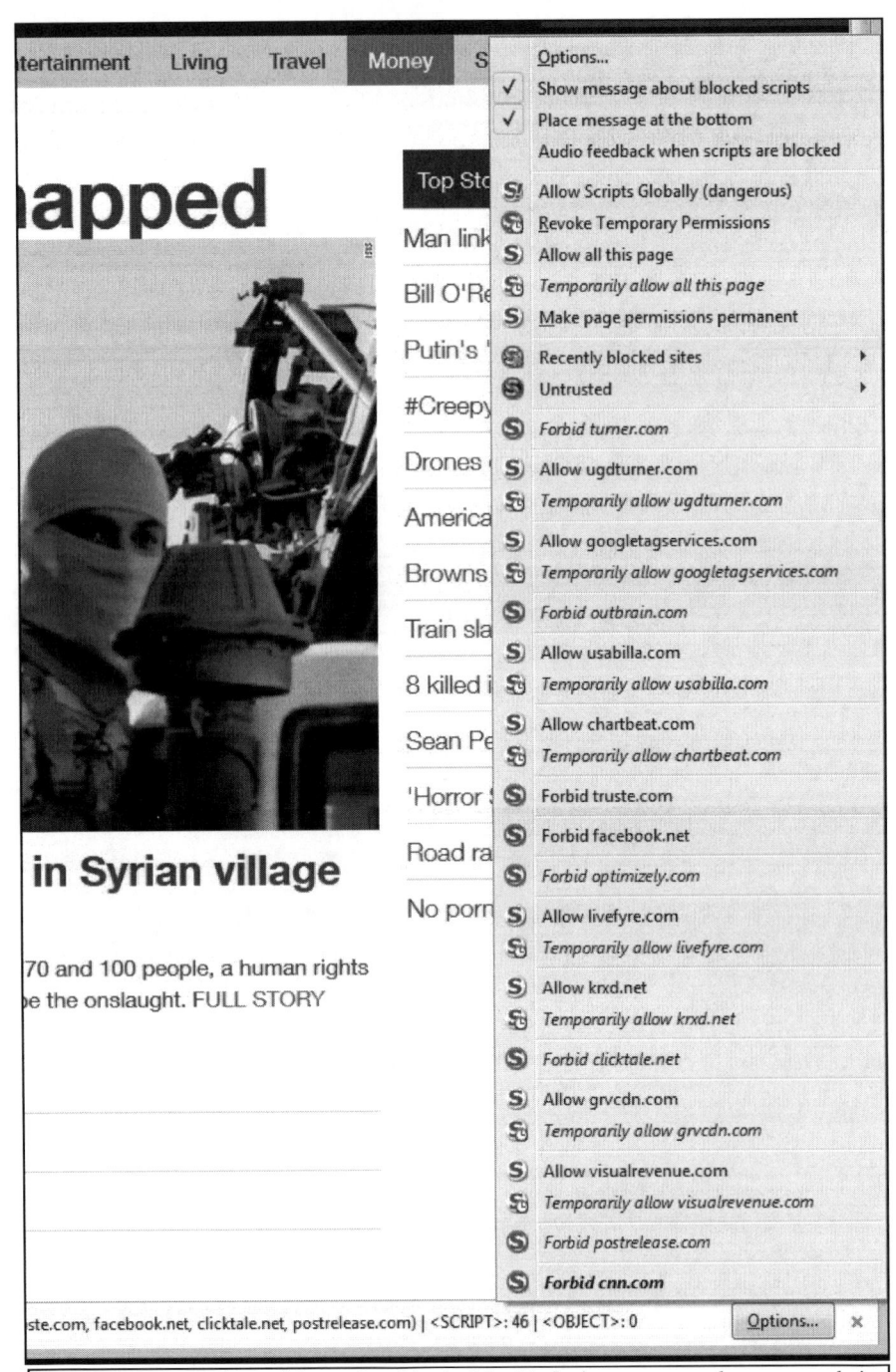

Figure 6.6: A portion of the scripts blocked by NoScript on a popular news website. Note that some of these scripts have been temporarily allowed to run. Some sites will attempt to execute scores of scripts.

EPIC PRIVACY BROWSER

If you do not want to take the time to set up Firefox, or if you prefer Chrome's interface and low system impact, consider using Epic Privacy Browser. Epic is a browser designed with privacy in mind and is based on Chromium (the same foundational code as Google Chrome). Unlike Chrome Epic Privacy Browser does not track or store any information about you. Epic also blocks third-party trackers and does not allow third-party cookies. Further, Epic offers a built-in proxy, the enabling of which masks your IP address (which may be used to reveal your physical location), encrypts your traffic, and routes all searches through the proxy, whether it is enabled or not. Epic even features "Encrypted Data Preference," a built-in function similar to HTTPS Everywhere that attempts to always force an HTTPS-encrypted connection where available.

Figure 6.7: The very clean interface of Epic Privacy Browser. Besides the privacy it offers this browser is desirable because of its light weight and good performance, though you may have to adjust some settings (such as allowing cookies) too make certain sites work.

Due to privacy concerns around most browser extensions (see sidebar on Page 138) Epic does not allow any add-ons to be installed. This is a good thing for users who would install privacy-compromising extensions but it does hamper the ability of the security-conscious user somewhat. I would use Epic almost exclusively if it had to ability to use the Mailvelope email encryption add-on (discussed in Chapter 7). I do appreciate that Epic Privacy Browser does make secure, private browsing a simple matter and I do use it quite frequently for casual browsing.

Epic Privacy Browser is free and available at: https://epicbrowser.com/

TOR

Though it is nearly impossible to be completely anonymous online, Tor is as close as you can get. No discussion of online privacy would be complete without mentioning Tor. I use Tor religiously and advise everyone to whom I talk to do the same. Tor prevents your internet service provider, third-party advertisers and trackers, and even governments from seeing what you're up to online. Developed by the US military, which continues to donate money to the project ($1.8 million in 2013, alone), and currently operated by a non-profit organization, the Tor Browser Bundle (Tor was formerly known as "The Onion Router") is a secure, anonymous web browser. Tor is free, open source, heavily audited for security holes, and frequently patched.

At this point a brief explanation of how Tor provides the anonymity it offers may be helpful. When using the Tor browser the traffic you request is not sent straight to and from the provider. Tor makes your traffic anonymous by routing it through three intermediary servers (called "nodes") prior to sending the request to the desired site. Your traffic is heavily encrypted within the Tor Network, which also contributes to your anonymity. When your request leaves your computer it is encrypted three times. The first node at which it arrives(called the "entry guard") can see that it came from you. Upon removing the first layer of encryption, it can "see" the next node in the network to which your traffic is to be sent. When your traffic arrives at the second node, it can see the node it was sent from and the node it will forward to, though it cannot tell that the request originated with you, or where the request is ultimately being sent. When your request arrives at the exit node the last layer of encryption is removed and your request is transmitted to its final destination.

For the disproportionate amount of privacy it offers Tor is now incredibly simple to use. Simply visit the site (https://www.torproject.org/) and download the Tor Browser Bundle. Once it has downloaded double click .exe file (the onion logo). This will extract a folder called Tor Browser. Within this folder is a file called "Start Tor Browser.exe." Installation is now complete. Because Tor runs as a portable application you simply double-click this file each time you wish to access the internet through Tor and Tor will begin constructing your circuit (the set of servers through which your traffic will be routed for the duration of your browsing session). Once your custom circuit has been built Tor will open its own browser, which is a highly customized version of Firefox and has the HTTPS Everywhere and NoScript add-ons already built in. You can then begin browsing with the closest thing there is to true online anonymity.

It is important to understand that Tor is not a panacea. Your anonymity can be compromised on Tor in any of several different ways. For example, if you make a purchase on Tor using your credit card or other financial information, your anonymity will be breached. Likewise if you log into an email, social media, ecommerce, or other site that is associated with your name, your true identity will be associated with that browsing session. If you open an application on your computer that has the ability to communicate with the internet (e.g., Microsoft Office or Adobe Acrobat) your anonymity may be compromised by information leaked through those applications. There are many other ways that the veil of anonymity Tor provides can be pierced and to be truly anonymous (or at least as anonymous as is possible) takes extraordinary effort. For more information on how to use Tor to achieve the maximum level of anonymity possible, visit the Tor Project's website at: https://www.torproject.org/download/download.html.en#warning

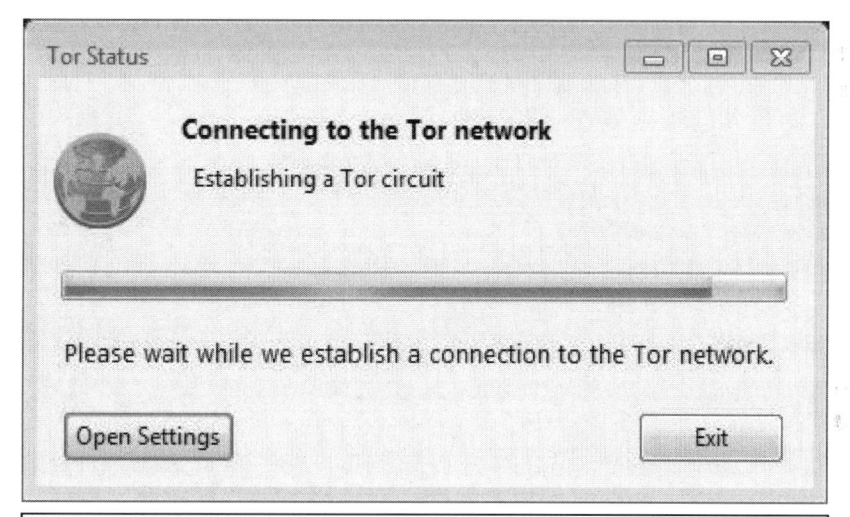

Figure 6.8: Upon opening the Tor Browser Bundle you will be presented with this dialogue as Tor builds your unique circuit.

In the interest of full disclosure, Tor is also inconvenient. By routing all your traffic through three intermediate servers prior to sending it to its destination Tor traffic is much slower. Each of the computers through which your traffic is routed may be much slower than your own, and so may be their individual internet connections. Second, some sites disallow logins from the Tor network. Further, many sites will require multiple captcha entries and are generally unfriendly to Tor. As I have said several times throughout this book, convenience and security are inversely proportional, but I believe this slight inconvenience is worth the security and privacy Tor provides.

Some interesting facts: All the Tor servers used to re-route communications are hosted by volunteers. The host of the final server your communications are routed through can monitor any transmissions that exit Tor in plaintext (though it would still theoretically be anonymous). Secondly, because of the anonymity provided by Tor, it is used extensively by the "dark web," the criminal element that deals in child pornography, online drug sales, etc. Because of this, Tor is extensively monitored by law enforcement and intelligence agencies (both domestic and foreign) that may be able to observe your traffic. Tor is not a perfect solution and can be broken by certain adversaries.

The Tor Browser Bundle is free and open source and available at: https://www.torproject.org/

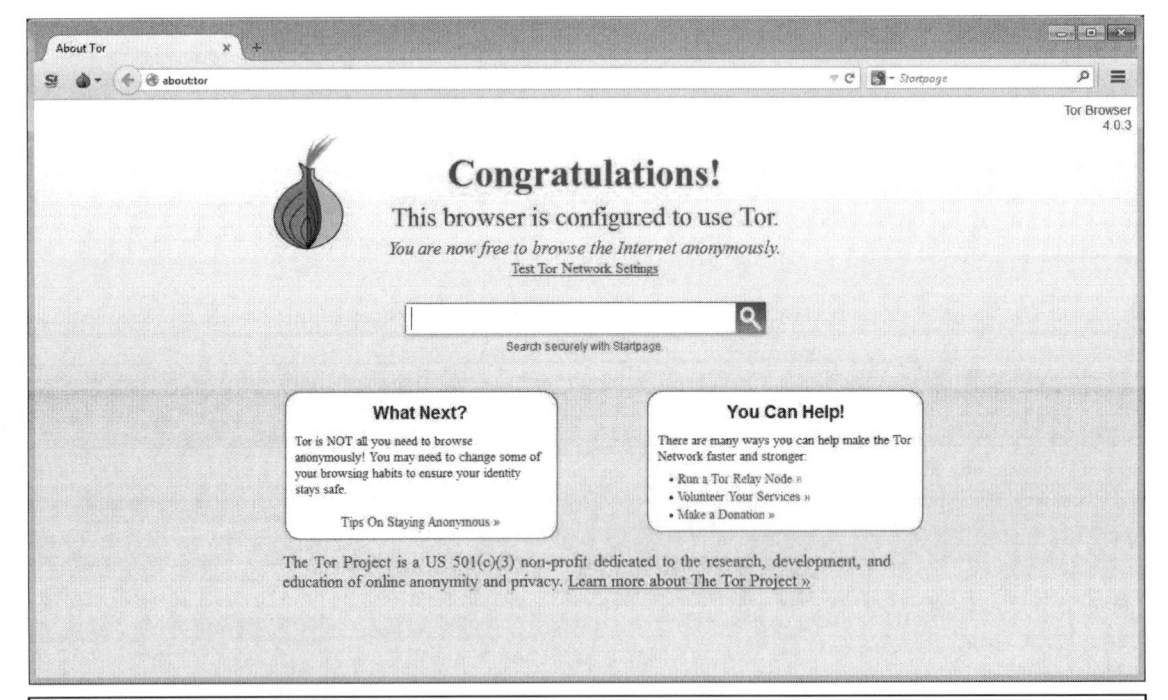

Figure 6.9: The Tor Browser upon establishing a secure network. The browser is based on Firefox and features HTTPS Everywhere and NoScript organically.

BROWSING BEST PRACTICES

All the security settings and add-ons in the world will not protect you if you practice poor Internet browsing hygiene. The best protection is the human element of security. Thoughtfulness, awareness, and patience are better than settings, add-ons, and anti-virus. Below are some browsing best practices that will make you much less likely to encounter malicious sites and make it much less likely that your machine will be compromised if you do.

Be careful what sites you visit: The beauty of the Internet is that it puts the world at your fingertips. Any interest you have can likely be explored and expounded upon on the Internet. Many (the vast, vast majority) of these sites do not have your best interests in mind and care little about your security or privacy. Websites are commonly used as attack vectors for malware, to track your browsing habits, or to get personal information from you. Thoughtfulness is required when browsing the Internet.

Pornography sites are notorious as being attack vectors for malware. Clicking on the wrong ad on a porn site can quickly lead to adware, nagware, ransomware, or worse. Pornography sites are not alone in this. Be careful about the sites that you visit and ask yourself: is the site full of pop-ups? Does clicking a link on the site cause a new, unrelated window to open? Does the site cleverly conceal links that end up opening a new page or a new window? If the answer to any of these questions is yes, the site is probably one you should avoid.

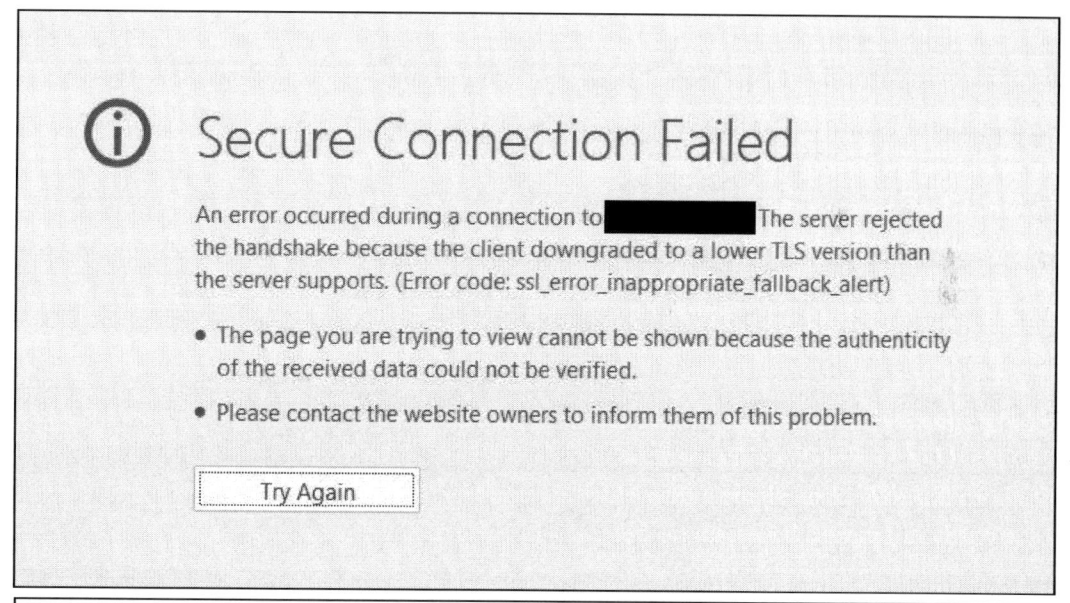

Figure 6.10: A warning from Firefox that a secure connection was not achieved. This can happen for a variety of reasons (malicious and benign alike) and should be taken seriously.

Don't ignore warnings: If you visit a website and receive a warning from your browser, your antivirus software, or from a browser extension like NoScript, it is probably a good idea to skip that site. There are a variety of warnings you may receive. If Firefox gives you a grey page letting you know that a site's SSL/TLS certificate is invalid, this could mean the site has a forged certificate (in which case the connection is not secure but is trying to make you think that it is), or it could mean that someone is interfering with you secure connection, also indicating that your visit is not secure and any credentials you transmit could be intercepted in plaintext. Take these warnings very seriously!

Firefox may also warn you that a site is attempting to install an add-on. This may be a "drive-by download." (A site attempting to install a malware application without your knowledge.) Unless you specifically visited that site with the hopes of downloading an add-on, do not allow it to be installed. As discussed earlier, even seemingly benign add-ons that are presented as a way to enhance your experience with a website often harvest a great deal of data about your browsing habits.

You may also receive warnings from NoScript that will warn you when a Cross-Site Scripting (XSS) attack is detected. Avast Free Antivirus will also warn you (alarming you with a siren sound if you have not disabled these audible indicators) that a site presents a potential threat to the well-being of your system. While it may be tempting to ignore warnings such as these, you do so at your own risk.

Don't download from untrusted sites: Be very careful about the sites from which you download files and applications. Though torrent sites are fun and many people use them to get free media, they are also rife with malware. If you download a free version of Microsoft Office, you have saved yourself a few dollars, but the risk of also downloading malware with it is very high.

You should scan any files that you download from the Internet with your antivirus and anti-malware scanners before attempting to open or execute them, even when downloading from trusted sources. This is no guarantee of protection, as the file(s) may be infected with a zero-day vulnerability that is not yet in your antivirus software's definitions, but it does provide some level of protection.

Use care when downloading applications: When downloading applications, you should always use extreme care. Applications can contain extensive malicious payload, and attention should be paid to the quality of the download you are getting. If at all possible, attempt to download programs directly from their source: the original developer's site. All of the applications in this book are accompanied by a link to a reputable site through which they can be downloaded. Where possible, these are all original developer pages. Where not possible, they are direct links to reputable sources such as Source Forge (www.sourceforge.net).

Also be aware that some sites may prompt you to download an application to enhance your experience on that site. Can't watch a video? No problem, download "our" video player. Beware of such enticements to download applications. If a video cannot be posted on a reputable video hosting site like Vimeo or YouTube it is probably an attempt to get you to install a malicious program of some sort.

SUMMARY

Internet browser selection and setup is an important part of good online security. Your Internet browser serves as your ambassador to the internet and should leak as little information about you as possible, while also protecting you from certain types of exploits, warning you about potential attacks, etc. In this chapter we covered:

- o Firefox setup for maximum security and privacy
- o Security- and privacy-enhancing add-ons for Firefox
- o Epic Privacy Browser
- o The Tor Browser Bundle and the benefits and risks inherent in using the Tor Network
- o Internet browsing best practices that will reduce your risk and exposure online

CHAPTER 7
SECURING ONLINE ACCOUNTS

Online account security concerns me greatly. This concern is largely the result of two facts. First, most online accounts that I have contain some personal information about me. Some of these accounts may contain financial information or other personal information like my home address, mailing address, etc. The second reason I am concerned by online accounts is that they exist on servers that I do not personally control—enemy territory if you will. Existing on the internet, these sites are vulnerable to attacks against me personally, attacks against the site the account is held with generally, and other forms of spillage.

Online data stands a statistically much greater chance of being exploited than data-at-rest on my machine, and for this reason, I take some special pains and considerations to ensure the security of online accounts. Some of these techniques have been covered elsewhere in this book. The use of password managers, strong passwords, unique usernames, and two-factor authentication were all covered in chapter two. Though these will be reiterated here, I will cover some other best practices for online accounts, and, ideally, make you reconsider the information you are putting online, whether through email, social media, other accounts, or into cloud storage.

ONLINE ACCOUNT SECURITY BEST PRACTICES

Online accounts are a common Achilles' heel of a good information security posture. Because they exist on computers over which you have no control (the servers owned by the account's host), you likewise have little control over how carefully your information is stored and how secure it is. There are, however, steps you can take to make your accounts more secure.

Use Accurate Information Sparingly: When signing up for a new online account, consider what information is really important and necessary to the creation of the account. When you sign up for an email account, does it really need your true date of birth? Probably not. E-commerce sites require your address to ship packages to you, but do they need your real name? Perhaps they do. When you create an online account with your bank, do you need to use complete and accurate information? Yes, you probably do.

When creating online accounts carefully consider the information that service or site really needs and do not give more information than necessary. Thoughtfulness is what I intend to encourage. If you are using completely accurate information it is collected and sold to marketers which is damaging to privacy. If someone is attempting to hack your account and they have accurate information about you it is more likely they will succeed. With that in mind, let's reconsider the above examples.

Though it might seem counterintuitive, some of these sites need far less information than you would imagine. Email accounts don't need your true birthday or sex. Though your birthday may be collected to ensure you are of age to view certain content the primary purpose of collecting such data is help them to build a profile on you. E-retailers need your home address but they don't necessarily need your real name (again, this information is collected so it can be used in a profile that is sold to data marketers) so long as you pay with pre-paid gift cards. On the other hand, some sites *do* require fully accurate information, and this is underscores the need to be thoughtful. It is a good idea to use accurate information with some sites like online banking or bill pay. Using false information on a bank account could be a crime and could result in you being locked out of your account.

Check the Status of Your Accounts: An early step in securing online accounts is to ensure they have not been breached. There are a couple of services that will offer you a bit of insight into this by allowing you to cross-reference your email address against lists of hacked accounts. Breachalarm.com (formerly shouldichangemypassword.com) allows you to input your email address, which it then cross-references against a list of hacked accounts. If your account has been hacked, change the password immediately. Notify your friends and family that you will be changing your email address and then migrate as quickly as possible to a new email account. Before closing the hacked one, delete all the emails, contacts, calendar entries, and other personal information from it.

Haveibeenpwned.com is a similar site that checks not only email addresses, but usernames, too. This site is relatively new and maintains a database of breached accounts. When you enter your email address or username it is cross-referenced against a list of known leaked usernames and passwords. If you find that your account information has been leaked, you should change the password on the account immediately (and perhaps close it and open a new one).

Keep in mind that services like these only track large breaches and should not be considered conclusive proof that your account is safe. However, checking your email address through one of these services does give some peace of mind that you are OK in the wake of big breaches.

Multiple Email Accounts: All of the techniques described above merely obscure your username and make it difficult for an attacker to locate your online accounts. If they all forward to the same address, the compromise of that one address could lead to a total compromise. Further, the email provider will still have a comprehensive picture of the "real" you if all the emails from all your online accounts forward to the same inbox. The best (but most time consuming and potentially frustrating) practice is to use multiple email accounts and assign only one or two online accounts to each email address. Admittedly this takes some patience and dedication and is not for everyone.

Figure 7.1: The results of a haveibeenpwned.com search. Though this will let you know if your account has been compromised, the results of such a search should not be considered conclusive proof your account has *not* been hacked.

Get Rid of Unused or Untrusted Accounts: If you have old online accounts that are no longer used close them down if possible. Some tools that can help you do this are Know 'Em (www.knowem.com), a tool that helps you find all the sites on which you have created accounts, and tools that help you close those accounts like Account Killer (www.accountkiller.com), WikiCancel (www.wikicancel.org), and Just Delete Me (www.justdelete.me). Account Killer and Just Delete Me will give you the links and helpful hints for removing online accounts and they also rate sites on the difficulty of deleting their accounts (it is a good idea to check this out before you build an account in the first place). If you cannot delete an account log into it and replace as much information as possible with disinformation by replacing your name (if possible) birthday, billing information, address, and other fields with false information. This will ensure that even if these old, unused accounts are breached they will not leak sensitive information about you.

Only Log in on Trusted Platforms: Uncheck the "remember me" box during login on the accounts that still offer this option. This option keeps you logged in by placing a cookie on your computer but it is too easy to forget to manually log off (especially on a public computer). If you are using a computer that you do not personally control consider whether you *really* need to enter login information on that device at all, or if it can wait. If you do not control the device it may be (wittingly or unwittingly) infected with key loggers or other malicious software that may harvest your login information.

ONLINE BANKING ACCOUNTS

Banking and ecommerce accounts are two very sensitive types of accounts and should be closely guarded. There are several best practices that can make these accounts more secure.

I personally refuse to bank with an institution that does not support two-factor authentication. With the prevalence of breaches occurring on a daily basis financial institutions have no excuse for not implementing this as a standard feature. If your bank does not support two-factor authentication, support one that does. Several major national banks do offer TFA including Bank of America, Chase, Discover, HSBC, and USAA. Bafflingly, several financial institutions that I have used in the past have severe password limitations (limiting passwords to as few as 8 characters in one instance). This makes two-factor authentication especially important.

E-COMMERCE ACCOUNTS

Shop reputable sites: Though I hate to encourage you to use the big-box online retailers they do typically offer excellent security. These large retailers characteristically have a lot more to lose if a breach occurs and more money to throw at the problem before it becomes a problem.

Check out as a guest: If you are using a site that you will not likely use again check out as a guest to avoid creating an account if at all possible. If you are required to create an account, do not save your credit card information. Though not a guarantee, this may somewhat limit the information that site maintains about you. More accounts equates to a larger attack surface, and more databases containing sensitive personal information.

If you are shopping with a smaller retailer that offers the option to (and many smaller retail sites do), consider using a digital wallet service like PayPal. PayPal offers excellent security features and supports two-factor authentication. The biggest benefit of using a service like this is that you don't have to enter your credit card or bank account information to the site with which you are transacting, and PayPal can serve as a single, unified payment service.

HTTPS: When shopping online, ensure that the site you are using is encrypted (https) on any page requesting credit card information. Though it is relatively rare to find a site that still permits transactions over insecure connections, they do still exist. Be especially aware of this when purchasing from less reputable websites. Firefox displays a padlock to the right of the URL bar when a secure connection has been made. A grey padlock indicates the site has been verified and the connection is encrypted; a green padlock means the same, and that an extended verification has been conducted by Mozilla to verify the authenticity of the site.

Figure 7.2: A secure connection in Firefox. The padlock (and the https:// prefix) indicates that the site has been verified and the connection is encrypted.

EMAIL ACCOUNTS

Email accounts contain a great deal of sensitive personal information. This information is often more starkly personal and potentially embarrassing than the details of your financial accounts, business interests, etc., though email can also contain these details. Your email is at risk on two fronts: from the interest of the email provider (if you use a free email provider, as even I do) who scans the content of your emails and serves you ads based on that content, and from hackers who would break into your account for various malicious purposes. Aside from the best practices that I continually preach throughout this chapter (use random usernames, long passwords, and two-factor authentication), there are several other best practices you can take to make your email accounts more secure.

Compartmentalize: This is probably the most onerous step to take but also the best one for improving the security of your email. Setting up multiple email accounts and linking your various other online accounts to these addresses takes time and remembering which one is which takes patience and energy. But consider this: if you have one email address to which all of your other online activities link, that email address is the lynchpin of your entire online security system. The breach of it could potentially lead to the breach of many of your other accounts because it is also likely used as your password reset mechanism.

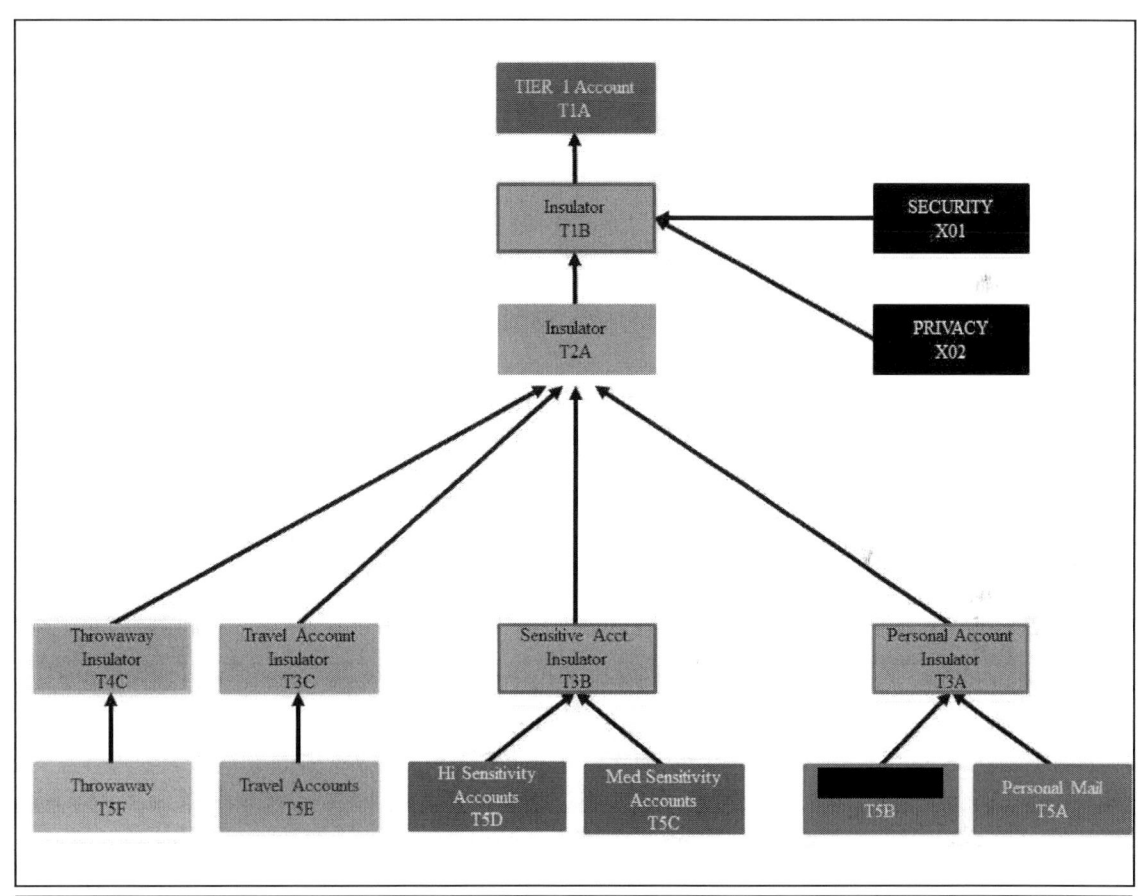

Figure 7.3: A portion of the author's grossly overcomplicated email forwarding scheme. A greatly simplified version of this system is described below.

For this reason I recommend using multiple email addresses. It has taken me a long time to get to this point but each email address I have is only linked to one or two other accounts. For example, I have one email address that my two bank accounts are associated with. That is all this email address is used for—I do not give it out to personal contacts and I don't use it for online shopping. In short, the only thing it is used for is to receive emails from my bank. This prevents the username of the account from becoming widely known information and reduces its attack surface, as well as limiting the information that could be retrieved from it were it breached.

This system may be overly complicated for all by the most security-conscious users. At the minimum, however, I recommend using at least five separate email accounts. My recommendations for what these accounts are used for are listed below but ultimately it is up to you to decide how they are organized.

- **Security Account**: this account should be used only for security-based subscriptions and logins such as your VPN service and cloud-based password manager.
- **High-Sensitivity**: the account that you use for your most sensitive financial and personal accounts, such as banking, mortgage, retirement, and investment accounts. Examples of extremely sensitive personal information are medical accounts
- **Medium Sensitivity**: this account should be used for things that contain some combination of personal information and financial information, such as utility bills, mobile phone bills, and online retail accounts.
- **Personal**: an account that you use strictly for personal communications. I do not associate this email address with any online accounts and I do not give it out for any purpose other than communicating with family and friends.
- **Throwaway Account**: the throwaway account is the email address you should use when you have to register for an online service, buy from an untrusted site that you do not wish to have your "real" e-commerce email address, and for retail store loyalty cards.

Additional accounts may be added as needed for forwarding purposes if you use this model. Some email service providers (see Gmail and FastMail below) offer the ability to forward multiple accounts to a single account. This requires you to log in to only one account, from which you can receive and send mail from all the other accounts (and to reply from the original accounts). This does create a single point of failure but if you are following all other security best practices and you never give out the address of the account to which all emails are forwarded it is relatively well-protected.

Though it may seem counterintuitive the throwaway account is the most important one in this list. By having an email address that contains no sensitive personal information (and very little accurate information at all) you can give out an address that, if compromised, would lead to no real damage to you. You can even add a layer of protection to this account by using 33mail.com or notsharingmy.info email addresses (see below) that forward to the throwaway account. The more exposure an email address gets, the greater the likelihood becomes that it will be hacked. I am extremely cautious about giving out my "real" email address(es) and try to protect them.

33mail.com: This is currently my favorite mail forwarding service. When you set up a 33mail account you choose an email address to which all mail is forwarded and a username. This username will be a suffix in all of your future forwarding addresses so choose it with care. Once you have created and verified your account you will be given a custom email domain that contains your username. For this book I set up a 33mail account using the username "example." Now I have a custom email domain called "@example.33mail.com".

When I am ready to begin giving out email addresses I can use any address I want as long as it terminates with "@example.33mail.com." If I want to register for a customer loyalty card at a retail store I will make up a custom email address on the spot: rewardscard@example.33mail.com. I do not have to set this email address up in 33mail ahead of time, either. Any email sent to any @example.33mail.com address will forward on to my "real" throwaway email account.

One of the great things about 33mail is the ability to organize email addresses. I can create a custom address for every single use, track what that email address is used for, and see if it is sold to a third-party. If in the future I find I am receiving too many emails from any particular 33mail email address I can log into my 33mail account and cancel forwarding for that address.

Notsharingmy.info: This is a service that lets you set up anonymous email addresses that will forward mail to your "real" address. These email addresses are six-digit, pseudo-random alphanumeric combinations that are perfect for use as an obscure username. I use this service to sign up for accounts that are unimportant but to which I need to provide an email address and forward it to my throwaway email account. Like 33mail, notsharingmy.info also allows you the ability to cancel forwarding if you no longer desire to receive emails from that address.

As a note of caution be aware that if you reply from your "real" address when using notsharingmy.info, the recipient will see your real/non-anonymous email address. Also, I would not use this service for accounts that are very sensitive or very important. If notsharingmy.info discontinues service or its servers go down you will have no way to receive emails for that account. Further, notsharingmy.info administrators may have some access to emails flowing through their servers.

Clicking links and opening attachments. One major problem with email is that it is very difficult to verify the sender of an email. If you receive an email from your friend Ethan it is usually pretty reasonable to assume that Ethan sent you an email. On the other hand, it is also possible that an attacker is spoofing Ethan's email address to make it look like Ethan sent the email. It is also possible that Ethan's email account was hacked and though the email is originating from his account, it is being sent by a malicious third-party.

Malicious links are a fairly common attack vector and can be used in any number of ways. One of the more benign ways a link may be malicious is by merely verifying the validity and use of an email address. By clicking the link, you alert the sender that the address is valid and used, which makes it more valuable to spammers. It is also possible to craft links through free services that will capture the IP address to which you were connected when you clicked the link, potentially revealing your geographic location. Finally, links may redirect you to disreputable websites (who hasn't gotten an email from a friend's hacked account with a link to "Cheap Electronics!!!" or some other scam site?) or to look-alike sites. The latter are used in an attempt to capture login credentials. The accompanying email will look like it came from a reputable site like your bank. The email will tell you that your account has been compromised and that you need to change your password, while helpfully providing a link to a look-alike login page that will capture your credentials, which will then be used or sold.

Malicious attachments probably represent a greater threat, generally speaking. If an attachment contains malicious code, downloading and attempting to open the attachment can run the code. Though malicious attachments are less common than malicious links because of the greater technical difficulty required in developing them, they are very dangerous and you should open attachments cautiously. I view any email attachment from anyone somewhat suspiciously.

For these reasons (and many more) it is important to think carefully about the links you click and the attachments you download in an email. If the body of the email seems to have a great deal of inside knowledge about you and your relationship to the sender, it is probably OK to open the attachment or click the link, but it also wouldn't hurt to verify via voice if you have any doubt whatsoever about the email's provenance.

Choose your email provider(s) carefully. The mainstream email providers vary pretty widely in the levels of security they offer, though all of them have implemented serious security upgrades in the last couple of years. Because of this, I recommend several providers below that offer good security or privacy (but usually not both). The four providers below are not comprehensive. Indeed, there are numerous other providers that offer built-in encryption, excellent security, and good privacy. The ones listed below are merely the ones with which I am most familiar.

Gmail: As mentioned before, privacy advocates sometimes bristle at the mere mention of Google products because of Google's large, profit-driven data collection. While I do not argue with this (Google does collect a great deal of data) one distinct benefit offered by Google products is excellent security. Gmail accounts are protected by very thorough, comprehensive security measures.

Google allows passwords up to 99 characters in length. This is in stark contrast to maximum password lengths of other mainstream email providers, some of whom cap passwords at an astounding 16 characters. Additionally, Google offers two-factor authentication through several means. The most common is the text/SMS method, followed by app-based TFA. Google also offers TFA through hardware-based tokens. The most convenient thing about Gmail is the ability to use app-specific passwords. App-specific passwords allow you to generate a simple (all lower case letters), short (16-character) passcode that can be used on one instance of a mobile device application. This is a boon to using a Gmail account on a mobile device where inputting a very complex, very long, randomly-generated password would be extremely frustrating. App-specific passwords only work if you have two-factor authentication enabled which makes enabling TFA worth it alone.

Google also does an excellent job of encrypting traffic. Gmail accounts are encrypted with HTTPS throughout the entire session, not just during the login. Google also takes this one step further, encrypting all traffic as it travels between servers internal to Google. This makes it very unlikely that your traffic could be intercepted.

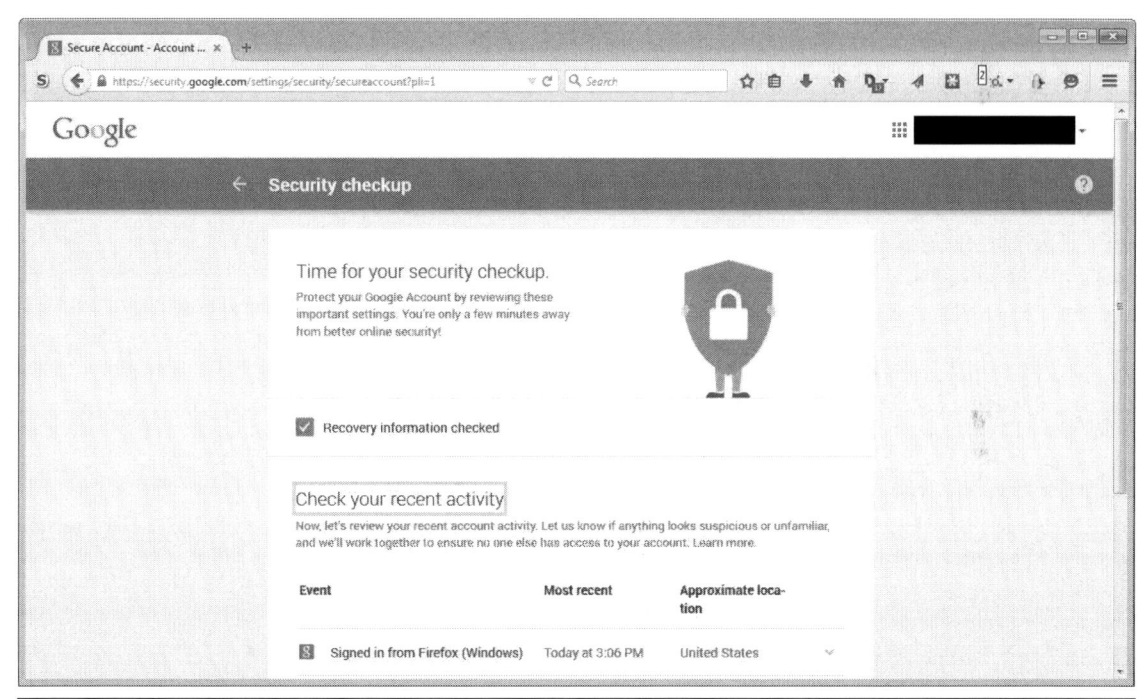

Figure 7.4: A portion of a Google "Security Checkup". This checkup verifies your alternate email address and telephone number(s), allows you to see your recent login activity, and update passwords and TFA options.

Finally, Google does a very good job of recording logins, noticing suspicious login attempts, and alerting the account owner of suspicious account activity. In Gmail you can view a log of login arranged in chronological order and containing an IP address. If any of these logins look suspicious it should be an indicator to change your password and monitor that account carefully in the future.

Google has done an excellent job at securing Gmail accounts and it stands far ahead of most of the competition.

Another benefit of Gmail that is not directly security-related is its ability to forward emails between accounts (see Figure 7.3). If you find the idea of checking five separate email accounts daunting you can set up a sixth account and have all of the emails from the other accounts forwarded to that single, unifying account. In each individual account you can modify the settings to have all emails deleted once they are forwarded, ensuring that if any of those accounts is breached there will be nothing in them. If you choose to do this never give out the email address for the central account that receives all of your emails, only the lower-level addresses that forward to it. By doing so you can keep the top-level account very low profile and reduce the risk it will be located and attacked. Obviously this has an inverse impact on privacy; now Google will know that all of these accounts belong to you so it is up to you to decide whether the security benefits outweigh the privacy concerns in a setup like this.

FastMail: FastMail is one of my new favorite new email services. With the exception of being free (it is not), FastMail is an extremely powerful email provider that offers many of the benefits of Gmail. FastMail allows you to use custom, domain name-based emails, the integration of multiple email accounts, and it supports business users as well as individuals.

One of be biggest benefits of FastMail is that although they offer many of the convenient features of Gmail they monetize directly and do not scan emails for advertising purposes. FastMail has a very transparent privacy policy, does not store deleted emails past one week, and does not sell user data to advertisers. Unfortunately, FastMail only allows passwords up to 50 characters, but they do support two-factor authentication via SMS and Yubikey. The Yubikey can also be used as the sole authentication token, allowing you to login from public computers without typing a password into the keyboard (it is transmitted from the Yubikey). Though this service is not invulnerable it may be worth considering if you frequently use public computers to access your email account.

FastMail is paid and available at: https://www.fastmail.com/

Kolab Now: Kolab is a Switzerland-based email service provider that has gained popularity as of late and markets heavily to privacy-minded users. Kolab is a paid subscription service. Because they monetize directly Kolab does not scrape data to sell to marketing companies. Further, I like to use providers who advertise privacy. If they are caught violating customer privacy their entire business model is in jeopardy which gives them very good incentive to do the right thing.

Just as Gmail is a tradeoff between security and privacy, so is Kolab. While Kolab offers excellent privacy, its security could be better. Kolab does not (at time of writing) offer two-factor authentication (if it did I would almost certainly use Kolab exclusively). For this reason, I strongly recommend using very long passwords (100+ characters) and changing them frequently. This minimizes the chances of your password being hacked and ensures that if it is it will only be good for a short period of time (though all the historical emails stored in the account would be compromised in the event of a breach).

Kolab Now email is paid and available at: https://kolabnow.com/

ProtonMail: There are several email providers that provide built-in encryption. Some of the best of these have been closed down in the last several years, possibly due to government pressure to turn over the encryption keys. Recently an upstart called ProtonMail has been creating an encrypted email service promising privacy and zero-knowledge (that is, the inability to access user emails). ProtonMail is still in beta at the time of this writing but so far it looks extremely promising.

Figure 7.5: A ProtonMail Account. Here the account holder is being prompted to enter the second of two passwords that must be entered to access the inbox. Though not as secure as true two-factor authentication this is a positive security feature.

When you set up a ProtonMail account you are prompted to enter two passwords. The first of these passwords is the standard login password. The second is your "mailbox" password. This is the password that allows you to use the private key that ProtonMail generates for you. ProtonMail allows you to communicate securely with other ProtonMail users and it allows you to send encrypted emails to non-ProtonMail users. Unfortunately when sending an email to a non-ProtonMail user you must have a way to securely get the password to the recipient to open the message. Additionally, the recipient will not be able to send an encrypted reply to you unless he or she is a ProtonMail user.

The primary benefit of ProtonMail is that it is user-friendly to those unfamiliar with asymmetric encryption. It is far easier to use even than Mailvelope (see next section), which is already a greatly simplified system. A downside to ProtonMail at the time of this writing is the inability to encrypt attachments. This is something that ProtonMail is working to resolve and according to their literature should have available by mid-2015. One other major drawback of ProtonMail at the time of this writing is the lack of a two-factor authentication system, but again, according to their documentation TFA is in the works. If these changes are implemented and ProtonMail receives a thorough external audit, they may very well become my sole-source solution for email encryption.

ProtonMail is free and available at: https://protonmail.ch

EMAIL ENCRYPTION

Email is not as private as many of us have long assumed it to be. For decades the assumption around email is that it is essentially a private communication between two parties. This myth has largely been dispelled by the Snowden leaks, and many average individuals are now much more aware of the lack of privacy inherent in email communication. Email is accessible to many, many parties between the recipient and the sender, including police and intelligence agencies, the email service provider, and perhaps the Internet service providers. For all intents and purposes, email should be treated by the sender as a matter of public record. I assume as a matter of course that my email is read by someone other than the intended recipient (or at least scanned by several computers) and as a result am very hesitant to send anything via email that I would not want the world to see.

One thing that does make me feel somewhat better about the emails I send is encryption. Email encryption has typically been very difficult and relies on a wholly different encryption model than that used to protect data-at-rest. Encrypting email and web traffic relies on asymmetric encryption (also known as public key encryption). One of the huge problems with encryption for email is key exchange. It would be simple to encrypt a file with TrueCrypt or 7-Zip and email it to another party, but it would be difficult to exchange the password for that file without sending it in *unencrypted* in some form or fashion. Sending it plaintext would leave the password vulnerable to intercept and compromise the integrity of the entire system.

Asymmetric encryption solves this problem rather elegantly by using a pair of keys instead of a single key that is used to both encrypt and decrypt (such as the symmetric keys used by TrueCrypt). A key pair consists of a public key and a private key and each has a separate and distinct purpose. The public key is used to encrypt messages to the recipient. For example, if I wanted to send an encrypted email to my friend Jason I would download his public key. I would then use *his* public key to encrypt the email to him. When he receives the email he must have his own *private* key and password to decrypt the message. When Jason responds to me, he will encrypt his response using *my* public key; his response can only be decrypted using my private key.

Because the public key can only be used for encryption it is not secret. In fact public keys can be posted on websites, on purpose-built key servers, or emailed freely. The interception of the public key makes no difference as it cannot be used to decrypt any information. The private key, on the other hand, is secret and should be very closely guarded. The private key can be used to decrypt anything encrypted with the public key, and the compromise of a private key can be used to compromise all your incoming messages that were encrypted with your public key.

This system of asymmetric encryption has been around for many years. Unfortunately, it has traditionally been difficult to implement for email. Until recently, email encryption has required a complicated process to set up and use. While this was not necessarily a problem for the security conscious and technically literate, it was difficult to convince *anyone else* to implement encryption. Email encryption requires participation on the part of both sender and recipient.

Mailvelope: Fortunately, a new browser add-on called Mailvelope has greatly simplified the process of asymmetric encryption and puts email encryption within the grasp of even casual users. Mailvelope is available for Chrome and Firefox and is fully integrated with Gmail, Microsoft, and Yahoo! email accounts. Once Mailvelope has been installed on your browser clicking its icon (a small padlock and key) will allow you to open its options. You must open these options and generate a key pair before using Mailvelope to encrypt your emails.

To generate a key pair, open the Mailvelope options. On the right-hand side of the screen select "Generate Key." Several fields will appear, the first of which is Name. Enter the name that you wish to have associated with that key. I would generally recommend using the name that is on the email account you intend to use with the key because this name will be visible to others using the key. Next, enter the email address with which the key will most commonly be used. Though you can use this key pair with any email address you wish that information will also be available to recipients of your public key.

Below the email address field select "Advanced." This will give you the option to select your desired key length. The default key length is 2048 bits. A 2048-bit key is considered to be superbly strong by today's standards but I prefer to err on the side of caution. I always make my key length the longest allowable: 4096-bit. Selecting this option will require more time for the program to generate your key but in my opinion this is time well spent (in practice it is only a couple of minutes). The last field that must be filled before generating your key pair is the password field. You should use a very strong password for your key pair. Once you have selected a password it can never be changed. For this reason, I probably go overboard; the passwords for my keys are randomly generated and in excess of 150 characters, but I have little concern that they will be broken. If you are using a password manager this should be a painless step as the manager does all the work for you.

After you have generated your key pair I recommend downloading it to a secure location. Mailvelope stores your keys (your personal key pair(s) and the public keys of everyone with whom you correspond using Mailvelope) in the local storage of the browser. If anyone has brief access to your computer in the decrypted state (because by now you are full-disk encrypted, right?) they can access all of your keys, public and private. Because your keys are only stored here, if your system crashes and you have to rebuild, you will also have lost all your keys. Storing a copy locally in your encrypted file that you backup regularly will ensure that you don't lose them.

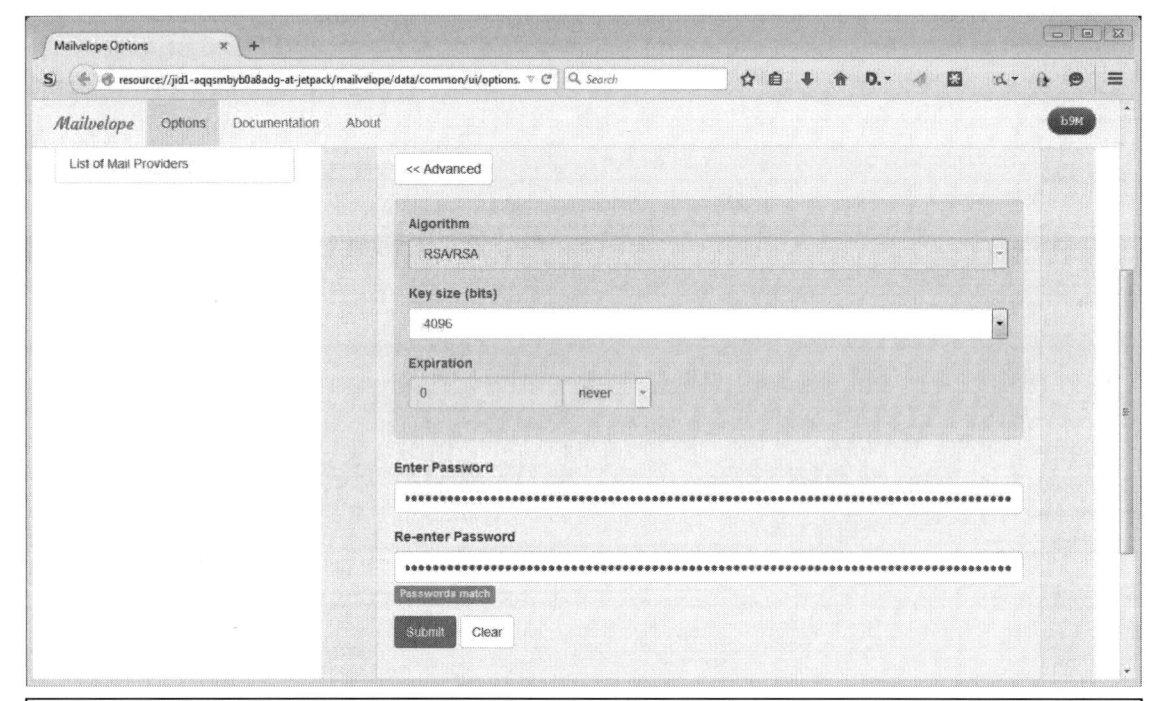

Figure 7.6: Generating a key pair in Mailvelope. I consider it important to use the strongest key length possible (4096 bit) and a very, very strong password as the password cannot be changed.

To download your keys open Mailvelope options. Right above your Key Ring (the list of keys you possess) is a blue button labeled Export. Clicking this button will reveal a number of options:

Display public key, Send public key by mail, Display private key, Display key pair, and Display all keys. To download your key pair click on the Export button and select Display key pair, and then click Create file. Save this file in a secure location. When you have exchanged keys with others, use the Display all keys option to save all of their public keys. I recommend doing this each time you exchange keys with someone to ensure your database is up to date.

Once you have generated your key pair and saved it in an encrypted location to your hard drive, the next step is to share your public key with others and import theirs. To share your public key you can copy it and paste it into the body of an email or download it as an .asc file that can be sent as an attachment. Regardless of which of these two methods you choose, be absolutely certain you are sending your public key ONLY.

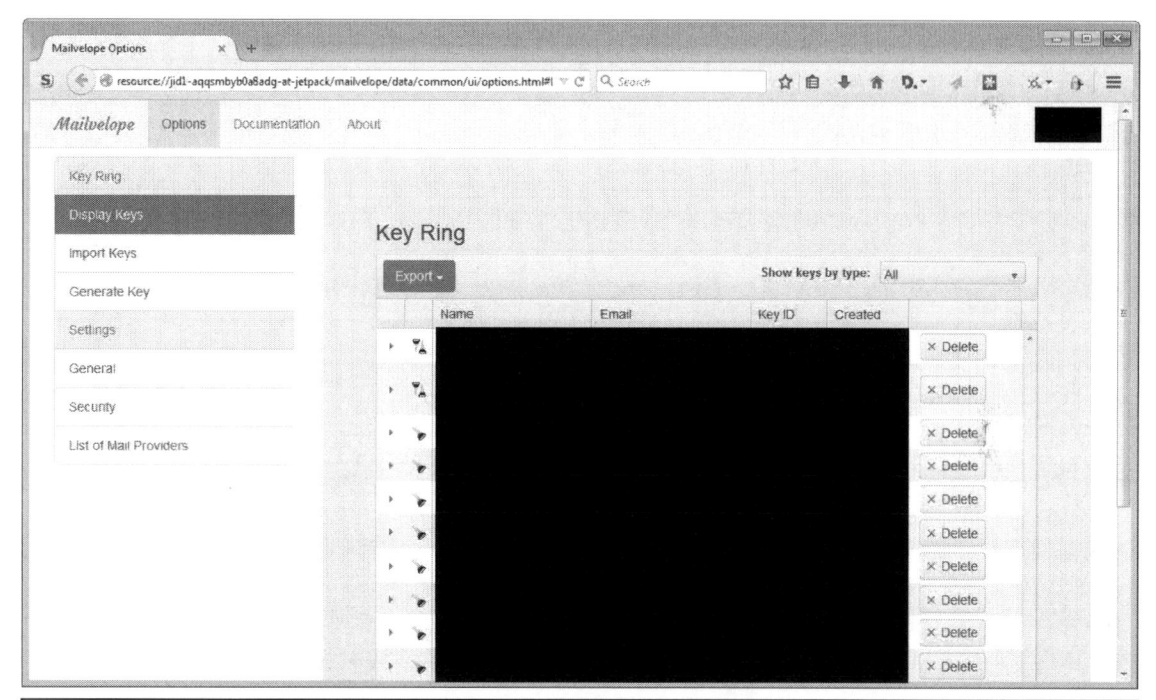

Figure 7.7: A Mailvelope Key Ring displaying all of the user's key pairs and public keys. The keys on the key ring should be backed up to an encrypted volume via the "Export" button.

When you receive a public key from another person, Mailvelope will usually recognize it as such, immediately upon opening the email and superimpose a blue box with a key over the body of the email. Clicking this blue box will automatically import the key. If, for some reason, Mailvelope does not recognize it as a key, or if you receive it in some other manner, it can still be imported. First, copy the public key. Next, open Mailvelope options and click Import keys, and paste the key into the field provided, then click Submit. If they key is valid Mailvelope will recognize it and import it.

Once you and others with whom you intend to communicate have shared keys you are ready to send and receive encrypted emails. When you log into your Gmail, Hotmail, or Yahoo! email account and click the "Compose" button to create a new email you will notice an icon in the composition window that looks like small envelope. Clicking this icon will open a new composition pane where you will type the content of your message. Typing it in this pane prevents the content of the message from being readable by the email provider.

When you have finished composing your message click the "Encrypt" button in the lower right-hand corner. A dialogue will appear with a drop-down menu allowing you to select the public key you wish to use to encrypt the message. Select the recipient's public key and click "Add." Next, click "OK" and the dialogue will disappear. Finally, click "Transfer" and the encrypted text will be transferred back to the mail provider's compose pane. Your message is now encrypted and ready to be sent.

TO WHOM DO YOU SEND ENCRYPTED EMAIL?

My answer is everyone! I am a huge advocate of encrypted communication and encourage you to convince as many people as possible to use it. This will require some patience on your part, as well as teaching a lesson or two in the ins and outs of using email encryption. Teach your friends and family, set it up for them, explain why encryption is important, and encourage them to use it. You may also be surprised to find that some of your friends already use email encryption.

I generally attempt to encrypt as much email as I possibly can. If I encrypt only one out of every hundred emails it is pretty easy to guess which of my emails are highly sensitive. If, on the other hand, half of all my emails are encrypted, it would be much more difficult to make this guess and harder to separate the signal of an email that is worth attempting to decrypt from the noise of scores of others that are not.

When you receive an encrypted message Mailvelope will recognize it as such. The message will appear superimposed with an envelope and a lock; your mouse pointer will look like a key when you hover over the message. Clicking this icon will prompt you to input your password. Entering the correct password will allow the message to be decrypted.

It is important to note that metadata about your communications is not encrypted. The email addresses with which you are communicating are visible, as are subject lines. For this reason it is imperative not to place any sensitive in the subject line. One major drawback of Mailvelope is that it currently does not support the encryption of attachments. Be aware that any attachments to an encrypted email will remain unencrypted.

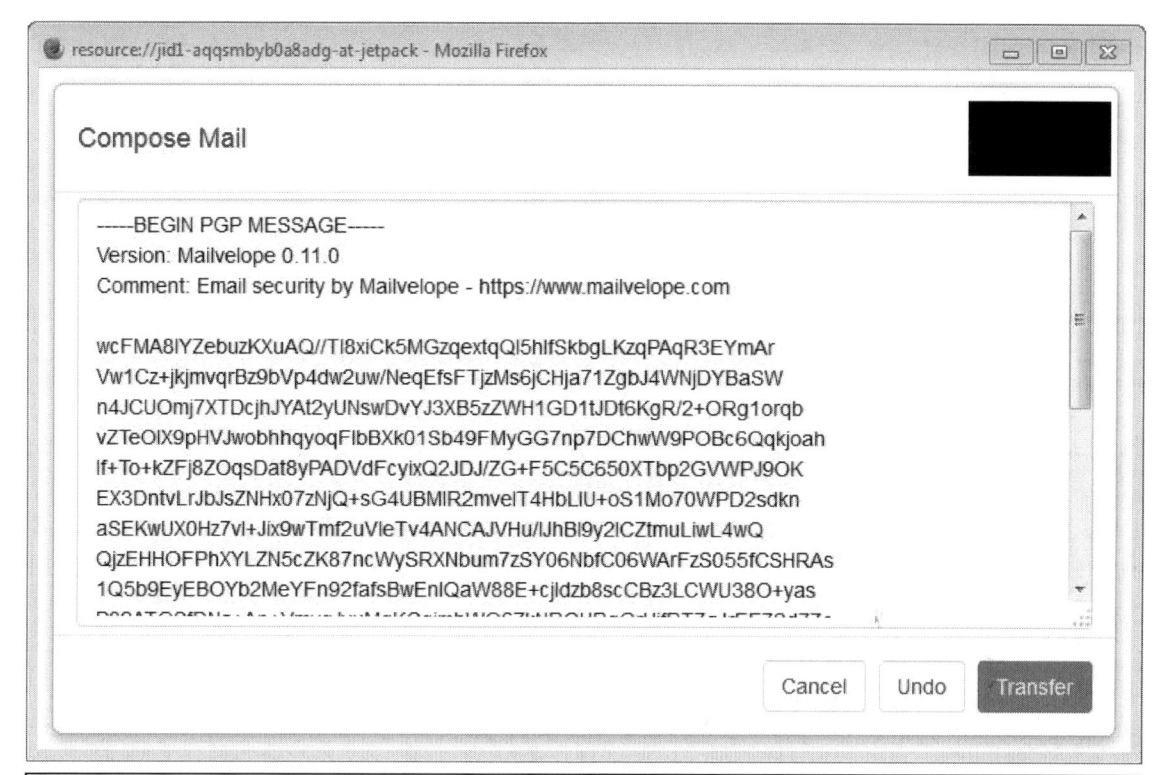

Figure 7.8: A Mailvelope Key Ring displaying all of the user's key pairs and public keys. The keys on the key ring should be backed up to an encrypted volume via the "Export" button.

Mailvelope is free and open source and available at: https://www.mailvelope.com/

Other email encryption options: Mailvelope is not the sole option for encrypted email. There are a number of other options available and I would be remiss if I did not mention them. As mentioned earlier in this chapter, ProtonMail offers free email accounts that are automatically encrypted using PGP (Pretty Good Privacy) and enjoy the tremendous benefit of requiring no working knowledge of public key encryption. ProtonMail is still relatively new on the block but does look very good.

Probably the most prevalent and popular option for years was (and perhaps still is) the Thunderbird/Enigmail/GPG4Win combination. Thunderbird is a desktop email client and is a product of Mozilla. Thunderbird performs like many other desktop email clients (such as Outlook) and allows you to use POP3 email, which downloads your emails from the server to your device where you can access them at your leisure without an internet connection. Like Firefox Thunderbird also allows you install add-ons.

Enigmail is a Thunderbird add-on that allows Thunderbird to use a PGP encryption implementation known as GPG4Win (Gnu Privacy Guard for Windows) that provides the encryption. Thunderbird provides the email and Enigmail is the middleman between the two. A major benefit to this system over Mailvelope is the ability to encrypt attachments. Though technically sophisticated users will have no problems with it, a major drawback to this system is the time and effort it takes to learn it, set it up, and use it. I use this system and have for years, but have failed in convincing a single person to use it on a regular basis. I am much happier showing my friends Mailvelope and much more successful at getting them to actually use it.

If you are interested in using this system rather than relying on Mailvelope or ProtonMail, numerous tutorials are available online. The best written tutorial I have seen online is part of the Electronic Frontier Foundation's Surveillance Self Defense series of articles and is available at https://ssd.eff.org/en/module/how-use-pgp-windows-pc

Thunderbird is free and available at: https://www.mozilla.org/en-US/thunderbird/
Enigmail is available at: https://www.enigmail.net/home/index.php
GPG4Win is free and available at: http://gpg4win.org/

SOCIAL MEDIA ACCOUNTS

The most important thing you should understand about social media is that nothing is truly private. Though social media sites have "privacy" settings, anything you post to a social media site should be considered to be fully within the public domain and a matter of public record. Resources such as Michael Bazzell's excellent *Open Source Intelligence Techniques* will show you how to quickly and easily bypass such "protections" and view anyone's private content on many popular social networks.

Further, when signing up for these services, in almost all cases you release the rights of the content to the service provider. This means that even if you do decide later that you no longer wish for your photos and other personal information to be online you have no choice in the matter: "your" content no longer belongs to you. Further, anything placed on the Internet will live on long after you wish it gone. The Internet never forgets and old versions of many sites are stored in caches by a number of databases and websites. *Open Source Intelligence Techniques* is also demonstrative of this fact showing you how to access archives that the content creators themselves have probably forgotten or assume to be long gone.

Rather than detail the largely useless steps of enabling privacy settings on the various social media platforms I will generally discourage the use of social media, period, saying simply: don't use it. I fully realize, however, few will take this advice. If you insist on voluntarily placing personal information on the Internet, use a good password, use two-factor authentication where it is available, and think carefully about the information post. Good luck.

CLOUD STORAGE ACCOUNTS

Cloud storage has become immensely popular in recent years (though trust in them has perhaps waned slightly, post-Snowden). Dozens of companies offer cloud storage services, allowing you to exchange the small monthly or annual fee you pay for a space on their server to store your files, and bandwidth over which you can upload and download those files. Cloud storage is tantalizingly convenient. You can upload a document to your cloud account from your work computer, download and edit it on your home computer, view it from your smartphone, or share it with another person or group of people.

Making these services even more enticing still is the fact that most offer a small amount of storage for free, generally 2-5 gigabytes, which may be a sufficient amount of storage for home users. This convenience comes at a cost, however. Anything stored on a server or device that you don't control is vulnerable to the terms of the provider. Cloud storage operators, if inclined, may inspect, edit, or delete (intentionally or accidentally) your documents as long as doing so does not violate the terms of the user agreement, and all of these things have happened. Further, if you store files with a cloud storage provider that does not provide secure storage, it negates a lot of the hard work you have done in securing your own system, as a hacked account could result in the spillage of sensitive data.

The greatest concern I have with files stored in the cloud is that they will be accessed by an unauthorized party, whether an employee of the provider (either for "legitimate" or illicit purposes in the case of a rogue employee), or a hacker who has gained unauthorized access to my account or the cloud provider's servers. This may sound slightly far-fetched, but as this book was being written a large data breach occurred that exposed nude photographs of several A-list celebrities, all of whom had their accounts hacked, and some of whom had "deleted" the photographs in questions months earlier. For these reasons, I use cloud storage only minimally and for completely non-sensitive data, and I do not recommend it. If you require this service, however, use the best practices discussed earlier in this book (obscure usernames, strong passwords, TFA) as well as those discussed below. Further, I will recommend what I feel to be the most secure providers and best practices.

BitTorrent Sync: BitTorrent Sync isn't truly a cloud-based service. BT Sync is a peer-to-peer file sharing service that allows you to sync multiple devices without ever uploading your data to a cloud storage provider. Though this information does flow from one device to another via the Internet (where it is potentially vulnerable to intercept), it is not stored on an external server.

BitTorrent Sync requires that one of your devices always be on, and online, if you wish to use it as a cloud service. There are numerous tutorials that show you how to build your own cloud storage with a network-attached storage device, a computer that you can leave on, and even with a Raspberry Pi (a very small, minimalistic computer processor). If you go this route you may wish to look further into also building your own encrypted virtual private network through which you can access the device. The major downside of a setup like this is that your "cloud" is in your home, so if you house burns down or falls victim to a natural disaster you have lost one of the major advantages of cloud storage. On the other hand, it is probably far more secure than placing it with a true cloud provider.

SpiderOak: SpiderOak is perhaps the most recommended cloud storage provider among the security conscious. This is primarily due to SpiderOak's "zero knowledge" claims. According to their website, SpiderOak has no access to (i.e., zero knowledge of) your data. Further, all data that is uploaded to SpiderOak's servers is first encrypted on your device *before* being uploaded.

SpiderOak does deem it necessary to make users aware that logging in via the Internet or on a mobile device, rather than from the SpiderOak desktop application, does place your password on SpiderOak's servers for the length of the session. SpiderOak claims that the password is encrypted and is destroyed on logout. I do not find this ideal, but I do appreciate their transparency. One other slight downside of SpiderOak is that they do not offer two-factor authentication for free accounts. If I were storing documents in the cloud I would find it incredibly important to make the account as difficult to get into as possible. SpiderOak does, however, offer a limited two-factor authentication system for paid account holders.

DropBox and Google Drive: DropBox and Google Drive are far more popular alternatives to SpiderOak. Both are usable across most platforms, both offer excellent security by way of strong encryption, have HTTPS connections when uploading and downloading, allow very long passwords (99+ characters), and support two-factor authentication. DropBox offers 2Gb of free storage, while Google Drive offers 15 Gb of free storage. Further, if sharing files with others is a priority, both of these providers enjoy the immense advantage of popularity. With convenience comes a cost, however. Reading through the privacy policies of both Dropbox and Google, it is clear that your data can be accessed at their discretion. If you opt to go with a cloud provider, I recommend understanding and implementing the cloud storage best practices that follow:

Dropbox is available at: https://dropbox.com
Google Drive is available at: https://drive.google.com

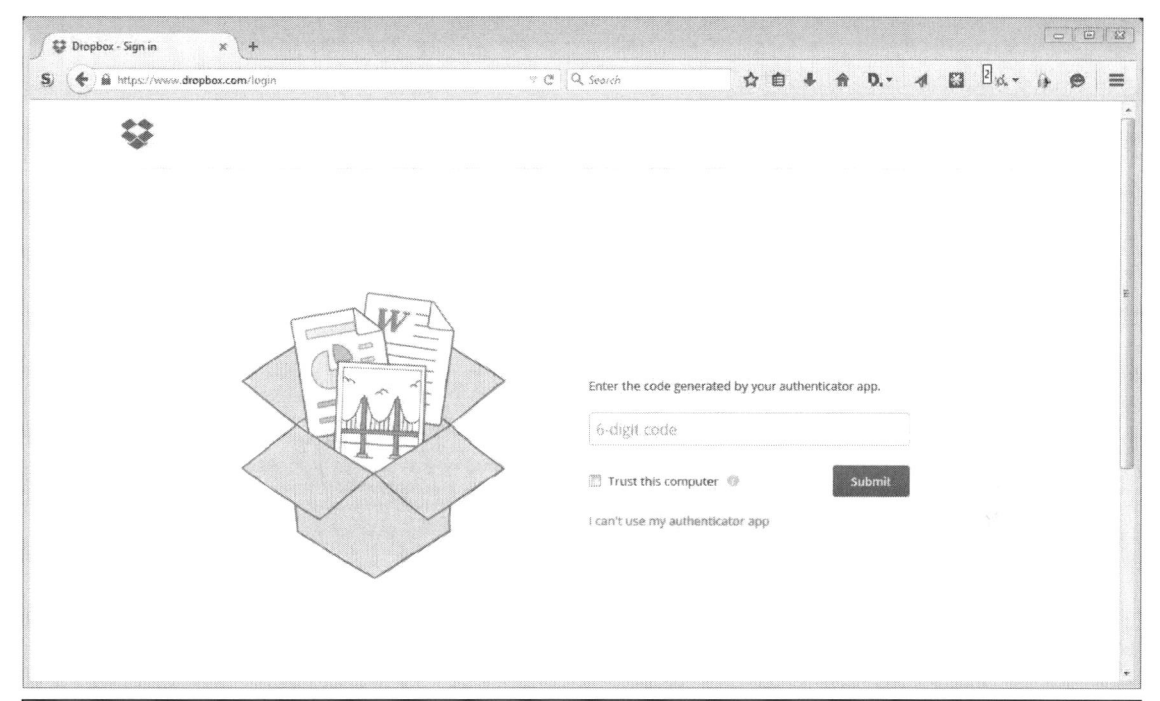

Figure 7.9: A prompt from Dropbox requiring the second authentication factor. This account is set up to use the authenticator app rather than SMS messages. Both Dropbox and Google Drive offer excellent security.

Read the ToS and Privacy Policy: The terms of service are an important part of any online service that the vast majority of users fail to ever examine. This document should always be read carefully, as it clearly outlines what the provider can do with your information. If reading through the legalese is too time consuming, there is a website that can help: https://tosdr.org. TOSDR (which stands for "Terms of Service, Didn't Read") attempts to simplify the terms of service from many popular websites into a small amount of easily understandable information, along with a letter grade (A through F).

Limit what you Store: You should carefully consider the items you store in the cloud. I have no problem with cloud storage if it is just used to conveniently access non-sensitive information. If the information you store would not leak data about you and does not contain information that would be financially or personally damaging, the risk is minimal. This is a very high bar, however, as just about anything would leak some information about you.

Encrypt Before Uploading: Even though cloud storage providers now take pride in the encryption they offer, it is possible that they possess the encryption keys. This could potentially give them access to your data. For this reason, it is a good idea to encrypt files locally with *your own* encryption before uploading them. I recommend using CryptSync, as described for backups in Chapter 3, though TrueCrypt or 7-Zip would both work equally well. This ensures that if the provider or a hacker does access your data, they will only be able to access an encrypted version. Admittedly, this likely makes your files inaccessible from your smartphone or computers without the software necessary for decryption, which defeats the convenience inherent in cloud storage. It still serves you well if the primary intended purpose of the account is as an offsite backup.

ONLINE MESSAGING SYSTEMS

I look at online messaging systems similar to the way I look at email: encrypt whenever possible. Also, because of the seemingly ephemeral nature of video and IM chats, I believe these forms of communication should be protected more strongly. When we engage in communications of this nature, the underlying assumption is that it's like an in-person ephemeral chat and that once the conversation is over, it's gone. This is not the case, nor are many of these systems very secure. Many claim encryption, and on the surface that may be true. But implementing good security is difficult and costly in time and money. Some messaging services do it well and some don't. So how do you choose?

The Electronic Frontier Foundation has recently published a Secure Messaging Scorecard that rates messaging systems of all types, including email, video chat, and text messaging services for all operating systems and all platforms. The Secure Messaging Scorecard gives indicators as to how secure a given messaging system is based on seven factors, and it does so in an easy green check mark/red caution sign format. The factors considered on the Secure Messaging Scorecard are:

o **Is the message encrypted in transit?** This is important for obvious reasons.
o **Is the message encrypted in a manner that prevents the provider from seeing it?** It is entirely possible for a provider to encrypt your messages in transit (protecting them from local attacks against you) while still leaving them the ability to view the messages. This compromises security because if they can access the messages, they can turn them over to law enforcement/intelligence agencies, they are accessible to rogue employees, and the company itself may be hacked and your information leaked. Further, the very presence of a backdoor is a security concern because it may be used by an actor other than the provider.
o **Can you verify contacts' identities?** This protects you from having a conversation with an imposter and revealing sensitive information.
o **Are past communications secure if your keys are stolen?** This is possible in some systems, but not possible in others. Encrypted email using typical public key encryption is

an example of a system where the compromise of your keys would lead to the compromise of historical communications.
- **Is the code open to independent review?** Closed cryptosystems that are not open to independent review are less trusted than systems that are open to review. If the code is not open to review, users must blindly trust that the provider is following through on any security claims that are made.
- **Is security design properly implemented?** Self-explanatory.
- **Has there been any recent code audit?** Code audits are necessary to validate the implementation, and are only possible when the code is open to independent review. Ideally, a code audit would occur each time an update was made to a secure messaging application but this is not always feasible due to the time and expense involved. When possible, select programs that have undergone a recent code audit.

I will not repeat the results of this scorecard here, but I will encourage you to take a look at it. Using this scorecard you should take a look at any messaging systems you currently use. If you find that the ones you currently use are not up to your security standard, consider switching (and getting your friends to switch) to ones that do. There are quite a few messaging systems out there that are very secure.

EFF's Secure Messaging Scorecard is available at: https://www.eff.org/secure-messaging-scorecard

SUMMARY

This final chapter covered securing your online accounts. I cannot overstate how important a step this is for security and privacy reasons. Poor practices online can have consequences in the physical world. There are hundreds of cases of people being stalked through their online activity, homes broken into when social media announced they were on vacation, and individuals who have been doxed (personal information like full name, home address, personal telephone number, and financial information posted online).

This chapter covered the broad-brush strokes of securing a variety of online accounts, and thoroughly reiterated the need for random usernames, strong passwords, and two-factor authentication. This chapter also covered:

- Basic best practices for all online accounts
- What to look for in online security for banking accounts, e-commerce accounts, and other accounts dealing with sensitive financial information

o Email account best practices, a rundown of email account providers, and email encryption using Mailvelope
o A warning about social media account insecurity
o Cloud storage account best practices and secure providers

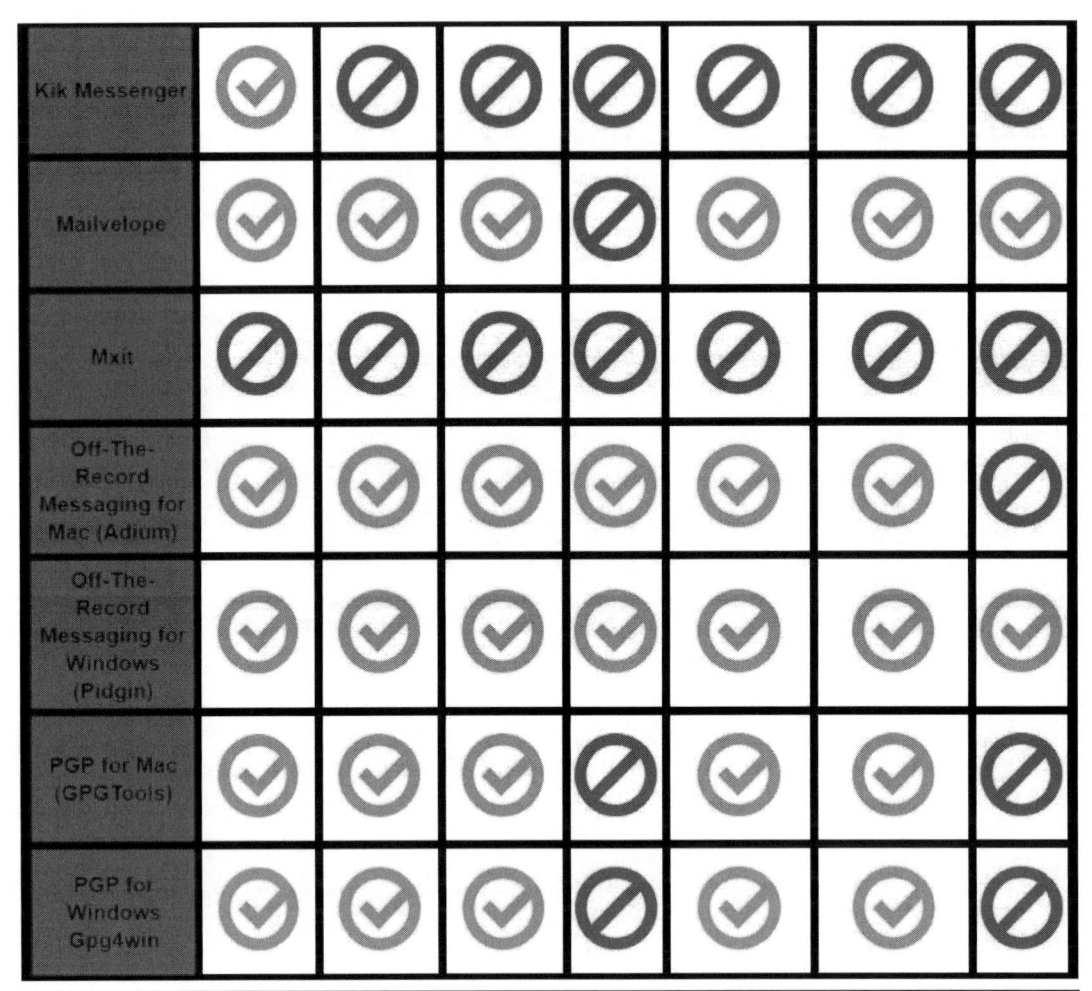

Figure 7.9: A portion of the EFF's Secure Messaging Scorecard. Courtesy of the Electronic Frontier Foundation; full scorecard available at: https://www.eff.org/secure-messaging-scorecard

CONCLUSION

After taking the simple steps outlined in this book, your computer will be significantly hardened against many threats. In fact, if most people took even the simplest of steps recommended here it is unlikely that malware would be anywhere near as prevalent or lucrative as it currently is. That being said, I am certain this book is not comprehensive or complete. A one hundred percent secure system does not exist, and computer security is an ongoing process that requires constant vigilance and attention. Just as most of the steps mentioned here require revisiting (updates, definition updates, etc.), so too does thorough computer security require an awareness of the constantly changing threat landscape.

As I mentioned at the beginning of this work, these techniques will not make you invulnerable to attacks. They will not make you totally secure against the incredibly powerful threats presented by the National Security Agency and other very well-funded and extremely sophisticated adversaries. It will make you a much harder target, however, and likely make all but the most determined cybercriminals and hackers move on to easier pickings. Even if you are specifically targeted, you are still very well-protected. All the security measures in this book, if taken, should provide you with an advance warning if you are being targeted.

Going forward, I encourage you to pass this information along to others. Hacked and infected computers affect us all, and the more secure we are as individuals, the more secure we become as a group. The more of us who use encryption, the more difficult it becomes to separate the signal from the noise. The more of us who demand two-factor authentication, the more services that will begin to offer it as a matter of course.

That is not to say that all others will be receptive, but someone will be. The more you encourage others, the more they will begin to think about things like encryption and the quality of their passwords, and perhaps a few of them will implement some of these techniques. Teach others. Loan this book to friends and family. Give it away. Donate it to a local library.

If you find yourself wanting to do more to increase awareness about computer security and personal privacy, consider joining or donating to the Electronic Frontier Foundation. The EFF is a non-profit organization and the premier advocate for civil liberties in the digital realm. More information on the EFF, its mission, and membership is available at: https://www.eff.org/

7-Zip	78
Anti-Malware	17
Comodo Cleaning Essentials	19
Malwarebytes	19
SpyBot Search and Destroy	19
Antivirus	15
AVAST	16
Bitdefender Free	16
Microsoft Security Essentials	16
Application Updates	14
AutoPlay	23
BIOS Security	33
BitTorrent Sync	167
Bloatware Removal	27
breachalarm.com	148
CCEnhancer	95
CCleaner	92
Certificate Authorities	106
Checksums	60
CHK Checksum Utility	61
Cookies	134
Cloud Storage	166
Best Practices	168
Dropbox	167
Google Drive	167
SpiderOak	167
CryptSync	80
Data Leakage, Managing	98
Defraggler	98
Decrap My PC	29
Disconnect	134
Disconnect Search	135
Disk Defragmenting	97
DiskCryptor	75
Dropbox	167
Email	151
33mail.com	153
Best Practices	151
Encryption	159
Gmail	155
FastMail	157
Kolab Now	157
notsharingmy.info	154
ProtonMail	158
Encryption	67
Algorithms	69
Email	159
File Level	67
Full-disk	68
Enigmail	165
Epic Privacy Browser	139
Eraser	89
FastMail	157
File Extensions, Displaying	24
Firefox	127
Gmail	155
Google Drive	167
GPG4Win	165
haveibeenpwned.com	148
Hibernate Mode	31
HTTPS Everywhere	136
Limiting Startup Applications	32
Mailvelope	160
Microsoft EMET	21
Microsoft Office	100
NoScript	136
Operating System Updates	12
Passwords	48
Across Multiple Accounts	53
First Letter Method	51
Lifespan/Fatigue	53
Passphrases	50
Recycling	54
Vulnerabilities	49
Password Managers	
Basic Information	36
Host-Based	37
LastPass	44

Password Safe	37	Transport Layer Security (TLS)	105
Web-Based	44	TrueCrypt	70
Patch My PC	14	Two-Factor Authentication	55
Principle of Least Privilege (PLP)	10	Authy	57
ProtonMail	158	Google Authenticator	57
Recuva	86	Grid	58
Removable Media, Scanning	26	Hardware Based	58
Revo Uninstaller	30	Text/SMS	56
Secunia PSI	15	USB Devices, Scanning	26
Secure Sockets Layer (SSL)	105	User Access Control (UAC)	10
Secure File Deletion	85	Usernames	45
Secure Messaging Scorecard	169	VeraCrypt	78
Sleep Mode	31	Virtual Private Networks (VPNs)	108
Shut Down	31	Wi-Fi	112
Social Media Accounts	165	Router Setup	115
SpiderOak	167	Untrusted/Insecure Networks	120
Start Menu (Privacy)	99	Windows 7 Settings	113
Thunderbird	165	Windows Firewall	20
TOR	140		

Printed in Great Britain
by Amazon.co.uk, Ltd.,
Marston Gate.